An Illustrated Guide to
Eighteenth–Century
English Drinking Glasses

by L M Bickerton
With a Bibliography of English Glass by D R Elleray

BARRIE & JENKINS
LONDON

To Mary, who shared the effort this volume entailed

First published in 1971 by
BARRIE & JENKINS LTD
2 Clement's Inn
London WC 2.

© Copyright
L. M. Bickerton 1971
Bibliography ©
Barrie & Jenkins 1971

Designed by Michael R. Carter
Setting in 'Monophoto' Bembo,
printing and binding by
Jarrold and Sons Limited,
Cowgate, Norwich

ISBN 0 214 65297 1

An Illustrated Guide to
Eighteenth–Century English Drinking Glasses

Contents

Acknowledgments

My first thanks must be accorded to Laurence Boreham for introducing me to the study and collection of English glass: the enthusiasm which he communicated was the starting-point of this volume. It was increased by the gift of a copy of E. Barrington Haynes's *Glass through the ages* from the Hon. Mrs. R. J. P. Wyatt from whom also I learned something of Hartshorne's own tireless researches and meticulous scholarship. My library was doubled by Derek Davis's gift of a copy of his book on the subject; from him I also gained, by his wise counsel, an appreciation of the quality, variety and craftsmanship of glass of the eighteenth century.

I am even more indebted to the owners of private collections listed below and to the curators of collections also listed for the opportunity they have given me of handling, photographing and studying thousands of specimens during the past few years. They have shown me kindness, hospitality and friendship; no words of mine can express sufficient thanks, nor can I even mention the names of many who, for obvious reasons, wish to remain anonymous. To one owner especially, Graeme Cranch, I must record my appreciation of his encouragement and belief that I could add something useful to the literature of the subject.

Finally, I have to thank two collaborators who have contributed directly to the production of this volume, my colleague Robert Elleray who has been responsible for the extensive bibliography which will undoubtedly prove to be one of its most important features, and my wife who accompanied me on most of my expeditions, took notes by the hour and was responsible for typing almost the entire manuscript. Additional typing was also undertaken by my secretary, Gillian Dodds, who also conducted for me a questionnaire on glass in public collections.

Mr. and Mrs. K. A. Alexander
Mr. L. C. Boreham
Mrs. Chevallier
Mr. and Mrs. A. G. Cranch
Mr. R. Lymbery

Mr. G. M. Pinker
Mr. W. A. D. Riley-Smith
Sir Ernest Taylor
Mr. C. P. C. de Wesselow
Mr. O. Wyatt

Author's Note

The purpose of this book is to provide a sufficient collection of illustrations of eighteenth-century drinking glasses to facilitate recognition of and reference to the majority of types likely to be encountered, to add brief descriptions according to a standard pattern and to suggest a classification which might be useful to collectors and curators.

The astonishing variety of glasses produced in the eighteenth century makes it impossible to cover the subject exhaustively in a single volume of this size, nor has it been possible to include coloured glass or more than a fraction of the engraved glasses of the period. On the other hand a few glasses for purposes other than drinking have been included to illustrate important features or because of their association interest.

A very full bibliography has been provided covering relevant literature in periodical and book form: ancient and foreign glass has been excluded. Similarly, the guide to public collections is primarily concerned with English glass since the seventeenth century, sufficient detail being provided to indicate the scope and importance of the collections.

Introduction

Since the publication in 1897 of Albert Hartshorne's monumental *Old English Glasses* there has been, first, a steady trickle, more recently such a flood of books on the subject that any addition to its spate demands explanation and justification. Many aspects of English glassmaking require further study, the whole question of provenance being the most intriguing and the most elusive; dating of glasses is also far from precise and much work needs to be done on the development of wheel-engraving, enamelling and gilding in England. Unfortunately, excavation of factory sites, which has yielded such important evidence in determining the provenance of pottery and porcelain, does not apply to glass since every scrap of waste from breakages or spoilages was used in succeeding batches. Cullet was, indeed, such an important ingredient that, as W. A. Thorpe[1] quotes, poor people earned a livelihood by collecting all kinds of broken glass for sale to makers. The alternative method of determining where glass vessels were made – by chemical analysis – is therefore rendered equally unreliable since the contents varied from pot to pot. Thorpe's conclusion remains unchallenged 'There is no type of eighteenth-century metal either in England or Ireland which can be ascribed to any particular glasshouse.'[2]

It is not the author's intention, however, to advance new theories: it is rather to compile a working manual which could be of assistance to collectors, students, antique dealers and museum curators by bringing together a series of illustrations of all types of eighteenth-century drinking glasses, providing a uniform system of describing them and adding an extensive bibliography. No single volume can hope to be exhaustive – indeed one of the attractions of the subject is its almost infinite variety – but it has been felt that within the scope of some eight hundred and fifty illustrations it will be possible to display most stem formations and types of bowl and foot commonly encountered and provide a convenient means of referring to them.

Mr. Elleray's bibliography used in conjunction with the general index, will direct the reader to sources of information on many aspects of English glass which are obviously beyond the scope of this guide. As the reader will

[1] Thorpe, W. A. *History of English and Irish glass*, p. 35, footnote.

[2] Ibid.

quickly perceive, the bibliography is far wider than the subject of the book: indeed it covers the whole field of English glass studies over the last hundred years.

It was, in fact, a strange coincidence which brought this about. In discussing with Mr. Elleray my own plans for a bibliography limited to items on eighteenth-century drinking glasses, I discovered that he had already assembled most of the material now published. He generously offered to make his work available to me but it seemed to me and to my publishers that this opportunity of making the fruits of Mr. Elleray's wider research available should not be missed. This decision was reinforced by the knowledge that no comparable, up-to-date bibliography is available elsewhere.

1 Classification

Any consideration of English drinking glasses produced throughout the whole of the eighteenth century involves some attempt at classification, for the dual purpose of ensuring that the author covers the subject systematically and that the reader is led through it in an orderly and intelligible progression, having a recognised skeleton upon which to append the information he gleans from this and other sources.

During the seventy years or so since Hartshorne[1] first attempted an appreciation of this hitherto unexplored subject, a classification has slowly evolved, that produced by Haynes[2] being one of his most valuable contributions to the study of glass. More than ten years have elapsed since *Glass through the Ages* was revised and those years have proved the soundness of the principle he adopted – classification by stem formation. Hartshorne, understandably, was groping in the dark: most of his sixteen groups were based on stem formation, but by no means all and certainly not in chronological order, 'Air-twisted stems and bell-shaped bowls' preceding 'Baluster stems', whereas champagnes, sweetmeats and tavern glasses formed other groups irrespective of type of stem.

In 1927 Thorpe[3] published the fruits of much research and scholarship and divided his subject into three divisions for the period prior to 1675, 'The age of adoption', 'The age of assimilation' and 'The Ravenscroft revolution', understandable enough for this historical section. For the period 1675 to 1850, however, he adopted three more divisions, partly stylistic, partly chronological, 'The age of design', 'The age of ornament' and 'The Anglo-Irish revival: cut glass', which summarise the main developments but give little help towards the presentation of a workable classification.

Ten years later Arthur Churchill Ltd produced a catalogue[4] which achieved a considerable advance, the arrangement being by stem formation in chronological order with the exception of subjects such as Lynn bowls, champagnes and sweetmeats, inserted illogically. However, as the following summary of its main divisions shows, an order was emerging and a chronology had been attempted:

[1] Hartshorne, A. *Old English glasses*, 1897.

[2] Haynes, E. B. *Glass through the Ages*, 2nd ed. 1959.

[3] Thorpe, W. A. *History of English and Irish glass*, 1927.

[4] Arthur Churchill Ltd. *Catalogue of old English glass*, 2nd ed. 1937.

1

1 Heavy balusters (1685–1710)

2 Silesian stemmed glasses (1710–20)

3 Light balusters (1720–40)

4 Plain and simply knopped glasses (1700–1800)

5 Air twists (1740–60)

6 Opaque twists (1760–80)

7 Colour twists (1770–80)

8 Facet-cut stems (1770–90)

Another eleven years elapsed before E. Barrington Haynes produced *Glass through the Ages* notable for the absence of cross-classification and reassessment of the dates suggested by Arthur Churchill Ltd. in 1937. The term 'balustroid' was introduced as an alternative to 'simply knopped glasses' and a useful section was included to embrace the heterogenous and numerous glasses with very short stems or no stems at all which defied inclusion in the other categories. It is a system which has so fully proved its soundness that only minor amendments are suggested to make it of even greater convenience and assistance to collectors.

Heavy balusters, for example, are again restored to the dignity of a separate class on the grounds that they are of distinctive form and are regarded by collectors as of much greater importance than the lighter glasses which followed. The balustroid section is retained but, as seems logical, now includes the Newcastle balusters. There seems little justification, either, for the provision of a separate class for hollow stems, a type comparatively few in number and satisfactorily accommodated as a subdivision of balusters and plain straight stems.

In suggesting the subdivisions enumerated below, the principle has been followed of proceeding from the simple to the more complex: thus, under 'Balustroids', arrangement has been from one to three or more knops; moulded pedestals have been arranged by number of sides from four to eight (equally tenable on chronological grounds) and air twists and opaque twists have been divided into the two main sections, first single, then double series, with subsections within them of increasing complexity. Whether or not it is possible to argue that development of air and opaque twists follows a chronological order, no proof is forthcoming and the probability is that the simple form preceded the complex.

For the sake of collectors fortunate enough to possess English glasses earlier than the heavy baluster a simple classification is suggested which provides for an arrangement according to the most prominent decorative feature.

Schedules have also been provided for those who wish to arrange engraved and enamelled glasses together, and are prepared to depart from the strict principle of classification by stem type for this purpose. The arrangement of glasses with rudimentary stems is another exception to the rule for reasons which are obvious. In some cases it would be possible to guess at a chronological order but guesswork is an unsatisfactory principle: the one employed, classification first by purpose and then by distinguishing feature may be empirical but will suffice until a chronology can be established.

Façon de Venise sixteenth and seventeenth centuries
  Hollow-blown knops
  Lions' mask knops
  Filigree-work
  Latticino
  Vetro de trina (lace-glass)
  Painting and gilding
  Other features
English glass of lead 1670–1700
  Hollow-blown knops
  Rope twists
  Prunts
  Gadrooning
  Pincered wings
  Flammiform decoration
  Other features

HEAVY BALUSTERS (c. 1685–1710)

Inverted baluster
Angular knop
Annulated knop
Drop knop
Ball knop
Mushroom knop
Acorn knop
Cylinder knop
Egg knop
Other knops

BALUSTERS (c. 1710–35)

Inverted baluster
True baluster
Angular knop
Annulated knop
Drop knop
Ball knop
Mushroom knop
Acorn knop
Cylinder knop
Egg knop
Other knops
Hollow knops

BALUSTROIDS (c. 1725–60)

Inverted baluster
True baluster
Other knops – single knop
Other knops – two knops
Other knops – three knops
Other knops – more than three knops (including bobbin knops)
Newcastle balusters

MOULDED PEDESTAL STEMS (c. 1715–65)

Four-sided
Six-sided
Eight-sided
Debased

PLAIN STEMS (c. 1730–75)

Two-piece stems
 Drawn trumpet bowls
 Drawn trumpet bowls with tears
 Other bowls
Three-piece stems
 Bell bowl
 Round-funnel bowl
 Ogee bowl
 Bucket bowl
 Cup bowl
 Ovoid bowl
 Other bowls
Collared stems
Hollow stems

AIR-TWIST STEMS (c. 1745–70)

Single series; two piece, unknopped
 MSAT without collars
 MSAT with collar
 Pair of corkscrews
 Other twists
Single series; two piece, knopped
 Single-knop MSAT
 Two or more knops MSAT
Single series; three piece, unknopped
 MSAT without collar
 MSAT with collar
 Pair of corkscrews

    Four corkscrews
    Spiral cable (single or pair)
    Other twists
  Single series; three piece, knopped
    Single-knop MSAT
    Single knop, other twists
    Two or more knops
  Double series; two piece, unknopped
  Double series; three piece, unknopped
    Pair spiral threads outside cable
    Four spiral threads outside cable
    Six- to twelve-ply spiral band outside cable
    Other twists
  Double series; three piece, knopped
  Triple series

INCISED-TWIST STEMS (*c.* 1745–65)

  Coarse twist, unknopped
  Coarse twist, knopped
  Fine twist, unknopped
  Fine twist, knopped

COMPOSITE STEMS (*c.* 1745–75)

  Plain section over air twist
  Air twist over plain section
  Plain section over opaque twist
  Opaque twist over plain section
  Plain section with air and opaque twists
  Plain section with mixed twist
  Knop over air twist
  Air twist over or divided by knop
  Knop over opaque twist
  Opaque twist over knop
  Any other two stem formations
  Three or more stem formations (other than plain section with air and opaque twists)

OPAQUE-TWIST STEMS (*c.* 1755–80)

  Single series; unknopped
    MSOT (multiple-spiral opaque twist)
    Corkscrew
    Lace twist outlined
    Spiral gauzes or cables
    Alternating twists
    Other twists

Single series; knopped
  MSOT
  Other twists
Double series; unknopped
  Ten- to twenty-ply spiral band outside pair spiral tapes or threads
  Solid spiral band outside pair spiral tapes or threads
  Four- to twelve-ply spiral band outside gauze
  Pair spiral threads outside gauze
  Three or four spiral threads outside gauze
  Four- to twelve-ply spiral band (or pair) outside lace twist or corkscrew
  Spiral threads outside lace twist or corkscrew
  Pair corkscrews outside spiral threads, cable or gauze
  Pair spiral threads outside cable
  Other twists
Double series; knopped
  Single knop; two to four spiral threads outside gauze
  Single knop; other twists
  Two knops
  Three knops
  Four or more knops
Triple series

MIXED AND COLOUR TWIST STEMS (*c.* 1755–75)

Single series; air alternating with opaque white
Double series; air outside opaque white
Double series; opaque white outside air
Single series; colour only
Single series; colour with air or opaque white
  Colour and air, unknopped
  Colour and opaque white, unknopped
  Colour and opaque white, knopped
Double series; colour and opaque white, unknopped
  Inner twist of opaque white
  Inner twist of opaque white and colour
  Inner twist of colour only
Double series; colour and opaque white, knopped
Single series; air, opaque white and colour
Double series; air, opaque white and colour

FACETED STEMS (*c.* 1760–1810)

Unknopped stems
  With diamond faceting
  Hexagonal faceting
  Vertical fluting
Knop at top of stem
  With diamond faceting
  Other facets

6

Centre-knopped stem
  With diamond faceting
  Other facets
Two or more knops

Persons
  Royalty
  Williamites
  Jacobites
  Titled families
  Commoners
  Corporate bodies
Public events
  Historical events: military
  Historical events: naval (including Privateers)
  Historical events: civil
  Politics and elections
  Other subjects
Private affairs
  Family occasions and events
  Friendship and conviviality
  Business
  Sports and recreations
  Other subjects (including Masonics)
Places
  Towns and villages: England
  Towns and villages: Holland
  Other towns and villages
  Imaginary scenes, e.g. Chinese gardens
  Individual buildings
Natural and geometric forms
  'Flowered' borders
  Hops and barley
  Fruiting vine
  Fruiting apple
  Other decorative forms
Myths and legends
Stippled decoration

DECORATION: ENAMELLING

Ownership (including armorials)
Portraits
Sports and pastimes
Pastoral scenes
Classical landscapes and ruins
Birds and insects
Fruit and trees
Hops and barley
Floral borders
Other subjects (including Masonics)

DECORATION: GILDING

2 Stem Formations

Venetian influences

The term 'façon de Venise', adopted in so many countries of Europe to describe glasses made in Venetian style, is testimony in itself to the influence of that great glassmaking centre on design and decoration during the fifteenth, sixteenth and seventeenth centuries. Delicacy, ingenuity, richness, fragility, are all terms which could be used of the wares exported by Venice and so highly prized by their eventual owners. Nevertheless, it is interesting to see from John Greene's drawings of the glasses which he ordered from Murano about 1670 that English taste was already in favour of the less flamboyant, more conservative shapes – a conical foot, simple hollow-knopped stem and conical bowl.

English glassmakers during the last quarter of the seventeenth century could not wholly escape from Venetian influence, however, and there were many Italian glassworkers employed in this country. Consequently, Venetian decorative effects persisted until about 1700 – rope twists, used in handles and stems; wings forming the stem or incorporated in a collar round the bowl; prunts with characteristic raspberry moulding applied as buttons on the stem; trailing seen as looped threads round body or foot of a bowl; flammiform gadrooning seen in spikes leaping outwards from the bowl; 'nipt diamond waies', frequently adopted by Ravenscroft himself and seen as diamond-shaped compartments made by pinching together the metal of a bowl whilst still soft enough to be worked.

Heavy balusters

By the turn of the century, Venetian effects had been abandoned in favour of the simple, solid, pure shapes of conical bowls, well-proportioned knops and workmanlike feet with folded rims to guard against accidental chipping. It cannot be said that such glasses were never decorated but the addition of

9

1 KNOP

2 FLATTENED

3 BALL

4 ANNULAR

5 ANNULATED

6 ANGULAR

7 MUSHROOM

8 ACORN

9 CYLINDER

10 BOBBIN

11 INVERTED
BALUSTER

12 TRUE
BALUSTER

13 DROP

14 CUSHIONED

15 EGG

16 BLADED

diamond-point or wheel-engraving was so rare that it is safe to assume that their makers and purchasers alike were as completely satisfied with them then as collectors are today.

This short period, from 1685 to about 1710, produced the finest drinking glasses this country has seen, pleasing to eye, comfortable to grasp, sturdy, strong, splendidly epitomising the qualities admired by an Englishman.

Light balusters

Before the end of the first quarter of the eighteenth century experimentation or perhaps the eternal search for novelty had resulted in a diversification of bowl shapes (the conical bowl with solid base being replaced by the bell, thistle and trumpet), and a more complex stem with lighter knops which gradually replaced those, such as cylinder, mushroom, acorn and egg, which demanded ample material for their execution.

Balustroids

The trend continued from 1725 until soon after the middle of the century when the baluster stem disappeared completely, knops being separated by lengths of plain stem giving an attenuated look which reached its climax in the type known as the 'Newcastle' baluster, that favourite vehicle for wheel-engraving, in which the stem was made thinner and longer than ever, broken by delicate knops, frequently beaded but, strangely enough, producing a glass which had its own distinctive charm and elegant appeal.

Balustroids abounded and are still among the most commonly encountered glasses to be found in the dealers' hands; suffering as they do in painful comparison with their stronger predecessors they are rather despised. The types of knop found in baluster and balustroid stems are illustrated.

Moulded pedestal stems

It seems rather pedantic to retain the description 'moulded pedestal stems' for glasses now commonly referred to as 'Silesian' but the doubtful origin of the latter term and its lack of reference to a distinctive method of manufacture make it unacceptable for every reason save brevity. No doubt its introduction was more or less contemporary with the accession of George I in 1714; a small number survive in the earliest, four-sided, form bearing the legend moulded round the top of the pedestal LONG LIVE KING GEORGE. Nevertheless, the distinguishing feature is the use of a mould in making the stem, first four-sided, then six- and eight-sided and finally becoming so debased, with rounded shoulders, that the distinctive moulded characteristic almost disappears. In its four- or six-sided form this type of stem applied almost exclusively to wines but after the introduction of eight-sided moulds, especially with the addition of collars above and below, it was most frequently used in the manufacture of sweetmeats and champagnes.

Plain stems

Though plain-stemmed glasses, many of them of simple, heavy manufacture for tavern use, persist throughout the middle fifty years of the century and form the least avidly collected group, they display surprising variety. The majority have trumpet bowls, the stem often enlivened by a long tear and occasionally by the addition of collars. No problems of description are encountered save that of distinguishing between two- and three-piece glasses. In the two-piece form the bowl and stem are clearly made from the same gathering of metal, no weld or joint between bowl and stem being either visible or possible.

Air-twist stems

It would be logical to assume that the air twist developed from the tear and this may well have been the method of evolution, since air twists are also formed from air trapped in the metal during stem manufacture. Two methods seem to have been used, (i) an indentation of a squat cylinder of metal by tool or mould, covering the indentations by another coating of glass and creating the twist by drawing out and twisting until the requisite pattern and thickness were achieved, or (ii) by pricking the top of a squat cylinder with pins set into a bobbin-shaped tool and thus forming regular patterns of air bubbles which become an air twist by drawing and twisting. The latter method was employed especially in the manufacture of multiple-spiral air twists, a term occurring so frequently that the abbreviation MSAT is used.

Since it is possible to create an air twist and then, after adding metal which increases the diameter, to repeat the process, the terms 'single series' (SSAT) and 'double series' (DSAT) are used to differentiate between them.

Strangely enough, although double-series air twists were much more complicated to make, single-series twists other than the MSAT are scarcer and of more interest to the collector, the most attractive of all being the so-called 'mercury twist'. This was produced by using two flat pins in the pricking tool so that when the stem was drawn out a series of wide corkscrews was created, reflecting the light so brilliantly that they appeared to be filled with quicksilver. There are, however, so many gradations between corkscrews with almost round section and the true 'mercury twist' that no attempt is usually made to differentiate between them. Readers should be aware that 'mercury twist' is often loosely used to describe any corkscrew and should note the difference between Plates 279 and 288. When the stem contains knops – and these can be from one to five – only two types of twist occur, the MSAT and a pair of corkscrews.

Incised-twist stems

Closely related to the air twist, indeed sometimes spoken of as the 'poor man's air twist', is the incised-twist or wrythened stem. The twist can be coarse or fine and coarse twists are found in soda glass also, when they are almost always associated with a waisted bell bowl and folded foot.

Composite stems

This most attractive section contains many interesting combinations of plain stem with air or opaque twists and occasionally a mixture of all three. Haynes's[1] definition of a plain section as one which exceeds half an inch in length avoids confusion with a normal trumpet bowl above a shoulder-knopped MSAT stem. Glasses in this section are particularly and consistently well made, almost as though the extra complexity of construction demanded extra care and craftsmanship.

[1] Op. cit., p. 241.

Opaque-twist stems

The opaque twist, introduced in 1755–60 (though Francis Buckley[2] records a dated specimen of 1747) owes much to the Venetian *latticino* technique of the early seventeenth century. In English stems it was formed by the introduction of opaque-white glass rods in the stem mould, the delicate patterns being produced by drawing and twisting and repeating the process for double-series twists. The results were ingenious and charming and evidently extremely popular, thousands having survived the vicissitudes of two centuries. As with air twists the single series (SSOT) are rarer and in greater demand than the double series (DSOT).

[2] Quoted in Thorpe, op. cit., p. 213.

Mixed and colour-twist stems

Instead of opaque-white rods, opaque rods in such enamel colours as red, blue, brown, green and pink and, rarely, yellow, were introduced, usually in combination with opaque white but occasionally alone. At the time of manufacture this was seen, no doubt, as a pretty but unimportant variation; those who adopted it could never have imagined the competition for their glasses today!

Another pretty combination was achieved by mixing air and opaque twists, an air twist within an opaque in a double-series stem or vice versa; less frequently an air twist alternating with opaque white in a single series. Rarest of all is the combination of air, opaque white and colour in the same stem.

Faceted stems

Cutting of bowls and stems of drinking glasses, as well as of larger vessels was practised many years before the date given for the commencement of this period but the early examples quoted by various writers represented occasional demonstrations of the art rather than a widespread fashion. It was the development of grinding techniques in Ireland and England which facilitated the production of faceted glasses and changed many of the features which had remained constant for so long. The conical foot tended to disappear, being replaced by the flat foot, the pontil-mark being ground out; many types of bowl, the trumpet and the bell bowl especially, were abandoned because they were unsuitable for faceting; a new attraction was added to the dinner-table – drinking glasses with stems brilliantly reflecting the light and matching the cut bowls, jugs and salts and candelabra which were already popular. The stem section is normally hexagonal, containing six to eight bands of diamond or hexagonal facets. A shoulder or central knop is often seen. A less frequently encountered feature is the alternation of vertical flutes and facets or notched flutes; after 1800, however, stems comprised of vertical flutes only supersede facets. Both facets and flutes can continue over the base of bowl (very rarely over the whole surface) and appear as bridge-flutes on the foot.

By the beginning of the last quarter of the century the faceted stem had almost completely captured the market: it reigned until the early years of the nineteenth century and was the last distinctive stem form in the history of English drinking glasses: since then we have seen many styles resurrected, attenuated and debased but the Victorians, for all their inventiveness, failed to find an equally popular successor.

Rudimentary stems

Throughout the eighteenth century a wide variety of small glasses was being produced with many purposes in mind – glasses for jellies, custard, sweetmeats of all kinds, glasses for short drinks, gins and drams, small footed bowls for salt or nuts or confectionery. In many of them can be seen characteristics which allow a reasonably accurate dating; others are extremely difficult to place in a chronological sequence. One characteristic they share, however; the stem is either almost or entirely lacking, automatically excepting them from a classification based on stem formation. They have their own fascination, however, and most collectors include a selection of interesting types in their cabinets: the simple classification suggested attempts little more than an obvious and simple order and certainly does not succeed in proving an evolutionary progression.

Engraved, enamelled and gilded glasses

Any attempt at chronology has been similarly abandoned in the case of engraved and enamelled glasses, in the belief that the subject of the decoration is of most importance.

3 The Bowl

Shapes

Within each stem group a further subdivision is possible according to type of bowl, this being the most distinctive feature after the stem. Its importance in the description of a glass is obvious, making necessary a key to bowl nomenclature. The twelve shapes most commonly encountered are illustrated.

During the heavy baluster period the pointed round-funnel and conical bowls with solid base predominated, bell and thistle shapes making up the remainder. The bell bowl persisted throughout all periods until the introduction of the faceted stem when the ovoid bowl became popular, no doubt because its shape was more suitable for bridge cutting.

The drawn trumpet bowl is particularly associated with plain stem glasses and the ogee and round funnel with opaque twists; similarly incised twists are mostly found in combination with a waisted bell bowl or a trumpet bowl. Otherwise there is a fascinating diversity of combinations of bowl and stem.

Many bowl shapes will be seen in elongated or waisted form, with everted or folded rim and with solid base. The commoner variations are: waisted bell or bucket bowls; solid base to conical, bell and thistle bowls; variations in depth and shape of the pan in pan-topped bowls, giving rise to such terms as 'saucer-topped' and 'cup-topped'.

Faceting often disguises the original shape making recognition difficult and there are other drinking glasses of the late eighteenth and early nineteenth centuries, especially rummers, found in many tantalising shapes. Although they are derived from the earlier styles exact terminology has not been developed to describe their precise shapes.

Decoration

Five forms of applied decoration are found on the bowl – diamond-point, wheel-engraving, enamelling, gilding and cutting – in addition to forms of

15

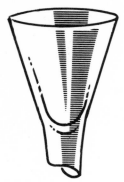

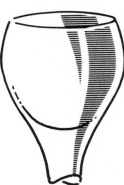

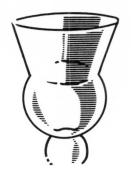

I FUNNEL
(*or CONICAL*)

2 BELL

3 THISTLE

4 TRUMPET

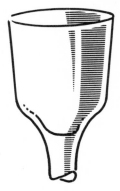

5 ROUND FUNNEL

6 POINTED ROUND
FUNNEL

7 OGEE

8 SQUARE BUCKET

9 CUP

10 OVOID

11 HEXAGONAL

12 DOUBLE OGEE
(*Variant of
PAN-TOPPED
ROUND FUNNEL*)

13 PAN-TOPPED ROUND
FUNNEL

14 STEPPED OR 'LYNN'

16

moulding and tooling which are part of the initial process of manufacture. Another decorative method, acid etching, must be mentioned but need not be enlarged upon as it was not a serious technique during the eighteenth century.

DIAMOND POINT Engraving scratched on the bowl by means of a diamond point is an ancient decorative technique particularly suited to the hard metal of soda glass. It is found on English glasses of the late sixteenth century (Verzelini goblets for example) and on such seventeenth-century specimens as the Exeter flute and the Royal Oak goblet, if indeed these can be regarded as of English manufacture, which many writers question. It was a technique less well suited to lead glass and during the eighteenth century found its exponents mostly among amateurs who wished to inscribe their own simple marks of ownership. Notable exceptions are the small group of 'Amen' glasses and a few other Jacobites. The diamond was also used for stipple-engraving, the chief exponents of this difficult technique being the Dutchmen David Wolff and Frans Greenwood who sometimes signed their work.

WHEEL-ENGRAVING The equally ancient technique of wheel-engraving, however, found its ideal medium in lead glass and was applied to many thousands of English glasses after about 1725. In many cases the decoration is nothing more than a simple floral border – advertised by sellers as 'flowered' glass – but in other cases the craftsmanship is of great delicacy and highest quality, low relief sculpture being exploited to produce light and shade. From the frequency with which these superlative engravings are accompanied by legends in Dutch and from our knowledge of individual Dutch engravers, it has been concluded that most, if not all, of the work of this quality was done in Holland, certainly the home of the renowned Jacob Sang whose signature appears on the foot or pontil-mark of some of the finest work of this period.

Flowered glasses, Jacobites, Williamites, Frigate glasses and those with simple inscriptions were almost certainly engraved in England since most of them demanded only modest skill and hardly justified the cost of transport to Holland. Surprisingly little is known, however, about English engravers or centres where engraving was practised until after 1800; after that date English craftsmanship was able to match the best in the world.

ENAMELLING Although the art of decorating glass in enamel colours, fused to the surface by firing, had been practised in Islamic countries in medieval times and in Venice and Germany in the sixteenth and seventeenth centuries, no attempt to pursue this art in England seems to have been made until after 1750. Dossie,[1] writing in 1758 says 'The practice of enamel-painting is of late introduction amongst us'; by 1760 it seems to have been flourishing in two centres at least, Bristol and Newcastle. Michael Edkins was certainly working in Bristol as a decorator of porcelain from about 1762, also painting glass, Delftware and even coaches in order to maintain his extraordinary family of thirty-three children.[2] Newcastle was the adopted home of the Beilby family, two, or possibly three, of whom were actively engaged in enamel decoration of drinking glasses from about 1760 to 1780. Some of their work is signed and, thanks to Thomas Bewick,[3] we have a detailed account of their activities from 1767 to about 1778 when the brother and sister chiefly concerned, William and Mary Beilby, seem to have left Newcastle for Fifeshire.

It seems reasonable to assume that the glasses decorated by the Beilbys were made locally, especially since the majority are opaque-white twists

[1] Dossie, R. *Handmaid to the arts*, 2 vols. 1758.

[2] Owen, H. *Two centuries of ceramic art in Bristol*, 1873, pp 330–2.

[3] Bewick, T. *Memoir of Thomas Bewick*, 1862.

characterised by a limited range of double-series patterns. The enamelling, too, has a uniformity of style and subject which allows one to attribute glasses to the Beilbys with reasonable certainty. Most work was in white enamel, the designs ranging from simple floral borders through a series of typically eighteenth-century scenes – shooting, fishing, Classical ruins, shepherds and shepherdesses – but occasionally more elaborate designs in a full range of enamel colours were undertaken. Their most spectacular, and probably William Beilby's earliest work, is seen in a series of goblets bearing the royal arms and commemorating the birth of the Prince of Wales (later George IV); these have become known as 'Royal Beilbys'.

It is not reasonable to assume, however, that all enamelling in white on clear glass was carried out by them, any more than one can assert that Michael Edkins was responsible for all enamel decoration on coloured glass. There are several glasses, for example, bearing enamelled portraits of the Young Pretender which can hardly be by the same hand as the Royal Beilbys! No doubt future research will reveal evidence of other enamellers of the period even though it is noticeably lacking at present.

GILDING Many glasses show traces of oil-gilding, that is, gilding applied by means of an oil adhesive. It was not fixed and was therefore relatively impermanent; however there are many examples extant on which the gilding is still intact, which suggests that some decorators mastered the art of firing. The patterns seen most frequently are fruiting vine decoration on wine glasses and hops and barley on ales. No doubt enamellers did their own gilding; there is little evidence of gilding specialists except Absolon at Great Yarmouth towards the end of the century and James Giles working at Bristol at about the same time. Giles's work reached a very high standard: he decorated decanters and bottles, usually of blue glass but sometimes of green or white, with exotic birds, fruit, landscapes and figures in gold with occasional use of coloured enamels. The Jacobs family worked in the same city, applying geometrical and floral designs to coloured glass. Neither Giles nor Jacobs appears to have decorated wine glasses but Absolon gilded rummers and goblets with such legends as A PRESENT FROM YARMOUTH or SUCCESS TO FARMING. His work is frequently signed under the foot.

CUTTING Apart from a few dated or engraved examples whose provenance or actual dates of cutting have been questioned, faceted English drinking glasses are not known before 1750 and there are very few which can be attributed with any certainty to a date earlier than 1760. The example quoted by Hartshorne in *Old English glasses*, Plate 47, and discussed by Haynes is reproduced as Plate 610; it could well be of German origin or faceted later than the period 1729–51 when Frederick Louis, eldest son of George II, was Prince of Wales. Stylistically the glass belongs to the first quarter of the century.

The Excise Act of 1745 encouraged the production of lighter glasses with thinner walls unsuited for cutting and the 1777 Act doubled the rate of tax. In 1780 free trade was permitted between England and Ireland. These fiscal measures had two effects: between 1745 and 1780 English glasses became lighter, with thin bowls unsuited to cutting and faceting: after 1780 many English glassmakers moved their works and their workmen to Ireland, producing there the heavier glass vessels which could then be shipped to England without tax or import duty. Cut glass became the vogue and drinking glasses and sweetmeats with faceted stems and cut bowls shared in the new fashion.

The faceted stem is often associated with additional engraving and cutting such as scalloping of the rim of the foot, scale-cutting of the bowl and decorating the bowl with stars and polished circles in a band below the rim as well as the engraving and stippling described earlier.

MOULDING The use of moulds in the manufacture of drinking glasses has already been remarked upon in describing moulded pedestal stems. It was a technique applied most attractively to glasses with other stem formations also, occurring most frequently at the base of wine glasses in the form of ribs or flutes or honeycomb moulding and frequently extending over the whole bowl as honeycomb or panel moulding, the decoration being repeated on the foot. This more extensive moulding is found most often on sweetmeats. Wrythen moulding, that is vertically moulded flutes given a twist by the glassblower, is found in late seventeenth-century ales and persists in similar glasses throughout the eighteenth century.

4 The Foot

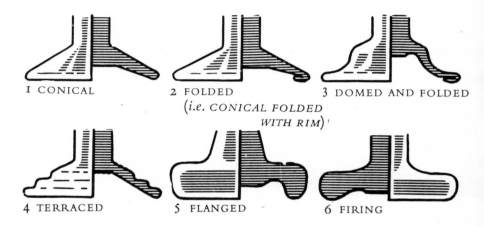

1 CONICAL   2 FOLDED   3 DOMED AND FOLDED
                (*i.e.* CONICAL FOLDED
                      WITH RIM)

4 TERRACED   5 FLANGED   6 FIRING

In the formation of the foot there is both variation and evolution. Its function is to give adequate support to the glass, allowing it to stand firmly on the table, a good general rule being that the diameter of the foot should at least equal that of the bowl. To this rule there are exceptions in both directions; massive feet are seen often enough to make one suspect that many glasses have been trimmed to remove chips; occasionally a glass with a large bowl has a considerably smaller foot, but if it is original (the rim folded for example) there can be no argument.

The shape of the foot is dictated by two other factors, the need to protect the table from the pontil-mark and any special function which demands modification. Throughout the first three-quarters of the eighteenth century the pontil-mark was rough and a conical foot necessary to give the required clearance. Until 1730 or 1740 a folded foot was normal, its abandonment being difficult to understand. The double thickness of a foot at the rim gives splendid protection against chipping, is an attractive decorative feature and used so little additional metal that saving weight could hardly be the reason for rejecting it. Perhaps folded feet were too robust and in their disuse we see an early example of built-in obsolescence?

The next significant change came about 1775 with the introduction of faceted stems, themselves the product of improved cutting and polishing techniques. Since stems could be ground so accurately and so cheaply, why not be rid altogether of the troublesome pontil-mark? Once it had been ground out there was no need for the conical foot, the firmer flat foot being preferable. It has become axiomatic that every glass of the eighteenth century will have either a pontil-mark or the evidence of grinding out: it is not equally true that every glass with a pontil-mark belongs to that century for there was a mid-nineteenth-century revival and there are many twentieth-century forgeries.

'Firing glasses', so called from the custom of rapping the table in concert after drinking a toast, thereby making a noise like the firing of a pistol, demanded sturdy feet, considerably thicker than usual and are normally appended to dram glasses; terracing allowed extra strength to be built into the construction of the foot, occasionally becoming such a decorative feature that it is appropriately described as a 'beehive' foot.

The domed foot is an alternative to the conical form frequently occurring in the first half of the century and usually with a folded rim; the helmet shape is a rare, more pronounced form of domed foot but is not to be confused with the exceptionally high dome characteristic of some baluster stems of German origin. Dram glasses are seen with flanged as well as firing feet; bonnet glasses are found with a variety of moulded, scalloped and square feet.

The square foot which became popular in the early years of the nineteenth century marked the first significant innovation after the ground-out pontil made the flat foot possible. It is found especially on rummers in combination with a moulded dome giving the characteristic 'lemon-squeezer' effect but is also seen on dwarf ales, salts and the bonnet glasses or Monteiths already mentioned.

5 Dating

Haynes's chronology has not been seriously challenged since the second edition of *Glass through the Ages* appeared in 1959 and it has been adopted here with very slight modifications. The periods quoted are simply those during which the styles were current since it would be manifestly impossible to say exactly when the first and last specimens were made. Dating is, indeed, an extremely difficult exercise and it will be useful to examine the evidence upon which a system can be based.

Few glasses bear a manufacturer's mark but some are found, notably the raven's head seal of Ravenscroft (accurately placing such glasses within the period May 1677 to May 1681) and the engraved marks on Waterford, Cork, Belfast and other Irish glass. Especially when the period of a factory's activities is brief, the dates of its products can be placed within those limits; when it survived for many decades and constantly repeated the same patterns, as was the case in the nineteenth century, such evidence is not very helpful.

[1] Reproduced in Hartshorne, op. cit., Plate 30, and in Thorpe, op. cit, Fig. 16.

[2] Buckley, F. *Old English glass*, 1925.

[3] Vol. 5, p. 300 (July 1928).

Documentary evidence is of great importance. John Green's designs[1] for glasses ordered from the firm Allesio Morelli in Venice between 1667 and 1672 are preserved in the Sloane MSS. in the British Museum and give us a clear indication of the styles current at that time. Francis Buckley's research[2] into advertisements appearing in eighteenth-century newspapers provides further information about the types of glass being sold, but unfortunately such general terms are employed that few inferences can be drawn. Thomas Bett's accounts, published by Buckley in *Glass*[3] are typical of another useful source. From the entry 'Wormed Egg Bowl Wine', for example, we learn that Thomas Bett was selling air-twist ('wormed') wine glasses at seven shillings per dozen; from another entry in 1757 we find that 'Enamelled Shank Flutes', that is ale glasses with opaque-twist stems, were already being made.

Engravings on glasses can give an approximate date if it is borne in mind that events and personalities continued to be of public interest for many years and that engravings of them could be applied to earlier glasses. Some engravings include a date and these are particularly valuable; the series of glasses, diamond-scratch engraved with descriptive scenes, mottoes and dates within the period of Verzelini's monopoly (1575–91) have been accepted as the products of his factory and as bearing contemporary dates; there are also glasses signed and dated by the engraver, providing a reliable indication of the date when the glasses were made; similarly Jacob Sang's signature can be linked with the dates between which he is known to have been working.

Such considerations do not apply, however, to all dated glasses; Williamites bearing the date 1690 are simply commemorating the Battle of the Boyne fought in that year, but the glasses were made half a century later; Jacobite engravings give no indication of date and continued to be made during the whole period from 1730 to 1800. Inferences can be drawn though, from the Frigate glasses, for the dates when the ships were operating are known and also those of their captains, so that we can safely date to 1757, for example, the opaque twists which were invariably used below bowls invoking success to the Eagle Frigate.

Similarly, we can link together the opaque twists which characterise the vast majority of the glasses decorated in enamel colours by the Beilbys at Newcastle on Tyne with the dates (c. 1760–78) during which they are known to have been engaged in this art. It is extremely likely that these glasses were manufactured locally and if so would be made in the Dagnia Glasshouse under the direction of John Williams or by Airey Cookson & Co. – thereby approaching an exact provenance for one group of glasses with more probability than any other group except the sealed glasses of Ravenscroft. Beilby decoration is found on other types of glasses – Silesian stems, air twists and, very rarely, incised twists – so that the possibility of earlier glasses being decorated to special order must not be overlooked.

Glasses and goblets are frequently encountered which contain coins sealed in the base. Rarely do these provide any evidence of date, the only fact proved being the date *after* which the glass must have been made. Sometimes the coins may be regarded as newly minted; Thorpe accepts the 1678[1] coin in a goblet in the British Museum as an accurate date but another glass, then in Wilfred Buckley's collection, he dates five years later than the 1680[2] coin it contains, whilst a third, in the Victoria and Albert Museum (Rees Price Collection), he evidently feels is considerably later than the 1664[3] coin it contains since he simply describes it as 'late 17th century'. Examples of Jacobite glasses of the eighteenth century which contain Stuart coins are well known and this use of coins a century earlier than the glasses themselves can be easily understood.

An interesting dating technique which has been exploited by Chambon[4] derives from the almost photographic attention to detail observed by Dutch painters of the seventeenth century. He has examined paintings of interiors and of still-life and has been able to show the forms of many glasses in use (not necessarily manufactured then but of no later date) at the time of the painting's execution. It is a line of inquiry which might possibly yield useful results if applied to English paintings and drawings; the well-known painting by Kneller, now in the National Portrait Gallery, of two members of the Kit-Kat Club taking wine from glasses which have derived their name from the Club, is an obvious example of material which might well merit further investigation along the lines already pursued by Frank Davis.[5]

[1] Thorpe, op. cit., p. 128.

[2] Ibid., Plate xxix.

[3] Ibid., Plate lxxvii.

[4] Chambon, R. *History of Belgian glass from the 2nd century to the present*, 1955.

[5] Davis, Frank. 'Kneller portrait illustrates fashions in 18th century glass', *Illustrated London News*, Jan 8th 1966, p. 27.

To conclude, then, it must be accepted that dating of eighteenth-century glasses on stylistic grounds will be vague: few thoroughly documented specimens are known and styles overlapped for many years. Nevertheless, the periods are sufficiently well defined to enable one to provide a workable chronology even though it is doubtful whether many writers would have the temerity to agree with Thorpe's statement that 'It is, I think, possible to date most glasses within ten years, and a good many as near as five.'

6 Values

Such are the fluctuations of market prices that any attempt to suggest, other than in the broadest terms, what one might expect to pay for drinking glasses would be confusing and misleading. During the past ten years prices have risen with a rapidity which collectors of the 1940s and 1950s find quite extraordinary and necessitate considerable caution in predicting the limits which will be reached in the next decade.

Museum directors as well as private collectors, interested in acquiring representative examples of eighteenth-century craftsmanship have begun to realise that the once-plentiful and rather despised drinking glasses of the period are rapidly disappearing from the dealers' cabinets and that the rarer types are increasingly difficult to find. Nevertheless, their prices are still (1971) considerably lower than those of any other craft product of the century – silver, porcelain, furniture and even fine earthenware – which are now beyond the reach of most purses. Plain-stemmed drinking glasses and the commoner opaque twists, however, can still be acquired for less than twenty pounds and jelly glasses may well be picked up for less than five.

At the other extreme it is possible to pay four figures for a superbly engraved or enamelled goblet and hundreds of pounds for a simple wine glass with a colour-twist stem: it is clear that the collector needs some guide to comparative values. Perhaps the most satisfactory indication of prices can be found by reference to a single sale since this indicates the date on which a glass had a definite market value though it must be borne in mind that if bought by a dealer it would retail at 20 or 30 per cent more.

The sale at Sotheby's of the Walter F. Smith collection was by far the most extensive and important of recent years, extending over four days in 1967 and 1968. Formed by the late Walter F. Smith Junior, of Trenton, New Jersey, acting upon expert advice, it contained superb examples in every category.

Among the early glasses there were numerous wrythen ale and wine glasses with flammiform and pincered decoration of the bowl and winged or baluster stems (Plates 25 and 553) which brought between £100 and £400, though £520 was paid for one with more pronounced Venetian character. A bobbin-knopped sweetmeat glass of about 1685 sold for £190 but a patch-stand or small tazza of the same period with a stem composed of eight graduated knops brought only £85. Another glass of this type but with a gadrooned bowl of goblet or mead-glass proportions (Plate 174) brought £470, however, and others of similar character realised from £85 to £300.

Heavy balusters dating to about 1700 hardly failed to exceed £100 for any perfect specimens and the rarer knops realised much higher prices. Examples of the commoner inverted baluster stems (Plate 28) realised £220 or £250; an angular knop (Plate 38) made £150, a drop knop (Plate 47) £135, another with a heavier knop £290; an annulated knop (Plate 42) with a slight chip on the rim made £150. The rarer knops referred to are the acorn, mushroom, cylinder and egg knops; acorn knops realised £400 and £550 (Plate 60); mushroom knops £180, £130, £200, £260 (Plates 55, 56 and 57) whilst for one magnificent glass with an acorn above a mushroom knop £520 was paid; early cylinder knops were generally more expensive still, £300, £460, £620 and, for a slightly heavier specimen than Plate 61, £310. Egg knops (Plate 63) are the rarest category of all, this great collection containing only one and that a modest six inches in height: it brought £460.

Silesian stems were made from about 1710, when they were four-sided and supported a funnel bowl, until well into the second half of the century when six or eight sides were the fashion and the sharp moulding had become rounded and debased. Of them all the rarest and most expensive is the four-sided stem which bears in moulded relief, a word on each side, the legend GOD SAVE KING GEORGE (Plate 188); the only example in the Smith sale realised £620. In striking contrast was the cut-glass sweetmeat with an eight-sided Silesian stem which brought only £22: a feature of the sale was the relatively low price realised by most sweetmeats, even the finest scarcely exceeding £100.

Not many balustroids were included unless they had the additional attraction of engraving and these will be referred to later. A few examples, however, will give some idea of prices obtaining for a class of considerable interest to those forming less ambitious collections. The inverted baluster was a popular eighteenth-century feature and one typical glass with bell bowl, IB knop, basal knop and folded foot (Plate 73) realised £35; another similar glass but with an annulated knop above the IB (Plate 99) made £42.

Plain-stemmed glasses, unengraved, realised the lowest prices of all, as one would expect, two drawn trumpets (Plate 223) making only £28 for the pair. A cordial, being rarer, (Plate 249) made £45 and had the added feature of a domed foot; a ratafia, perfectly plain but even rarer still sold for £145! A toasting glass (Plates 221 and 222) realised £30 and the unusual feature of a double collar below a trumpet bowl (Plate 258) attracted a final bid of only £22. Ale glasses, if plain, made £18 for one and £30 for a pair but another specimen with tall round-funnel bowl engraved with hops and barley and a domed and folded foot, made £42.

Glasses with air-twist stems normally command relatively modest prices unless the twist is exceptionally rare or the number of knops more than three. A cordial with the rare combination of an eleven-ply spiral band outside a single mercurial corkscrew reached £95 and another cordial with deceptive trumpet bowl and a double-series twist made £130. A glass with five knops and a bucket bowl (Plate 334 has similar stem but a bell bowl with

26

Jacobite engraving) sold for £290 and one with four knops (Plate 333) and a domed foot made £300. A more common type of multiple-spiral air twist – an ale glass engraved with hops and barley on a two-knopped stem (Plate 324) – sold for £75 and this price was about average for air twists with some particularly attractive feature.

Next to plain stems the opaque twist with an ordinary ogee or round-funnel bowl is the commonest and least expensive. Features which made them more attractive were cordial bowls, one with a round funnel (Plate 424) bringing £65; another with a double-ogee bowl and a mixture of an air spiral cable and spiral opaque thread made £150 and a ratafia (Plate 468) with normal double twist but a deceptive bowl sold for the even higher price of £175. At the lower end of the scale was £34 for a simple round-funnel bowl with a double-series twist, the bowl being engraved with fruiting vine and a moth: £50 and £55 were paid for sweetmeats with double-ogee bowls and single and double opaque twists respectively.

Closely allied with opaque twists and almost always in association with them are colour twists, one of the most desirable classes of eighteenth-century drinking glasses and one of the classes most fraught with danger, for high prices have encouraged late copies and many genuine glasses of the period are in soda metal and of continental origin. Red, green and blue are found most often and are very desirable in good strong colours; yellow (canary) is the most sought after and any good specimens bring very high prices. One with a pair of opaque-white corkscrews enclosing a yellow spiral centre (Plate 516) realised £300 and was the only canary twist in the sale; a firing glass (Plate 505) with alternate white and green threads outside a spiral gauze reached £270 and a glass with engraved bell bowl and the rare combination of spiral air cable and single pale green spiral thread (Plate 499) brought £240. An unusual glass with slender trumpet bowl and a stem comprising an opaque-white spiral thread outside an opaque-white lace twist edged with red and green (Plate 513 but this edged with red and turquoise) made £400, the highest price in this category except for a fine goblet with a white corkscrew edged with orange and green which exceeded it by £20 and a candlestick with an opaque-white lace twist encircled by a blue and white spiral thread which realised £1,350. None failed to exceed £100, a typical and more frequently encountered combination of bell bowl, opaque-white corkscrew spiral edged with brown and green (Plate 510 but this also has a pair of white spiral threads) bringing £120.

Faceted stems, dating to the last quarter of the century and for that reason in less demand realised comparatively modest prices, unless enhanced by engraving or rare bowl formation. A set of three, cut all over the bowls with diamond facets which continued down the stems (Plate 533) made only £50 and a cordial with double-ogee bowl (Plate 523 but this is a wine) brought £45. Among the sweetmeats the faceted examples brought the lowest prices, one with scalloped rim and knopped stem (Plate 548 but this has an ogee bowl) realising £28.

Finally, there is the large class of engraved and enamelled glasses which, if of good quality, bring uniformly high prices, whatever the stem formation. Although this sale did not contain a parallel the addition of a stipple-engraved portrait by David Wolff to a single-faceted stem (Plate 730), for example, would increase its value at least tenfold and probably twentyfold. The most superb eighteenth-century engraving was done in Holland, many consignments of Newcastle glasses being shipped there for engraving before sale either on the Continent or in England. It would appear that most of them were to satisfy specific commissions – especially for family coats of arms – rather than as speculative risks by the glass-dealer. Large quantities of English glasses, however, especially those with tall, slender knopped stems associated with Newcastle, remained in Holland and were engraved for Dutch customers with a wide variety of scenes and mottoes of their own country – canals, gardens, ships, drinking scenes, portraits, emblems of friendship, arms of the House of Orange, Dutch cities and private families, executed with incomparable skill and not infrequently signed. So many specimens were included in the Smith sale that it is impracticable to review them here and a few typical examples must suffice. Generally prices ranged from just below £100 to £1,100 for a portrait glass of Prince Charles Edward beneath the motto AUDIENTOR IBO (Plate 642) and £1,800 for the rarest engraving of all, an 'Amen' glass (Plate 607), so called because they were characterised by the royal cypher JR and, in diamond point, either two or four verses of the Jacobite version of the National Anthem:

God Save the King I pray,
God bless the King I pray,
God Save the King;
Send Him Victorious
Happy and Glorious
Soon to Reign Over us
God Save the King.

God Bless the Prince of Wales
The true-born Prince of Wales
Sent us by Thee
Grant us one favour more
The King for to restore
As Thou has done before
The Familie.

God Bless the subjects all
And save both great and small
in every station
That will bring home the King
Who has best right to reign
It is the only thing
Can save the Nation.

God Save the Church I pray
And Bless the Church I pray
Pure to remain
Against all Heresie
And Whigs Hypocrisie
Who strive maliciously
Her to defame.

Less exotic Jacobites also commanded good prices, a typical example having a trumpet bowl engraved with a rose and two buds, an oak leaf and the motto FIAT (Plate 636) on a multiple-spiral air-twist stem which sold for £240. A very attractive and rarely seen example of the 'Boscobel oak' Jacobite on a Kit-Kat stem (Plate 628) made £440. Of the two Williamites in the sale one was extraordinary in that the engraving (on a bell bowl above a true baluster stem) showed a continuous scene of William III with cavalry and infantry crossing the River Boyne in the middle of which was a riderless horse. Above the scene was, in script, IN GLORIOUS MEMORY OF THE CROSSING and below it the date (of the battle, not the glass), 1690. It compares with Plates 618 and 616 which are the more usual representations of the subject. The Smith glass made £420 despite a small chip in the foot.

Among the portrait glasses was one with an engraving in profile of the Duke of Cumberland with his full title engraved round it to form a circular medallion (Plate 661). The Duke's career as a military commander was erratic but when he defeated the Jacobites at Culloden he was a popular hero and these glasses would have been used to drink many a toast in his name. This example sold for £170 and the same price was obtained for a portrait glass of Sarah Siddons (Plate 668).

Many Newcastle light balusters are found engraved with the arms of Dutch cities, this sale including specimens with the arms of Amsterdam (£220), of Holland (stipple-engraved) (£300), Rotterdam (£240), Delft (£170) and Overyssel (£170) (Plate 716). As will be seen, stipple-engraved glasses bring particularly high prices, whatever the stem formation, authentic specimens by such artists as David Wolff (Plate 730) or Frans Greenwood always arousing great interest; a glass attributed to another stipple-engraver, J. Van den Blyk, sold for £300.

Privateer glasses were engraved to commemorate the success of privately owned frigates which, in the mid 1700s harassed the French to great effect. Most privateers sailed from Bristol and the most famous of all was the Eagle Frigate commanded by Captain Dibden (*London Chronicle*, Apr 11th 1757) and later by Captain Knill. The fact that they are associated with an opaque-white twist comprising a pair of spiral gauzes (Plates 676, 678 and 679) suggests that they were made by a glasshouse in Bristol. This sale yielded one of the rarest engravings SUCCESS TO THE LYON PRIVATEER of which only one other example is known and was bought for £500.

Enamelled glasses form another attractive and expensive section and enamelled glass, in the absence of indications to the contrary, is synonymous with the work of the Beilby family. The art of enamelling, usually in white but, exceptionally, in a full range of colours for the armorial and signed royal goblets which are probably the most highly prized of all eighteenth-century glasses, was perfected by William and Mary, two of the seven children of William Beilby Senior who was a jeweller and silversmith in Durham. The family moved to Newcastle shortly before William Senior died in 1765. Another brother, Ralph, a skilled engraver of heraldic subjects, no doubt supervised the accuracy of the armorial designs.

The bulk of their work, however, consisted in the decoration of small wines (most frequently ogee or round-funnel bowls on double-series opaque-white twist stems, supporting the theory that these were stock lines of the glasshouses in the Newcastle area) with simple floral designs or charming country scenes with shepherds and shepherdesses tending their flocks; another series depicted such sports as skating and wildfowling, representations of Classical ruins forming a further large group. Although opaque twist stems are most frequently found in association with enamelling, it is found occasionally on air twists, Newcastle light balusters, plain stems, incised twists and even Silesian stems. No important specimens were included in this sale but consistently high prices were realised for even the simplest decoration; a band of fruiting vine on a very ordinary opaque-twist wine glass made £95 (Plate 789, but this has a bell bowl instead of a round funnel) and £250 was paid for a goblet with plain stem and an ogee bowl decorated in white enamel with a growing vine (Plate 779 shows the identical design on a dram glass).

As a rough guide to 1969 prices the following table might be useful but should be regarded only as an indication of price levels. Rarity of bowl formation, addition of engraving or enamelling or an unusual stem feature can considerably increase their value; conversely, defects such as chips on rim or foot will inevitably reduce their value.

Under £10	Jelly glasses, wines after 1800, rummers.
£10–£20	Plain-stemmed glasses with drawn trumpet or bell bowl.
£20–£30	Opaque twists, faceted stems, balustroids with simple knops; unknopped multiple-spiral air twists.
£30–£40	Air twists with more interesting twists and single-knopped multiple-spiral air twists; balustroids with a series of simple knops; Silesian stemmed and faceted sweetmeats; opaque twists with knops.
£40–£60	Air twists with two knops; incised twists, engraved rummers and goblets, sweetmeats with knopped stems.
£60–£100	Ratafias and cordials; sweetmeats with attractive features; 'Newcastle' light balusters and air twists with some engraving; glasses with very simple enamel decoration; light balusters with good knops – Kit-Kat, annulated, etc.; wine glasses with Silesian stem; mead glasses, early wrythen ales.
£100–£200	Heavy balusters; colour twists; attractively engraved 'Newcastle' balusters and air twists; Jacobites; Beilby enamelled glasses; good ratafias; Lynn glasses; sweetmeats with heavy knops.
£200–£400	Rare heavy balusters – cylinder, acorn, mushroom; bobbin knops; important Jacobite and Williamite engravings; stipple engraving; armorial engravings; rare colour twists; air twists with more than three knops.
£400 and over	Superb cylinder, acorn and egg knops; signed Dutch engravings; superb enamelled glasses; rare colour twists; rare Jacobites; Anglo-Venetian glasses; perry or cider glasses; 'Amen' glasses; Privateers.

7 Reproductions, Soda Glasses and Forgeries

Books cannot be infallible guides: they serve as a valuable introduction to a subject and can impart a great deal of useful information. In most subjects connoted by 'Applied arts', however, they should lead to handling of the specimens themselves, a maxim certainly true of glass. No amount of reading can completely equip one to distinguish between the genuine and the spurious, between the original and its copy. Nevertheless, photography does help to bridge the gap between verbal description and specimen: to find an illustration which closely parallels a glass which is offered for sale encourages the prospective purchaser to treat the offer seriously and to make further inquiries. Even from photographs one can learn to look suspiciously upon glasses with a very high domed foot or upon specimens purporting to date to about 1700 which do not have a folded rim.

Such facts will soon be apparent to the collector with only modest experience: it is by no means so easy to recognise the glasses of the mid-nineteenth century, made after the patterns of the eighteenth century, complete with pontil-mark, folded foot and decorative twists and intended to demonstrate the glassmaker's mastery of his craft. The first differentiating characteristic is design, for the glassmaker of 1851 has unconsciously absorbed the feeling of his period and his trumpet bowl will tend to flare out in sympathy with its flamboyance; the second lies in construction, the 1851 glass being markedly freer from the slight imperfections, the stresses and striations and tool marks to be seen in glasses of a century earlier.

Fakes and forgeries

Photography will not completely protect the collector from the forgeries, many of them imported from the Continent, which are the inevitable consequence of rising prices. Hundreds of these have appeared in this country of recent years and many dealers and collectors have been deceived. Passing them on to the antique trade has become a highly developed sales technique, usually following a familiar pattern. A country gentleman in well-worn tweeds enters an antique shop and asks whether there would be any interest in a few old glasses which he has in a shopping-basket. He is clearing up the estate of an aunt and has found half a dozen in a cupboard. They looked rather old and might be worth a few pounds. The dealer releases them from the amateurish packing and to his delight finds that they are a set of mixed twists – cotton and air – very desirable and selling at upwards of forty pounds each. The country gentleman wonders whether they would be worth five pounds apiece, the glasses have pontil-mark, folded foot and striated bowls and the dealer is only too ready to conclude the purchase at the suggested price.

It is not long before he discovers that the glasses are virtually worthless but before then he may well have sold some to unsuspecting collectors – a friend of mine keeps a row of his 'mistakes' in the cloakroom – and either his purse or his reputation will have suffered. Where has he made his mistake? He certainly could not have learned to detect such fakes from photographs, but even a slight experience of handling genuine glasses would have taught him that these were much too light in weight and that they lacked the ring, colour and quality of lead glass. Photographs might have warned him that these were too good to be true, for folded feet are only infrequently found with air twists, very rarely indeed with opaque twists and not at all with mixed twists. Finally, he ought to have been very suspicious about any set of glasses of that date. Fortunately forgers frequently overreach themselves!

Soda glasses

Mention of weight and ring leads to a brief consideration of another type of glass which comprises neither copies nor fakes but which sometimes confuses the inexperienced collector. This is soda glass, light in weight, the metal containing seeds and blemishes and usually associated with small, poor-quality versions of lead glasses. Most stem formations can be found in soda glass except mixed twists and faceted stems, the Silesian and coarse incised-twist stems being most frequently encountered; it is thought that these glasses were made for export: they were certainly intended for a cheaper market. There should be little difficulty in recognising soda metal but in case of doubt physical and chemical tests are possible. Since glass fluoresces under ultra-violet light according to the elements of its composition, a distinction is easily seen between lead and soda glass, the former emitting a barely discernible blue light, the latter having a yellow content clearly seen on the rim. The chemical test demands extremely careful application. If a minute spot of hydrofluoric acid is applied to an unimportant part of the glass such as the pontil-mark and a second spot of sulphide of ammonia is superimposed the reaction will produce either a black or a white mark; black indicates the presence of lead, white the presence of soda. The chemicals should be washed off immediately after the test, and the hydrofluoric acid which is corrosive and highly dangerous should be handled and stored with great care.

Such tests are not normally required but there are cases such as colour twists, for example, where differentiation between a genuine lead glass and its contemporary continental counterpart or modern reproduction is all-important in determining its value. Fakes and forgeries do not always involve the metal of the glass but are usually related to value; whenever prices become exceptionally high the forger is quick to take advantage of demand; heavy balusters, mixed and colour twists, Jacobite, Williamite and 'Amen' glasses all need to be examined expertly before purchase. Engraving is all too easily applied to genuine glasses of the correct type but recent engraving is raw and white and the skill of the forger is rarely equal to the exact reproduction of the work of the eighteenth-century craftsman.

Repaired glasses

A number of firms specialise in the repair of broken glasses and are so skilful that it is extremely difficult to detect the replacement of a broken bowl with another of the same period or to be sure that stem, foot and bowl are parts of the original glass. The important test is that of balance and grace; ugly glasses were rare in the eighteenth century. Many glasses have been slightly altered to disguise a chip on the rim of either bowl or foot and until recently such repairs have reduced the value to less than half. Even today imperfect specimens are shunned by many collectors but they find a much readier market than ten years ago, presumably among collectors who can no longer afford the very high prices of the rarer types in perfect condition. Most repairs fall into two categories – trimming or flattening. The only remedy for a chip on the rim of the bowl is to remove a sufficient depth by grinding down. This can alter the balance of the glass and can also be detected by the elimination of the rounded contour of the original rim caused by reheating the sheared-off bowl in the mouth of the furnace. This was necessary for pleasant drinking and will be found in all eighteenth-century glasses in original condition. A sharp, ground-off edge is evidence either of repair or later date. Chips on the foot can be treated in the same way and if the chip is large enough the reduction in diameter of the foot can make the glass look top-heavy; if only one side of the foot is ground down the stem will no longer be in the centre. The normal rule that the radius of the foot should not vary and that its diameter should at least equal that of the bowl is a good guide. Alternatively, if the chip is on the underside of the foot only it can be removed by flattening, that is by polishing it out. Such flats are readily seen by examination in a good light – indeed the difference in thickness will be felt simply by passing the rim of the foot through thumb and finger.

Notes on the Plates

Descriptions

Descriptions of the glasses follow a regular pattern, each entry being divided into eight parts which are always enumerated in the same order.

- (*a*) Purpose of glass (wine, cordial, ale, etc.)
- (*b*) The bowl (shape, moulding, decoration, engraving)
- (*c*) The stem (knops in order from the top, the outer twist followed by the inner in the case of double-series twists)
- (*d*) The foot (shape, if other than conical, moulding, decoration)
- (*e*) Height in inches
- (*f*) Approximate date
- (*g*) Provenance (if other than English) and Collections (where known)
- (*h*) Present owner (public collections only)

The figure and plate numbers given in the captions to photographs of glasses from the Hartshorne Collection refer to those of Hartshorne's own book, *Old English Glasses*, details of which appear in the bibliography.

Abbreviations

Some abbreviations are already well established in glass literature, MSAT for multiple-spiral air twist, for example; several others listed below have been devised to avoid wearisome repetition in the captions. General acceptance of them would provide writers with a useful series of shorthand descriptions of particular value in cataloguing.

DF	Domed foot
D & FF	Domed and folded foot
DSAT	Double-series air twist
DSOT	Double-series opaque twist
FF	Folded foot

34

IB	Inverted baluster
MSAT	Multiple-spiral air twist
MSOT	Multiple-spiral opaque twist
OW	Opaque white
RF	Round funnel
SSAT	Single-series air twist
SSOT	Single-series opaque twist

Terminology

Most of the terms used in the captions and in the classification will be self-evident or readily understood by reference to the appropriate plates or line-drawings. A few require definition, however, if readers are to be saved the trouble of constant reference to other works: if fuller information is required reference to the Index will direct the reader to relevant entries in the Bibliography.

ALE: a glass of 3–5 oz capacity on stems of varying lengths; the bowl is in most cases the elongation of an ogee or round-funnel wine.

BALUSTER: strictly the form of knop illustrated in Plates 76–85 but loosely employed to describe a stem with any of the knops in sections 2 and 3.

BALUSTROID: a stem containing knops of small and relatively insignificant character.

CHAMPAGNE: a glass of 4–6 oz capacity, the bowl being wide and relatively shallow, most frequently of double-ogee form. It must be suitable as a drinking glass. The term is of doubtful authenticity as there is no proof that this shape of bowl was used for champagne in the eighteenth century.

COLLAR: a sharp-edged flange frequently occurring between bowl and stem and between stem and foot. The decorative bands encircling stems, especially of air twists, e.g. vermiform (if wavy) or coiled, are also referred to as 'collars'.

CORDIAL: a glass of 1 oz capacity on a tall, stout stem.

DEBASED PEDESTAL STEM: a stem in which the moulding has become indefinite, the shoulders rounded.

DRAM GLASS: capacity up to 3 oz; short or rudimentary stem.

FLAMMIFORM: a decorative effect achieved by forming spikes of glass protruding from the bowl and usually at the termination of wrythen moulding.

FLUTE CORDIAL: see Ratafia.

GADROONING: a decorative effect obtained by pinching the glass into ribs, at the base of a bowl for example.

GIN GLASS: a miniature wine glass.

GOBLET: a glass with large bowl.

JELLY GLASS: short glasses with rudimentary stem or set directly on the foot, intended for jellies or ices; often with single or double handles.

KNOP: a protuberance in the stem of a glass.

MEAD GLASS: an early glass with cup-shaped bowl which is gadrooned at the base: a term of doubtful authenticity.

MONTEITH: small glass with double-ogee or cup-shaped bowl, rather wider than a jelly glass and intended for salt or, possibly, for sweetmeats.

'NIPT DIAMOND WAIES': a decorative effect formed by pinching the glass, at the base of a bowl for example, into diamond-shaped compartments: the phrase is taken from Ravenscroft's usage in 1675.

POSSET GLASS: a low cylindrical vessel equipped with handles and a spout.

PRUNT: a circular or oval blob of glass added for decorative purposes and impressed to give dimpled (raspberry) effect.

RATAFIA: (also known as a 'flute cordial'): capacity 1–1½ oz; characterised by very narrow bowl.

RUMMER: capacity more than 4 oz: a term applied to small goblets after *c.* 1780.

SWEETMEAT: similar in form to champagne but unsuited for drinking by reason of dentated, cut or otherwise irregular rim. Possibly all so-called 'champagnes' were for sweetmeats.

TOASTING GLASS: having an exceedingly slender stem, easily snapped between the fingers.

TOASTMASTER'S GLASS: a cordial or dram glass with deceptive bowl.

I
Venetian
Decorative
Features

Soda Glass

1 Wine glass, 'Façon de Venise'; RF bowl; three hollow-blown knops of 'artichoke' design between collars; FF. Ht 10⅛ in. *c.* 1670. Flemish; soda glass. Harvey's Wine Museum, Bristol

2 Wine glass, 'Façon de Venise'; conical bowl; two hollow-blown knops between collars; FF. Ht 6⅞ in. *c.* 1680. Netherlands; soda glass. [Walter F.] Smith Collection. Harvey's Wine Museum, Bristol

3 Wine glass, 'Façon de Venise'; conical bowl with 'nipt diamond waies'; hollow-blown quatrefoil knop between collars; radially moulded FF. Ht 5¼ in. *c.* 1680. Netherlands; soda glass. Smith Collection. Harvey's Wine Museum, Bristol

4 Wine glass, 'Façon de Venise'; funnel bowl; double collar above hollow-blown quatrefoil knop; FF. Ht 5¼ in. *c.* 1665. Soda glass. Pilkington Glass Museum, St Helens

5 Wine glass, 'Façon de Venise'; square bucket bowl; hollow-blown knop moulded with lions' masks. Ht 5¾ in. *c.* 1630. Netherlands; pale amber soda glass. Smith Collection. Harvey's Wine Museum, Bristol

6 Wine glass, 'Façon de Venise'; pointed RF bowl with trailed threads and spiked gadrooning; two hollow-blown knops between collars flanked by scroll handles; FF. Ht 7⅞ in. c. 1670. Netherlands; soda glass. Harvey's Wine Museum, Bristol

7 Wine glass; pointed RF bowl; latticino stem and foot, stem comprising two hollow-blown knops between collars. Ht 5 in. c. 1680. Anglo-Venetian; soda glass. Harvey's Wine Museum, Bristol

8 Wine glass, 'vitro di trina'; RF bowl; hollow-blown flattened and IB knops between collars; FF. Ht 6⅛ in. 16th/17th century. Venetian; soda glass. Harvey's Wine Museum, Bristol

9 Wine glass, 'vitro di trina'; RF bowl; hollow-blown flattened and IB knops between collars; FF. Ht 6½ in. 16th/17th century. Venetian; soda glass. Harvey's Wine Museum, Bristol

10 Bottle decanter; lipped pan; spherical body decorated with 'nipt diamond waies'; swan-neck handle; FF. Ht 7⅞ in. c. 1665. English; brownish soda glass. Pilkington Glass Museum, St Helens

English Glass of Lead

11 Wine glass; RF bowl with spiked gadrooning and engraved in diamond-point with deer-hunt below inscription DEGESONT HEYT VAN DE HEER VAN YERFT (To the health of the Master of Yerst); hollow-blown quatrefoil knop between collars; basal knop; engraved FF. Ht 6 in. *c.* 1681. Probably from the Savoy Glasshouse; engraved in Holland. Pilkington Glass Museum, St Helens

12 Wine glass after Greene pattern; pointed RF bowl; hollow-blown knop between collars; FF. Ht 7 in. *c.* 1680. Thin, slightly opaque-white metal. Hartshorne Collection

13 Wine glass; conical bowl, solid base; hollow-blown quatrefoil knop between collars; FF. Ht 5¾ in. *c.* 1680. Smith Collection. Harvey's Wine Museum, Bristol

14 Wine glass; RF bowl with spiked gadrooning: hollow-blown quatrefoil knop; FF. Ht 7 in. *c.* 1675. Hawley-Bishopp period

15 Goblet; pointed RF bowl; hollow-blown knop (containing two silver Maundy 4*d.* pieces of 1677 and 1682) between collars; basal knop; FF. Ht 9⅛ in. *c.* 1690. Pilkington Glass Museum, St Helens

16 Goblet; pointed RF bowl; hollow-blown knop (containing silver 6d. dated 1703) decorated with five raspberry prunts, above a hollow IB knop; FF. Ht 8⅝ in. c. 1705. Cecil Higgins Museum, Bedford

17 Wine glass; bucket bowl; rope twist round a raspberry prunt between two small knops; basal knop; FF. Ht 7 in. c. 1700. Hartshorne Collection

18 Bowl and cover; pear-shaped body with band of trailed loops and 'nipt diamond waies'; pair of ribbed handles; cover similarly decorated and terminating in rope-twist handle above a frilled collar. Ht 9 in. c. 1690. Cecil Higgins Museum, Bedford

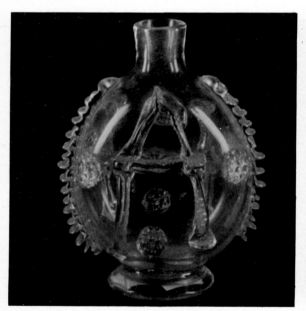 

19 Flask; ovoid body with pinched strapwork and raspberry prunts; trailed monogram A H (*Aqua Hierosolymurum*=Jerusalem water?). Ht 4¾ in. c. 1700. Hartshorne Collection

20 Reverse of 19 showing trailed letter H

21 Decanter-jug; vermicular collar at base of conical neck; onion-shaped body with wrythen gadrooning; pinched swan-neck handle; stopper tooled to match gadrooning. Ht 5⅛ in. *c.* 1685. This specimen appears to be the only one to survive. Pilkington Glass Museum, St Helens

22 Bowl and cover, both gadrooned; the bowl has threaded decoration below rim; the cover terminates in a beaded knop. Ht 6¼ in. *c.* 1700. Compare with posset pot in Thorpe, *English and Irish Glass*, Plate lxxvi

24 Bowl and cover; cup-shaped body with band of trailed loops and 'nipt diamond waies' which extend to D & FF; cover decorated to match terminating in crown knop with four pinched strapwork loops and trefoil pincered finial. Ht 15 in. *c.* 1675. Ravenscroft period. Hartshorne Collection

23 Mead glass; cup bowl with gadrooned base; double knop above plain stem; basal knop; FF. Ht 5¼ in. *c.* 1700. Smith Collection. Harvey's Wine Museum, Bristol

25 Dwarf ale glass; part wrythen bowl; collar, pincered winged knop and basal knop; FF. Ht 5½ in. *c.* 1700

26 Dwarf ale glass; part
wrythen bowl with
flammiform fringe; collar,
five-winged pincered knop and
basal knop; FF. Ht 5¾ in.
c. 1700. Cecil Higgins Museum,
Bedford

27 Dwarf ale glass; part
wrythen bowl with
flammiform fringe; wrythen
knop; FF. Ht 6 in. *c.* 1700.
Smith Collection;
S. G. Hewlett Collection.
Harvey's Wine Museum,
Bristol

II
Heavy Balusters

28 Goblet; conical bowl; solid base; IB with tear; FF. Ht 6¾ in. *c.* 1700. Hartshorne Collection

29 Goblet; funnel bowl, solid base with tear; IB with tear; D & FF. Ht 8 in. *c.* 1700

30 Wine glass; funnel bowl, solid base with tear; IB with tear; basal knop; FF. Ht 5¾ in. *c.* 1710

31 Wine glass; cup-topped bowl; IB knop with tear; FF. Ht 5¼ in. *c.* 1700

32 Goblet; RF bowl; round knop, IB and basal knop, all teared; FF. Ht 11¼ in. *c.* 1700. Pilkington Glass Museum, St Helens

33 Wine glass; bell bowl, solid base; IB with tear and basal knop; FF. Ht 5½ in. c. 1710

34 Wine glass; funnel bowl, solid base with tear; elongated teared IB; FF. Ht 5¾ in. c. 1700. Cecil Higgins Museum, Bedford

35 Goblet; RF bowl; IB and basal knops with tears; FF. Ht 8½ in. c. 1720

36 Wine glass; RF bowl, solid base; wide angular and basal knops, both teared; D & FF. Ht 5¾ in. c. 1700

37 Goblet; RF bowl, solid base; wide angular and basal knops, both teared; FF. Ht 8¼ in. c. 1710

38 Wine glass; conical bowl, solid base; wide angular and basal knops, both teared; FF. Ht 7¼ in. c. 1700

39 Wine glass; bell bowl, solid base; flattened knop above teared wide angular and basal knops; FF. Ht 6¼ in. c. 1715

40 Wine glass; funnel bowl, solid base with tear; collar above wide angular knop and teared swelled knop; FF. Ht 5⅜ in. c. 1700

41 Wine glass; funnel bowl, solid base, cushioned; angular knop above teared swelled knop; terraced foot. Ht 5¼ in. c. 1725

42 Wine glass; bell bowl, solid base; 7-ringed annulated knop over small baluster; FF. Ht 6 in. c. 1725

43 Sweetmeat glass; panel-moulded bowl; 5-ringed annulated knop over ball and basal knops; domed and terraced foot. Ht 5½ in. c. 1725

44 Goblet; funnel bowl, solid base with tear, cushioned; 3-ringed annulated knop above teared IB; FF. Ht 9 in. c. 1715

45 Wine glass; bell bowl, solid base; 5-ringed annulated knop over true baluster. Ht 7 in. c. 1715

46 Dram glass; funnel bowl, solid base with tear; 3-ringed annulated knop; basal knop; DF. Ht 5¼ in. c. 1715

47 Wine glass; tulip bowl, solid base; drop knop; D & FF. Ht 6½ in. *c.* 1710

48 Wine glass; tulip bowl, solid base; teared drop knop; D & FF. Ht 6¾ in. *c.* 1700. Smith Collection. Harvey's Wine Museum, Bristol

49 Wine glass; lipped bucket bowl; flattened knop above teared drop knop and basal knop; D & FF. Ht 5⅞ in. *c.* 1710

50 Wine glass; bell bowl, solid base; drop knop above squat true baluster; D & FF. Ht 7 in. *c.* 1710

51 Wine glass; bell bowl, solid base; drop knop; DF. Ht 5¾ in. *c.* 1710

52 Wine glass; funnel bowl, solid base with tear; teared ball knop; FF. Ht 6¾ in. *c.* 1700

53 Dram glass; RF bowl, solid base; ball knop and basal knop; FF. Ht 4¼ in. *c.* 1700. Hartshorne Collection (Fig. 305)

54 Wine glass; funnel bowl; two ball knops and basal knop; FF. Ht 5¾ in. *c.* 1715

55 Goblet; round funnel bowl; teared mushroom knop over tear basal knop; FF. Ht 9½ in. c. 1710

56 Goblet; round funnel bowl, solid base; mushroom knop over basal knop; FF. Ht 7¼ in. c. 1700

57 Wine glass; thistle bowl, solid base; teared mushroom knop over basal knop; FF. Ht 7½ in. c. 1710

58 Wine glass; round funnel bowl, solid base; teared acorn knop over basal knop; FF. Ht 5½ in. c. 1700

59 Wine glass; pan-topped bowl, solid base; teared acorn knop over basal knop; FF. Ht 5⅜ in. c. 1710

60 Goblet; thistle bowl, solid base; acorn knop over basal knop; FF. Ht 8½ in. c. 1710

61 Wine glass; bell bowl, teared solid base; flattened knop and collar above teared cylinder knop with cushion knop and basal knop; D & FF. Ht 6⅝ in. c. 1710. Cecil Higgins Museum, Bedford

62 Wine glass; bell bowl, teared solid base; flattened knop and collar above teared cylinder knop; basal knop; FF. Ht 7 in. c. 1710. Smith Collection. Harvey's Wine Museum, Bristol

63 Wine glass; funnel bowl,
solid base; teared egg knop;
FF. Ht 5⅞ in. c. 1700

64 Ale glass; funnel bowl,
solid base; cushioned knop
over ball knop; DF. Ht 6¾ in.
c. 1700

65 Goblet; conical bowl;
teared cushioned knop and
basal knop; FF. Ht 9¾ in.
c. 1710. Smith Collection.
Harvey's Wine Museum,
Bristol

III
Balusters

66 Wine glass; bell bowl, solid base; IB knop with large tear; basal knop; FF. Ht 7 in. c. 1730

67 Wine glass; waisted bell bowl, solid base; flattened, IB and basal knops; FF. Ht 6 in. c. 1730. Hartshorne Collection

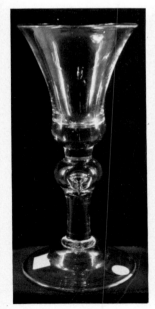   

68 Wine glass; bell bowl, solid base; IB knop with tear; DF. Ht 7 in. c. 1730 Hartshorne Collection (Fig. 195)

69 Wine glass; waisted bell bowl, solid base; annular knop over teared IB; basal knop; D & FF. Ht 6¾ in. c. 1730

70 Toastmaster's glass; deceptive waisted bell bowl; collar above teared IB and basal knops; FF. Ht 6 in. c. 1730

71 Wine glass; bucket bowl; teared IB and basal knops; FF. Ht 7 in. c. 1720. Cecil Higgins Museum, Bedford

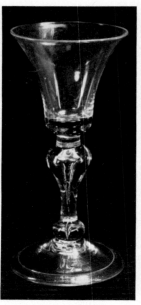

72 Champagne glass; cup bowl with everted rim and engraved border; IB knop; D & FF. Ht 4¼ in. *c.* 1730

73 Wine glass; waisted bell bowl, solid base; teared IB and basal knops; FF. Ht 6½ in. *c.* 1730

74 Wine glass; RF bowl; angular knop above cushioned IB. Ht 7 in. *c.* 1730

75 Champagne glass; pan-topped RF bowl, everted rim; collar above beaded ball knop, teared IB and basal knops; DF. Ht 6½ in. *c.* 1730

76 Wine glass; waisted bell bowl, solid base with tear; 4-ringed annulated knop over true baluster and basal knops. Ht 6⅞ in. *c.* 1730

77 Wine glass; waisted bell bowl; collar and flattened knop over true baluster and basal knop; FF. Ht 5¾ in. *c.* 1730. Worthing Museum

78 Wine glass; trumpet bowl, solid base; collars and flattened knop over true baluster and basal knop; FF. Ht 6½ in. *c.* 1730. Hartshorne Collection (Plate 41)

79 Wine glass; trumpet bowl, solid base; collar and flattened knop over true baluster; DF. Ht 7 in. *c.* 1720

80 Wine glass; trumpet bowl, solid base with tear; collar, flattened knop, true baluster and basal knop; FF. Ht 7½ in. *c.* 1720. Smith Collection. Harvey's Wine Museum, Bristol

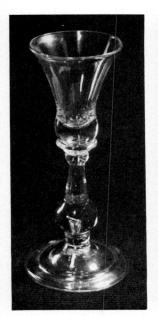

81 Wine glass; waisted bell bowl, solid base; collar, small round knop, true baluster and basal knop; FF. Ht 7 in. *c.* 1730

82 Cordial glass; trumpet bowl, solid base; collars, flattened knop, true baluster and basal knop. Ht 6½ in. *c.* 1720

83 Wine glass; pointed RF bowl, solid base; angular knop over true baluster. Ht 6 in. *c.* 1730

84 Cordial glass; trumpet bowl, solid base with tear; collar over round knop, true baluster and basal knop. Ht 6½ in. *c.* 1720

85 Wine glass; waisted bell bowl, engraved floral border below rim, solid base; two true balusters in tandem; basal knop. Ht 6¾ in. *c.* 1730

86 Wine glass; lipped RF bowl; ball knop over angular knop, teared true baluster and basal knop; D & FF. Ht 7¼ in. *c.* 1730

87 Wine glass; thistle bowl engraved with Baroque border below rim and birds in flight, solid base; angular knop between two ball knops, all teared; FF. Ht 6⅞ in. *c.* 1730. Smith Collection. Harvey's Wine Museum, Bristol

88 Wine glass; pointed RF bowl; ball knop over teared angular and basal knops; D & FF. Ht 7¼ in. *c.* 1730. Hartshorne Collection (Fig. 175)

89 Wine glass; bell bowl, solid base; angular knop over semi-hollow ovoid knop; D & FF. Ht 6 in. *c.* 1715

90 Wine glass; waisted bell bowl, solid base; 5-ringed annulated knop, teared angular knop and basal knop. Ht 6¾ in. *c.* 1730

91 Wine glass; moulded trumpet bowl; triple collar above 3-ringed annulated knop, smaller annulated knop and basal knop; similarly moulded D & FF. Ht 7 in. *c.* 1730. Pilkington Glass Museum, St Helens

92 Ale glass; waisted bell bowl, solid base; 5-ringed annulated knop; basal knop; FF. Ht 7⅛ in. *c.* 1730. Cecil Higgins Museum, Bedford

93 Wine glass; conical bowl 'nipt diamond waies' type decoration; triple collar over two 3-ringed annulated knops and basal knop; D & FF, moulded to match bowl. Ht 6½ in. c. 1730. Hartshorne Collection (Fig. 171)

94 Gin glass; bell bowl, solid base; flattened knop, 3-ringed annulated knop, basal knop; FF. Ht 4¾ in. c. 1720. Hartshorne Collection (Fig. 294)

95 Wine glass; waisted bell bowl, teared solid base; 3-ringed annulated knop, teared stem and basal knop; FF. Ht 6½ in. c. 1720. Hartshorne Collection (Fig. 196)

96 Wine glass; lipped square bucket bowl; 3-ringed annulated knop with tear; basal knop; D & FF. Ht 6 in. c. 1720

97 Wine glass; bell bowl, solid base; 3-ringed annulated knop over teared IB; basal knop; DF. Ht 6½ in. c. 1730

98 Sweetmeat glass; pan-topped moulded RF bowl; 3-ringed annulated knop over teared IB; basal knop; radially moulded D & FF. Ht 5 in. c. 1730

99 Wine glass; waisted bell bowl, solid base; 3-ringed annulated knop over teared IB and basal knops; FF. Ht 6¾ in. c. 1730

100 Wine glass; bell bowl, solid base; 3-ringed annulated knop over teared IB; basal knop. Ht 6½ in. c. 1730. Smith Collection. Harvey's Wine Museum, Bristol

101 Wine glass; waisted bell bowl, solid base; flattened and annular knops above ball knop; basal knop. Ht 6½ in. c. 1730

102 Wine glass; bell bowl; two ball knops; DF. Ht 7¾ in. c. 1730

103 Sweetmeat glass; cup bowl, folded rim; double ball knop; FF. Ht 4¼ in. c. 1730

104 Sweetmeat glass; panel-moulded pan-topped RF bowl; beaded ball knop over IB; panel-moulded D & FF. Ht 5½ in. c. 1730. Hartshorne Collection

105 Champagne glass; ogee bowl, everted rim; double collar above teared ball knop, 3-ringed annulated knop and teared IB; domed and terraced foot. Ht 5½ in. c. 1730

106 Champagne glass; pan-topped RF bowl, everted rim; collars above teared ball knop and small plain knop; domed and terraced foot. Ht 6 in. c. 1730. Hartshorne Collection

107 Wine glass; trumpet bowl; flattened knop, ball knop; FF. Ht 6¾ in. c. 1725

108 Wine glass; panel-moulded cup bowl; beaded ball knop; radially moulded foot. Ht 6½ in. c. 1735

109 Sweetmeat glass; pan-topped RF bowl; beaded ball knop; DF. Ht 4¾ in. c. 1735

110 Sweetmeat glass; honeycomb-moulded cup-topped RF bowl; ball knop; D & FF moulded to match. Ht 7 in. *c.* 1735

111 Wine glass; conical bowl; mushroom knop and basal knop, both teared; FF. Ht 5½ in. *c.* 1715

112 Goblet; RF bowl; hollow acorn and basal knops; FF. Ht 7 in. *c.* 1715

113 Wine glass; oval pan-topped RF bowl, engraved floral border; solid base; acorn knop between small ball knops; DF. Ht 6¾ in. *c.* 1730

114 Wine glass; bell bowl, solid base; flattened knop and collar over cylinder knop; basal knop; FF. Ht 6½ in. *c.* 1720. Smith Collection. Harvey's Wine Museum, Bristol

115 Wine glass; bell bowl; flattened knop over teared cylinder knop; basal knop; FF. Ht 5½ in. *c.* 1730. Worthing Museum

116 Wine glass; waisted bell bowl, solid base; flattened knop; collar, teared cylinder and basal knops; FF. Ht 7 in. *c.* 1730

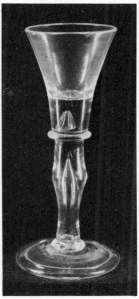

117 Wine glass; bell bowl, solid base; flattened knop, cylinder and basal knops, all teared; FF. Ht 6¾ in. *c.* 1715. Cecil Higgins Museum, Bedford

118 Wine glass; bell bowl, solid base; teared dumb-bell knop; basal knop; FF. Ht 8⅝ in. *c.* 1720

119 Wine glass; bell bowl, teared solid base; teared swelled knop; basal knop; FF. Ht 5¼ in. *c.* 1720

120 Cordial glass; trumpet bowl, solid base with tear; collar, teared swelled knop; FF. Ht 6¾ in. *c.* 1715

121 Toastmaster's glass; deceptive waisted bucket bowl; collar above swelling knop; basal knop. Ht 6¼ in. *c.* 1715

IV
Balustroids

122 Wine glass; bell bowl, solid base; IB. Ht 7 in. *c.* 1740

123 Wine glass; trumpet bowl; teared IB at centre. Ht 7 in. *c.* 1750. Hartshorne Collection (Fig. 190)

124 Wine glass; trumpet bowl; teared IB at centre; FF. Ht 6 in. *c.* 1750

125 Wine glass; trumpet bowl; teared IB at base; FF. Ht 7 in. *c.* 1750. Hartshorne Collection

 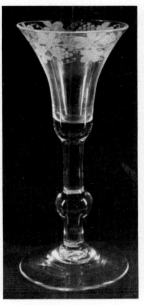  

126 Wine glass; waisted bell bowl; thin teared stem above teared IB; basal knop; FF. Ht 6¾ in. *c.* 1750

127 Wine glass; bell bowl, engraved fruiting vine below rim, solid base; IB at base. Ht 7¼ in. *c.* 1740. Portsmouth City Museums

128 Wine glass; trumpet bowl; IB at base; basal knop; DF. Ht 7¼ in. *c.* 1750. Hartshorne Collection (Fig. 189)

129 Ale glass; bell bowl, solid base; IB at base; DF. Ht 8 in. *c.* 1750

130 Sweetmeat glass; pan-topped RF bowl, dentated rim; IB shoulder knop; radially moulded foot. Ht 3¾ in. *c.* 1740

131 Wine glass; bell bowl, engraved fruiting vine border below rim; knop at shoulder, true baluster at base; basal knop; FF. Ht 6½ in. *c.* 1750. Hartshorne Collection

132 Wine glass; RF bowl; knop at shoulder; FF. Ht 6 in. *c.* 1750

133 Gin glass; bell bowl; knop at shoulder; FF. Ht 4¼ in. *c.* 1740. Soda glass

134 Ale glass; bell bowl; wide annular knop over teared swelled knop; FF. Ht 5¾ in. *c.* 1740

135 Wine glass; funnel bowl; acorn-type knop at shoulder. Ht 6 in. *c.* 1730

136 Wine glass; trumpet bowl, solid base; collar between pair of flattened knops; FF. Ht 7 in. *c.* 1730

137 Wine glass; ogee bowl; centre knop; FF. Ht 5½ in. *c.* 1750. Worthing Museum

138 Ale glass; pan-topped RF bowl, engraved border of hops and barley below rim; centre knop. Ht 7⅞ in. *c.* 1740. Cecil Higgins Museum, Bedford

139 Cider glass; waisted bell bowl, solid base, engraved decoration of fruiting apple branch; centre knop; DF. Ht 8 in. *c.* 1740

140 Wine glass; ribbed cup bowl, everted rim, swelled centre knop. Ht 7¼ in. *c.* 1740

141 Wine glass; drawn trumpet bowl, engraved flower and moth; centre knop. Ht 6¾ in. *c.* 1750

142 Goblet; double–ogee bowl; centre knop and basal knop; radially moulded foot. Ht 7½ in. *c.* 1740. Worthing Museum

143 Cordial glass; bell bowl, solid base with tear; teared swelled centre knop; basal knop. Ht 6¾ in. *c.* 1735

145 Wine glass; tulip bowl, solid base; basal knop. Ht 7½ in. *c.* 1740. Portsmouth City Museums

144 Wine glass (?); bell bowl with pair of applied B–handles; collar; basal knop. Ht 6½ in. *c.* 1735

146 Wine glass; trumpet bowl; thinning stem; ball knop above basal knop; DF. Ht 6¾ in. *c.* 1740. Hartshorne Collection (Fig. 198)

147 Wine glass; drawn trumpet bowl; cushioned knop over basal knop; DF. Ht 6½ in. *c.* 1735

148 Wine glass; bell bowl, solid base; flattened knop; cushioned knop at base. Ht 6 in. *c.* 1730

149 Wine glass; bell bowl, solid base; cushioned knop at base; FF. Ht 7¼ in. *c.* 1740

150 Wine glass; pointed RF bowl; knops at shoulder and centre; FF. Ht 6⅛ in. *c.* 1750

151 Wine glass; ogee bowl; annular knops at shoulder and centre; small basal knop; FF. Ht 5¼ in. *c.* 1750. Hartshorne Collection

152 Wine glass; RF bowl; flattened knop, teared stem and annular knop; FF. Ht 6 in. *c.* 1750

153 Wine glass; RF bowl; flattened knop, teared stem and bladed knop; FF. Ht 5¾ in. *c.* 1750

154 Wine glass; pan-topped RF bowl, engraved floral border below rim; flattened knop, teared stem with bladed knop; small basal knop; FF. Ht 6 in. *c.* 1750

155 Wine glass; RF bowl, moulded base; annular shoulder knop, wrythen ball knop at centre; FF. Ht 5¾ in. *c.* 1750

156 Wine glass; RF bowl; knops at shoulder and base; teared stem between; FF. Ht 6⅜ in. c. 1750

157 Gin glass; bell bowl; annular and basal knops; FF. Ht 4⅛ in. c. 1740

158 Wine glass; bell bowl, solid base; annular knop over beaded IB; FF. Ht 7 in. c. 1730

159 Wine glass; bell bowl, solid base; beaded ball knop over teared IB. Ht 6¾ in. c. 1750

160 Wine glass; ogee bowl; hollow knop between collars with four raspberry prunts and containing silver coin of George III dated 1766; teared IB; basal knop. Ht 6¼ in. c. 1766 (!)

161 Detail of 160 showing hollow knop and coin

162 Wine glass; cup-topped RF bowl, solid base; bladed knop, teared stem and basal knop; FF. Ht 6 in. c. 1750

163 Wine glass; bell bowl, solid base; drop knop over IB. Ht 7 in. *c.* 1730

164 Mead glass; cup bowl with gadrooned base; cushioned knop, teared stem and basal knop; FF. Ht 4½ in. *c.* 1720

165 Wine glass; RF bowl, slightly everted rim; flattened knop between two angular knops; DF. Ht 7 in. *c.* 1740

166 Wine glass; bell bowl; three knops; FF. Ht 6 in. *c.* 1750

167 Wine glass; moulded cup bowl, everted rim; double knop over IB and basal knop; panel-moulded DF. Ht 7 in. *c.* 1740

168 Wine glass; RF bowl; annular knop, teared swelled and basal knops; FF. Ht 6 in. *c.* 1750

169 Ale glass; trumpet bowl; two 3-ringed annulated knops over a true baluster; terraced foot. Ht 7¾ in. *c.* 1730

170 Mead glass; cup bowl, gadrooned base; flattened knop, teared knop and slight basal knop; FF. Ht 4¾ in. *c.* 1730

171 Wine glass; bell bowl; flattened, 3-ringed annulated, IB and basal knops; FF. Ht 7 in. *c.* 1730. Hartshorne Collection

172 Wine glass; bell bowl, solid base; collars over swelled and cushion knops; DF. Ht 6½ in. *c.* 1730

173 Wine glass; bell bowl; pair of true balusters in tandem, both teared, over basal knop; FF. Ht 5 in. *c.* 1730

174 Mead glass; cup bowl, gadrooned base; semi-hollow bobbin-knopped stem (four diminishing knops); basal knop; FF. Ht 5 in. *c.* 1720. Hartshorne Collection

175 Sweetmeat glass; triple-ogee bowl; bobbin-knopped stem (six knops); DF. Ht 4½ in. *c.* 1720

176 Sweetmeat glass; double-ogee bowl; bobbin-knopped stem (eight knops). Ht 6⅝ in. *c.* 1720. Cecil Higgins Museum, Bedford

177 Wine glass; pointed RF bowl with Baroque engraved border below rim; 'Newcastle' light baluster stem including teared swelled knop; FF. Ht 6⅝ in. c. 1750. Smith Collection. Harvey's Wine Museum, Bristol

178 Wine glass; trumpet bowl with engraved border of fruiting vine below rim; 'Newcastle' light baluster stem including beaded acorn knop and IB. Ht 7 in. c. 1750. Hartshorne Collection (Fig. 192)

179 Wine glass; pointed RF bowl, engraved floral border below rim; 'Newcastle' light baluster stem including IB; foot engraved with matching border. Ht 7½ in. c. 1750. Smith Collection. Harvey's Wine Museum, Bristol

180 Wine glass; trumpet bowl with engraved border of fruiting vine; 'Newcastle' light baluster stem including beaded acorn and IB knops. Ht 6⅞ in. c. 1750. Smith Collection. Harvey's Wine Museum, Bristol

181 Wine glass; RF bowl; 'Newcastle' light baluster stem including two beaded knops. Ht 7½ in. c. 1750

182 Wine glass; pointed RF bowl, engraved border of foliate branches below the rim; 'Newcastle' light baluster stem including 3-ringed annulated knop. Ht 8¼ in. c. 1750. Worthing Museum

183 Wine glass; trumpet bowl; 'Newcastle' light baluster stem including beaded acorn knop and swelled knop. Ht 7¼ in. c. 1750

184 Wine glass; bell bowl; 'Newcastle' light baluster stem including angular and IB knops; FF. Ht 8½ in. c. 1750

185 Wine glass; RF bowl,
engraved key pattern band
below rim; 'Newcastle' light
baluster stem including annular
knop between opposing
balusters; DF. Ht 7 in. *c.* 1750

186 Wine glass; pointed RF
bowl; 'Newcastle' light baluster
stem including teared annular
and angular knops; FF.
Ht 8¼ in. *c.* 1750. Worthing
Museum

187 Wine glass; RF bowl;
'Newcastle' light baluster stem
including beaded shoulder
knop and IB. Ht 7 in. *c.* 1750

V
Moulded Pedestal
Stems

188 Wine glass; conical bowl, solid base; four-sided teared pedestal stem ('Silesian'), moulded crowns on shoulders and moulded legend GOD SAVE KING GEORGE; FF. Ht 6¼ in. *c.* 1715. Hartshorne Collection

189 Wine glass; conical bowl, solid base; four-sided teared pedestal stem with rounded shoulders; FF. Ht 5¾ in. *c.* 1720. Soda glass

190 Wine glass; conical bowl, solid base; four-sided teared pedestal stem with diamonds on shoulders; FF. Ht 7¼ in. *c.* 1720

191 Wine glass; thistle bowl, solid base; four-sided pedestal stem with crowns on shoulders; FF. Ht 6¼ in. *c.* 1720

192 Wine glass; RF bowl, solid base with tear; four-sided pedestal stem with lobed ribs on each side and diamonds on shoulders; FF. Ht 6½ in. *c.* 1705. Smith Collection. Harvey's Wine Museum, Bristol

193 Wine glass; bell bowl, solid base; ball knop over four-sided pedestal stem with rounded shoulders and long tear. Ht 6⅜ in. *c.* 1720

194 Wine glass; thistle bowl, solid base; collar over four-sided pedestal stem with rounded shoulders and tear; collar; FF. Ht 6½ in. *c.* 1710

195 Toastmaster's glass; deceptive trumpet bowl engraved with rose and butterfly (Jacobite); four-sided pedestal stem with rounded shoulders; FF. Ht 5¼ in. *c.* 1715. Hartshorne Collection (Fig. 306)

196 Wine glass; conical bowl, solid base; six-sided pedestal stem with stars on shoulders; FF. Ht 6⅞ in. *c.* 1715. Smith Collection. Harvey's Wine Museum, Bristol

197 Wine glass; pointed RF bowl, solid base; six-sided teared pedestal stem, diamonds on shoulders; FF. Ht 7½ in. *c.* 1720

198 Wine glass; pointed RF bowl, solid base; flattened knop above six-sided teared pedestal stem; FF. Ht 5¾ in. *c.* 1730. Soda glass

199 Sweetmeat glass; saucer-topped honeycomb-moulded cup bowl; six-sided pedestal stem between collars; D & FF, moulded to match. Ht 5¾ in. *c.* 1740

200 Wine glass; pointed RF bowl, solid base, on cushion knop; eight-sided pedestal stem, diamonds on shoulders; FF. Ht 5¾ in. c. 1725

201 Wine glass; bucket bowl; eight-sided pedestal stem, diamonds on shoulders; collars. Ht 7¼ in. c. 1745. Harvey's Wine Museum, Bristol

202 Champagne glass; ogee bowl, everted rim; eight-sided pedestal stem, diamonds on shoulders, between collars; FF. Ht 6¼ in. c. 1745

203 Champagne glass; panel-moulded ogee bowl, everted rim; eight-sided pedestal stem between collars; panel-moulded D & FF. Ht 6¾ in. c. 1745

204 Champagne glass; double-ogee bowl, everted rim; eight-sided pedestal stem, diamonds on shoulders, between collars; D & FF. Ht 6½ in. c. 1745

205 Sweetmeat glass; honeycomb-moulded double-ogee bowl, everted rim; eight-sided pedestal stem between collars; D & FF to match. Ht 6½ in. c. 1745

206 Sweetmeat glass; honeycomb-moulded double-ogee bowl, everted rim; eight-sided pedestal stem between collars; D & FF to match. Ht 7¼ in. *c.* 1745. Worthing Museum

207 Sweetmeat glass; honeycomb-moulded double-ogee bowl, everted rim; eight-sided pedestal stem between collars; DF to match. Ht 6 in. *c.* 1745

208 Sweetmeat glass; panel-moulded double-ogee bowl with everted rim and diamond-studded base; eight-sided pedestal stem with diamond shoulders, between collars; DF to match. Ht 6¾ in. *c.* 1745

209 Champagne glass; panel-moulded double-ogee bowl with diamond-studded base; slightly twisted eight-sided pedestal stem between collars; DF to match. Ht 5½ in. *c.* 1750

210 Sweetmeat glass; panel-moulded double-ogee bowl with everted rim; eight-sided pedestal stem between collars; D & FF to match. Ht 6½ in. c. 1750

211 Champagne glass; double-ogee bowl, slightly everted rim; eight-sided pedestal stem, diamonds on shoulders, collared base; DF. Ht 7 in. c. 1750

212 Champagne glass; cup-topped RF bowl; angular knop above eight-sided pedestal stem, diamonds on shoulders; basal knop; D & FF. Ht 6¾ in. c. 1745

213 Champagne glass; double-ogee bowl, slightly everted rim; eight-sided pedestal stem, diamonds on shoulders, between collars; D & FF. Ht 6½ in. c. 1745

214 Champagne glass; panel-moulded double-ogee bowl; eight-sided pedestal stem, diamonds on shoulders; basal knop; DF to match. Ht 7 in. c. 1745

215 Champagne glass; panel-moulded cup bowl; eight-sided pedestal stem between collars; DF to match. Ht 6 in. *c*. 1755. Smith Collection. Harvey's Wine Museum, Bristol

216 Wine glass; trumpet bowl, solid base; collars above attenuated four-sided pedestal stem with long tear; basal knop. Ht 7½ in. *c*. 1760. Hartshorne Collection (Fig. 90)

217 Wine glass; hammered RF bowl; debased eight-sided pedestal stem, rounded shoulders, collared base; FF. Ht 6¾ in. *c*. 1760

218 Sweetmeat glass; panel-moulded cup bowl, everted rim; debased eight-sided pedestal stem, rounded shoulders; FF to match. Ht 4¼ in. *c*. 1760

219 Goblet; cup bowl, band of finely cut vertical flutes; debased eight-sided pedestal stem between collars; DF. Ht 7 in. *c*. 1765

VI
Plain Straight
Stems

220 Toasting glass; drawn trumpet bowl, flared. Ht 7 in. *c.* 1750

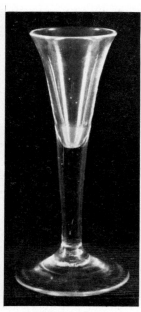

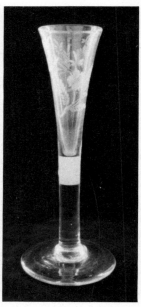

221 Toasting glass; drawn trumpet bowl. Ht 7¾ in. *c.* 1750. Hartshorne Collection (Fig. 89)

222 Wine glass; drawn trumpet bowl. Ht 5 in. *c.* 1750. Hartshorne Collection

223 Wine glass; drawn trumpet bowl; D & FF. Ht 8¼ in. *c.* 1740. Smith Collection. Harvey's Wine Museum, Bristol

224 Ratafia; drawn trumpet bowl, engraved with floral spray. Ht 7⅛ in. *c.* 1750. Smith Collection. Harvey's Wine Museum, Bristol

225 Ratafia; waisted bell bowl; plain stem; FF. Ht 8 in. *c.* 1740. Ipswich Museum

226 Short ale glass; drawn trumpet bowl, engraved with hops and barley. Ht 6 in. *c.* 1750. Hartshorne Collection

227 Short ale glass; funnel bowl, engraved with hops and barley; FF. Ht 6 in. *c.* 1740. Worthing Museum

228 Gin glass; fluted ovoid bowl; FF. Ht 3¾ in. *c.* 1740. Hartshorne Collection

229 Gin glass; vertically moulded drawn trumpet bowl; FF. Ht 3¾ in. *c.* 1740

230 Gin glass; drawn trumpet bowl, engraved festoons below rim; FF. Ht 4⅜ in. *c.* 1740. Hartshorne Collection (Fig. 20a)

231 Wine glass; drawn trumpet bowl, teared stem; FF. Ht 7¼ in. *c.* 1740

232 Ale glass; drawn trumpet bowl, engraved with hops and barley; teared stem; FF. Ht 7½ in. *c.* 1740. Hartshorne Collection (Fig. 273)

233 Wine glass; drawn trumpet bowl; teared stem; FF. Ht 6 in. *c.* 1740. Soda glass

234 Firing glass (?); drawn trumpet bowl; teared stem. Ht 5 in. *c.* 1750

235 Wine glass; drawn trumpet bowl; teared stem; FF. Ht 6½ in. *c.* 1740. Hartshorne Collection

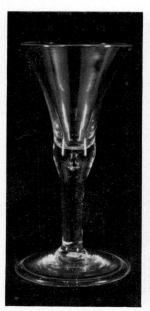

236 Wine glass; waisted bell bowl with tear in solid base; FF. Ht 8 in. *c.* 1740

237 Wine glass; waisted bell bowl with tear in solid base; FF. Ht 5½ in. *c.* 1740. Hartshorne Collection

238 Dram glass; fluted ovoid bowl. Ht 3½ in. *c.* 1750. Hartshorne Collection

239 Dram glass; ogee bowl, engraved fruiting vine and bird in flight; terraced foot. Ht 5½ in. c. 1740. Hartshorne Collection

240 Wine glass; RF bowl. Ht 5¾ in. c. 1750

241 Wine glass; ogee bowl, engraved in Jacobite manner; FF. Ht 5¼ in. c. 1740

242 Wine glass; ovoid bowl; FF. Ht 6 in. c. 1740

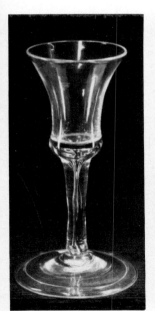

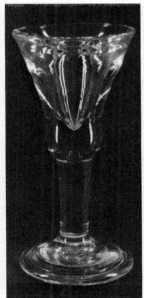

243 Wine glass, waisted bell bowl, solid base; teared stem; FF. Ht 6 in. c. 1740. Hartshorne Collection (Fig. 201)

244 Toastmaster's glass; deceptive bell bowl; FF. Ht 7 in. c. 1740

245 Ale glass; waisted bell bowl, engraved hops and barley; FF. Ht 7½ in. c. 1740. Hartshorne Collection (Fig. 272)

246 Ale glass; vertically moulded bell bowl; D & FF. Ht 6¾ in. c. 1740. Hartshorne Collection

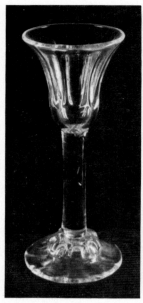

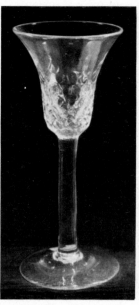

247 Wine glass; vertically
moulded bell bowl; moulded
domed foot. Ht 5⅞ in. *c.* 1750

248 Wine glass; hammered
bell bowl. Ht 7½ in. *c.* 1750

249 Cordial glass; RF bowl,
solid base. Ht 6½ in. *c.* 1750

250 Wine glass; RF bowl,
fluted base; FF. Ht 6 in. *c.* 1740

251 Ale glass; RF bowl; FF.
Ht 6 in. *c.* 1740

252 Wine glass; ogee bowl;
fluted base. Ht 6½ in. *c.* 1750

253 Goblet glass bowl;
FF. Ht 6¾ in. *c.* 1726.
Hartshorne Collection

254 Wine glass; bucket bowl.
Ht 6 in. *c.* 1750

255 Wine glass; cup bowl; FF. Ht 7¼ in. *c.* 1740

256 Wine glass; ovoid bowl, moulded base and engraved floral border below rim; FF. Ht 5⅝ in. *c.* 1740

257 Champagne glass (?); slightly waisted pan bowl; D & FF. Ht 6½ in. *c.* 1740

258 Wine glass; trumpet bowl; collar. Ht 7 in. *c.* 1750

259 Wine glass; bell bowl; thin stem between triple and quadruple collars; FF. Ht 6¾ in. *c.* 1740

260 Wine glass; ogee bowl, engraved sprays of flowers; collar; FF. Ht 5½ in. *c.* 1740

261 Wine glass; bell bowl, solid base; tapering stem between collars; D & FF. Ht 7 in. *c.* 1740. Cecil Higgins Museum, Bedford

262 Dram glass; vertically moulded conical bowl; collar. Ht 4 in. *c.* 1750

263 Wine glass; ogee bowl; hollow stem. Ht 4¾ in. *c.* 1760

264 Wine glass; trumpet bowl; hollow stem; FF. Ht 6¾ in. *c.* 1750. Smith Collection. Harvey's Wine Museum, Bristol

265 Wine glass; RF bowl, engraved fruiting vine and butterfly; hollow stem; D & FF. Ht 6½ in. *c.* 1745. Pilkington Glass Museum, St Helens

266 Wine glass; trumpet bowl; hollow stem; FF. Ht 6¼ in. *c.* 1745

267 Sweetmeat glass; lipped RF bowl; semi-hollow swelling stem between collars; high conical foot. Ht 7 in. *c.* 1750 (Unfinished glass?)

VII
Air-Twist Stems

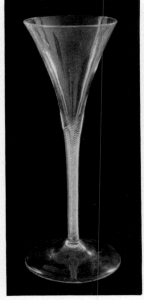

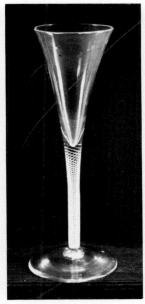

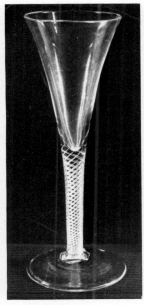

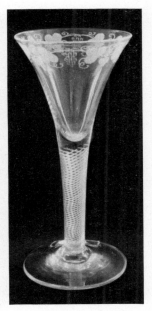

268 Toasting glass; drawn trumpet bowl; MSAT. Ht 7⅞ in. *c.* 1750. Smith Collection. Harvey's Wine Museum, Bristol

269 Wine flute; drawn trumpet bowl; MSAT. Ht 7¾ in. *c.* 1750

270 Wine flute; drawn trumpet bowl; MSAT; FF. Ht 7¼ in. *c.* 1750

271 Wine glass; drawn trumpet bowl, engraved fruiting vine below rim; MSAT. Ht 7 in. *c.* 1750. Harvey's Wine Museum, Bristol

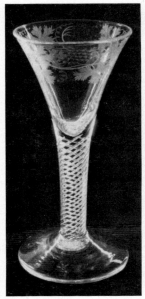

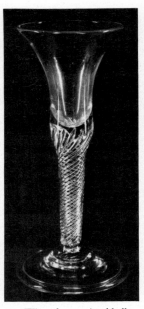

272 Wine glass; drawn trumpet bowl, engraved fruiting vine; MSAT. Ht 6½ in. c. 1750

273 Wine glass; waisted bell bowl, solid base; MSAT. Ht 6¾ in. c. 1750

274 Wine glass; waisted bell bowl; MSAT, the twist extending into base of bowl; FF. Ht 6½ in. c. 1745

275 Firing glass; bell bowl, solid base; MSAT, the twist extending into base of bowl. Ht 4 in. c. 1750

276 Wine glass; RF bowl, hammered base; MSAT; DF. Ht 6 in. c. 1750. Ipswich Museum

277 Wine glass; pan-topped RF bowl; MSAT. Ht 6½ in. c. 1750. Ipswich Museum

278 Wine glass; bucket bowl; MSAT. Ht 7¼ in. c. 1750

279 Ale glass; RF bowl, engraved hops and barley; MSAT. Ht 7⅞ in. c. 1750

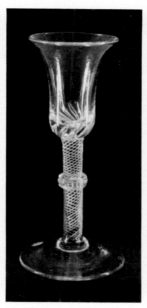
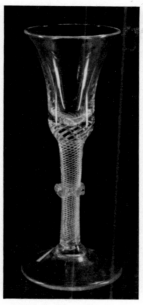
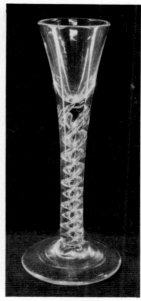

280 Wine glass; bell bowl, solid base; MSAT with central coil collar. Ht 6⅞ in. *c.* 1750

281 Wine glass; bell bowl, solid base; MSAT, the twist extending into base of bowl; central collar. Ht 6¼ in. *c.* 1750

282 Wine glass; bell bowl, solid base; MSAT, the twist extending into base of bowl; central vermiform collar. Ht 6¾ in. *c.* 1750. Hartshorne Collection (Fig. 188)

283 Cordial glass; drawn trumpet bowl; SSAT stem – pair of corkscrews ('mercury twist'). Ht 7 in. *c.* 1750

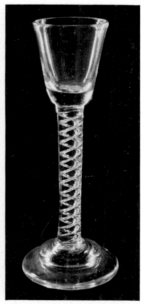

284 Champagne glass; lipped pan-topped RF bowl; collar; MSAT with central double-ringed collar; moulded domed foot. Ht 5⅞ in. *c.* 1750

285 Cider glass; bucket bowl, engraved border of apple branch below rim; SSAT – pair of corkscrews ('mercury twist'). Ht 6½ in. *c.* 1750. Hartshorne Collection (Plate 51)

286 Cordial glass; RF bowl; SSAT – pair of corkscrews; DF. Ht 6⅞ in. *c.* 1750. Smith Collection. Harvey's Wine Museum, Bristol

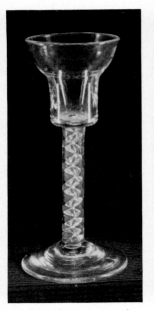

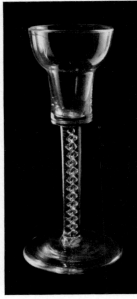

287 Wine glass; ogee bowl; SSAT – pair of corkscrews. Ht 6 in. *c.* 1750

288 Ale glass; RF bowl; SSAT – pair of corkscrews. Ht 7¾ in. *c.* 1750

289 Wine glass; pan-topped bucket bowl; SSAT – pair of corkscrews. Ht 6 in. *c.* 1750. Hartshorne Collection

290 Wine glass; pan-topped bucket bowl; SSAT – pair of tight corkscrews. Ht 6¼ in. *c.* 1750

291 Cordial glass; lipped RF bowl; SSAT – four corkscrews; annulated collar. Ht 7 in. *c.* 1755

292 Wine glass; pointed RF bowl; SSAT – four corkscrews. Ht 5¾ in. *c.* 1750. Hartshorne Collection

293 Wine glass; RF bowl, engraved floral design; SSAT – spiral cable. Ht 6¼ in. *c.* 1750

294 Wine glass; pointed RF bowl, engraved fruiting vine; SSAT – spiral cable. Ht 6 in. *c.* 1750

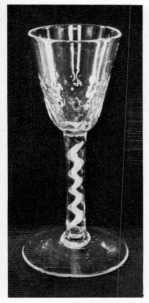

295 Wine glass; pointed RF
bowl, honeycomb-moulded
base; SSAT – spiral cable.
Ht 6⅝ in. *c.* 1750

296 Wine glass; pan-topped
RF bowl; SSAT – spiral cable.
Ht 6¼ in. *c.* 1750. Hartshorne
Collection

297 Wine flute; trumpet bowl;
SSAT – spiral cable. Ht 7½ in.
c. 1750. Portsmouth City
Museums

298 Wine glass; moulded RF
bowl; SSAT – pair spiral
cables. Ht 6 in. *c.* 1750

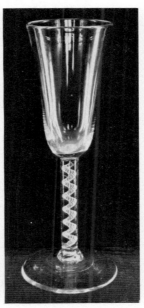

299 Wine glass; pan-topped
RF bowl with moulded base;
SSAT – pair spiral cables.
Ht 6½ in. *c.* 1750

300 Cordial glass; waisted
bucket bowl, engraved border
of fruiting vine below rim;
double collar; SSAT – spiral
gauze; basal knop. Ht 6⅜ in.
c. 1750. Cecil Higgins Museum,
Bedford

301 Ale glass; RF bowl; SSAT
– spiral gauze. Ht 7¾ in. *c.* 1750

302 Wine glass; pointed RF
bowl; tapering stem with
SSAT – pair spiral gauzes.
Ht 6 in. *c.* 1750

303 Wine glass; ogee bowl, moulded base; shoulder-knopped MSAT. Ht 6¼ in. c. 1750. Smith Collection

304 Wine glass; RF bowl, moulded base; shoulder-knopped MSAT. Ht 6 in. c. 1750. Hartshorne Collection

305 Wine glass; RF bowl, engraved moth and honey-suckle (? Jacobite); shoulder-knopped MSAT. Ht 5¾ in. c. 1750

306 Wine glass; RF bowl, moulded base; shoulder-knopped MSAT. Ht 6 in. c. 1750

307 Wine glass; pointed RF bowl, moulded base; shoulder-knopped MSAT. Ht 7 in. c. 1750

308 Wine glass; pointed RF bowl, moulded base; shoulder-knopped MSAT. Ht 6½ in. c. 1750

309 Wine glass; pointed RF bowl, moulded base; shoulder-knopped MSAT. Ht 5½ in. c. 1750

310 Wine glass; bell bowl; shoulder-knopped MSAT. Ht 6½ in. c. 1750. Hartshorne Collection

311 Wine glass; bell bowl, solid base; shoulder-knopped MSAT. Ht 6¾ in. *c.* 1750

312 Ale glass; bell bowl; shoulder-knopped MSAT; DF. Ht 8¼ in. *c.* 1750. Hartshorne Collection

313 Wine glass; vertical rib-moulded waisted bell bowl; shoulder-knopped MSAT; DF to match. Ht 5¾ in. *c.* 1750

314 Wine glass; RF bowl, engraved fruiting vine; MSAT with central swelling knop. Ht 6½ in. *c.* 1750

315 Wine glass; pan-topped RF bowl; MSAT with central swelling knop. Ht 6 in. *c.* 1750

316 Wine glass; pan-topped, vertically moulded RF bowl, engraved floral band below rim; MSAT with central swelled knop. Ht 5⅞ in. *c.* 1750

317 Ale glass; pan-topped RF bowl; MSAT with central swelled knop. Ht 8¼ in. *c.* 1750

318 Toastmaster's glass; deceptive funnel bowl; 3-ringed collar; MSAT with central swelled knop; D & FF. Ht 7 in. *c.* 1750. Cecil Higgins Museum, Bedford

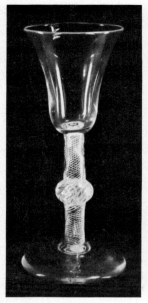

319 Wine glass; bell bowl; MSAT with central ball knop. Ht 6½ in. c. 1750

320 Sweetmeat glass; double-ogee bowl; 3-ringed collar; shoulder-knopped SSAT with pair of corkscrews ('mercury twist'); D & FF. Ht 7¼ in. c. 1745

321 Wine glass; RF bowl, engraved moth and lilies-of-the-valley; shoulder- and centre-knopped MSAT Ht 6 in. c. 1750

322 Wine glass; cup bowl, moulded base; shoulder- and centre-knopped MSAT. Ht 6½ in. c. 1750. Worthing Museum

323 Ale glass; RF bowl; shoulder- and centre-knopped MSAT. Ht 7¾ in. c. 1750

324 Ale glass; RF bowl, engraved hops and barley; shoulder- and centre-knopped MSAT. Ht 7¾ in. c. 1750. Hartshorne Collection (Plate 50)

325 Wine glass; pan-topped RF bowl; shoulder- and centre-knopped MSAT. Ht 6¼ in. c. 1750

326 Wine glass; waisted bucket bowl; shoulder- and centre-knopped MSAT. Ht 6 in. c. 1750

327 Ale glass; waisted bucket bowl, engraved hops and barley; shoulder- and centre-knopped MSAT. Ht 8 in. c. 1750

328 Wine glass; bell bowl, engraved Baroque border below rim; shoulder- and centre-knopped MSAT. Ht 7½ in. c. 1750. Hartshorne Collection (Fig. 178)

329 Wine glass; pointed RF bowl; MSAT with shoulder and basal knops. Ht 6 in. c. 1750

330 Wine glass; bucket bowl, engraved floral design; MSAT with shoulder and basal knops. Ht 6½ in. c. 1750

331 Wine glass; RF bowl; MSAT with three knops. Ht 6¾ in. c. 1750

332 Wine glass; waisted bucket bowl; MSAT with four knops; DF. Ht 6½ in. c. 1750. Smith Collection. Harvey's Wine Museum, Bristol

333 Wine glass; bell bowl; MSAT with four knops. Ht 6¼ in. c. 1750

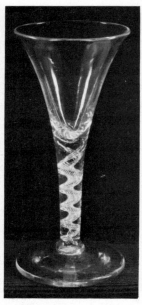

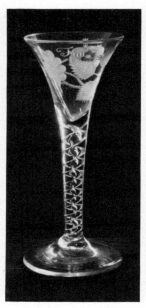

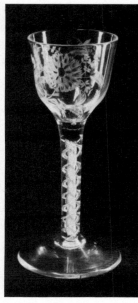

334 Wine glass; bell bowl with Jacobite engraving; MSAT with five knops. Ht 6 in. *c.* 1750

335 Wine glass; trumpet bowl; DSAT – multi-ply spiral band outside cable. Ht 7 in. *c.* 1750

336 Wine glass; trumpet bowl with Jacobite engraving and inscribed FIAT; DSAT – pair of corkscrews outside pair of spiral threads. Ht 7½ in. *c.* 1750

337 Wine glass; ogee bowl engraved in Jacobite style; DSAT – pair of corkscrews outside cable. Ht 5½ in. *c.* 1750

338 Wine glass; rib-moulded RF bowl; DSAT – pair of corkscrews outside cable. Ht 6 in. *c.* 1750. Worthing Museum

339 Wine glass; pan-topped RF bowl; DSAT – pair of corkscrews outside cable. Ht 6 in. *c.* 1750. Hartshorne Collection

340 Goblet; ogee bowl with faintly moulded flutes; DSAT – pair of corkscrews outside cable. Ht 7 in. *c.* 1750

341 Ale glass; RF bowl; DSAT – pair of corkscrews outside cable. Ht 7½ in. *c.* 1750

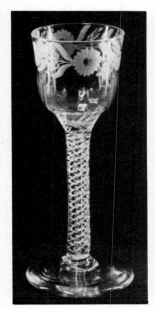

342 Wine glass; ogee bowl with basal flutes and engraved floral band below rim; DSAT – four spirals outside cable. Ht 6 in. c. 1750

343 Wine glass; ogee bowl with basal flutes and engraved formal band below rim; DSAT – four spirals outside cable. Ht 5⅞ in. c. 1750

344 Wine glass; ogee bowl; DSAT – 7-ply spiral band outside thin spiral cable; DF. Ht 6½ in. c. 1750. Worthing Museum

345 Cordial glass; bucket bowl; DSAT – 4-ply spiral band outside spiral cable. Ht 6¾ in. c. 1750

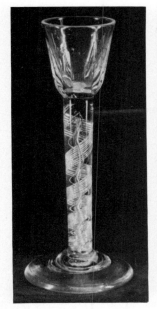
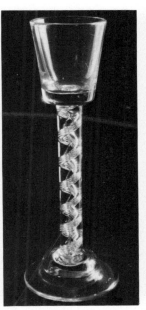

346 Cordial glass; fluted RF bowl; DSAT – 9-ply spiral band outside thin spiral cable. Ht 6½ in. c. 1750

347 Cordial glass; bucket bowl; DSAT – 4-ply spiral band outside loose spiral cable; DF. Ht 6½ in. c. 1750

348 Cordial glass; bucket bowl; DSAT with shoulder and basal knops – MSAT outside thin cable. Ht 6¼ in. c. 1750. Worthing Museum

VIII
Incised-Twist
Stems

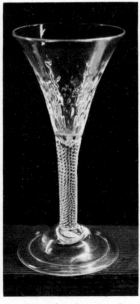

349 Wine glass; hammered trumpet bowl; coarse incised twist; DF. Ht 7 in. *c.* 1755

350 Wine glass; hammered trumpet bowl; coarse incised twist; D & FF. Ht 6½ in. *c.* 1755

351 Wine glass; hammered trumpet bowl; coarse incised twist. Ht 6¾ in. *c.* 1755

352 Wine glass; hammered RF bowl; coarse incised twist. Ht 5½ in. *c.* 1755

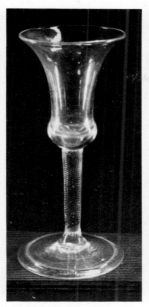

353 Goblet; RF bowl; coarse incised twist. Ht 8⅞ in. c. 1760. Smith Collection. Harvey's Wine Museum, Bristol

354 Wine glass; RF bowl; coarse incised twist; DF. Ht 5⅜ in. c. 1760

355 Wine glass; waisted bell bowl, solid base; coarse incised twist; FF. Ht 6½ in. c. 1755. Soda glass. Hartshorne Collection

356 Wine glass; hammered RF bowl; shoulder-knopped coarse incised twist. Ht 6½ in. c. 1760

357 Wine glass; large RF bowl with basal flutes; fine incised twist. Ht 5½ in. c. 1760

358 Wine glass; RF bowl; fine incised twist. Ht 6 in. c. 1760

359 Ale glass; hammered bell bowl; fine incised twist. Ht 7 in. c. 1760

IX
Composite Stems

360 Wine glass; trumpet bowl; plain section over shoulder-knopped MSAT. Ht 6¾ in. *c.* 1750

361 Ale glass; trumpet bowl; plain section over shoulder-knopped MSAT. Ht 9 in. *c.* 1750

362 Wine glass; trumpet bowl; plain section over MSAT with shoulder and swelled centre knops. Ht 6½ in. *c.* 1750

363 Wine glass; bell bowl; plain section over MSAT with shoulder and swelled centre knops. Ht 6⅞ in. *c.* 1750. Portsmouth City Museums

364 Wine glass; bell·bowl; hollow knop (containing Charles II 6d. dated 1687) between collars, over double-knopped MSAT. Ht 6¾ in. c. 1750. Hartshorne Collection (Plate 37)

365 Wine glass; bell bowl, solid base; MSAT over annulated knop; DF. Ht 6¾ in. c. 1750

366 Wine glass; trumpet bowl; MSAT over collar and basal knop; D & FF. Ht 7¼ in. c. 1750

367 Wine glass; tulip bowl; MSAT over IB knop; DF. Ht 6 in. c. 1750

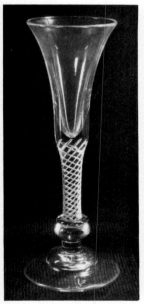

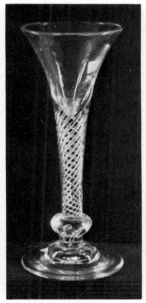

368 Ale glass; waisted bell bowl; MSAT over cushioned knop; DF. Ht 9¼ in. c. 1750

369 Wine glass; trumpet bowl; MSAT over beaded knop; DF. Ht 7 in. c. 1750. Hartshorne Collection

370 Wine glass; wide pointed RF bowl; MSAT over beaded IB knop; DF. Ht 6½ in. c. 1750. Hartshorne Collection

371 Ale glass; long bucket bowl; MSAT over beaded knop; DF. Ht 7½ in. c. 1750

372 Wine glass; trumpet bowl; MSAT over collars and beaded knop; DF. Ht 6⅝ in. *c.* 1750

373 Wine glass; bell bowl; annulated knop between two opposing MSAT balusters. Ht 6¼ in. *c.* 1750

374 Wine glass; RF bowl; beaded knop between two opposing MSAT balusters. Ht 6¾ in. *c.* 1750

375 Wine glass; bell bowl, engraved with band of fruiting vine below rim; beaded knop over SSOT – multi-ply corkscrew; DF. Ht 7 in. *c.* 1765

376 Wine glass; RF bowl; faceted knop over DSOT – four spiral threads outside gauze. Ht 6 in. *c.* 1770

377 Detail of a goblet showing composite stem comprising multi-ply spiral OW band between collars above a beaded knop and short plain section. Ht of goblet 10½ in. *c.* 1765

X
Opaque-
Twist Stems

378 Wine glass; stepped RF ('Lynn') bowl; MSOT; FF. Ht 5½ in. c. 1760. Hartshorne Collection (Fig. 218)

379 Wine glass; trumpet bowl, border of fruiting vine in white enamel ('Beilby'); MSOT. Ht 7 in. c. 1765. Hartshorne Collection

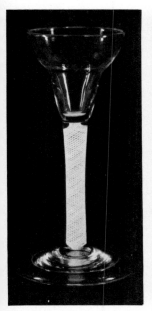

380 Wine glass; pan-topped RF bowl; MSOT; FF. Ht 5¾ in. c. 1760

381 Wine glass; RF bowl; MSOT. Ht 6 in. c. 1765

382 Wine glass; bell bowl with floral engraving; SSOT – single corkscrew. Ht 6½ in. c. 1765

383 Wine glass; pointed RF bowl with hammered base and 'flowered' engraved border; SSOT – single corkscrew. Ht 6 in. c. 1765

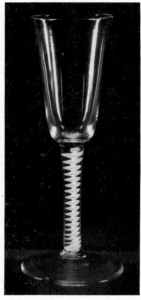

384 Ale glass; RF bowl; SSOT – single corkscrew. Ht 8¼ in. c. 1765

385 Wine glass; fluted ogee bowl; SSOT – single loose corkscrew. Ht 6 in. c. 1765

386 Cordial glass; RF bowl; SSOT – single loose corkscrew. Ht 7¼ in. c. 1765

387 Ratafia glass; trumpet bowl, hammered base, gilded rim; SSOT – single loose corkscrew. Ht 7½ in. c. 1765

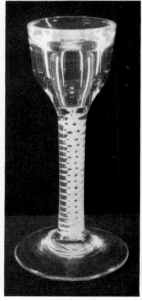

388 Sweetmeat glass; double-ogee bowl with looped arcading terminating in eight prunts on the rim; SSOT – single corkscrew, between collars; D & FF. Ht 6 in. c. 1760. Cecil Higgins Museum, Bedford

389 Ale glass; pointed RF bowl, engraved hops and barley; SSOT – four corkscrews. Ht 7½ in. c. 1765. Hartshorne Collection

390 Toastmaster's glass; deceptive ogee bowl; SSOT – four corkscrews. Ht 5¾ in. c. 1765

391 Wine glass; ogee bowl, spirally moulded base; SSOT – lace twist outlined. Ht 6 in. *c.* 1760

392 Wine glass; RF bowl; SSOT – single spiral gauze. Ht 5¾ in. *c.* 1760. Hartshorne Collection

393 Wine glass; trumpet bowl, engraved rose, two buds and moth (Jacobite); SSOT – single spiral cable. Ht 6¾ in. *c.* 1760. Hartshorne Collection

394 Wine glass; ogee bowl, engraved fruiting vine; SSOT – single spiral cable. Ht 6 in. *c.* 1760

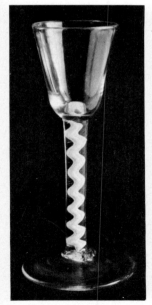

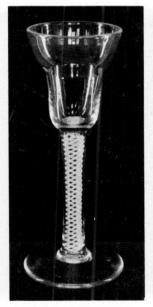
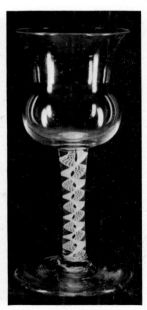

395 Wine glass; RF bowl; SSOT – single spiral gauze with core. Ht 6 in. *c.* 1760

396 Wine glass; waisted bucket bowl, engraved fruiting vine; SSOT – pair of spiral gauzes. Ht 6½ in. *c.* 1760

397 Wine glass; pan-topped RF bowl; SSOT – four spiral gauzes. Ht 6 in. *c.* 1765

398 Wine glass; large tulip bowl; SSOT – corkscrew alternating with spiral gauze. Ht 7¾ in. *c.* 1765

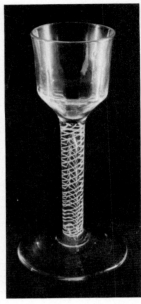

399 Wine glass; saucer-topped bucket bowl; SSOT – corkscrew alternating with spiral gauze. Ht 6 in. *c.* 1765

400 Wine glass; ogee bowl decorated in white enamel with fishing scene; SSOT – pair of heavy spiral threads alternating with spiral gauze. Ht 5⅜ in. *c.* 1770. Attributed to Beilby

401 Wine glass; ogee bowl; SSOT – four heavy spiral threads outside long tear. Ht 5¾ in. *c.* 1765

402 Sweetmeat glass; cup bowl with dentated (or 'cogwheel' or 'pincered') rim and OW vertical stripes; MSOT stem with shoulder and basal knops; panel-moulded foot. Ht 4 in. *c.* 1760

403 Sweetmeat glass; double-ogee bowl with dentated rim; shoulder-knopped MSOT; radially moulded foot. Ht 3¾ in. *c.* 1760

404 Sweetmeat glass; panel-moulded double-ogee bowl with dentated rim; MSOT stem with shoulder and basal knops; radially moulded foot. Ht 4 in. *c.* 1760

405 Wine glass; trumpet bowl; shoulder-knopped MSOT. Ht 6 in. *c.* 1760

406 Wine glass; waisted bell bowl, solid base, engraved fruiting vine; MSOT with shoulder and basal knops. Ht 6¾ in. *c.* 1760

407 Wine glass; bell bowl, engraved rose, two buds and moth (Jacobite); shoulder-knopped MSOT. Ht 6½ in. *c.* 1760. Hartshorne Collection (Plate 44)

408 Wine glass; ogee bowl; centre-knopped MSOT. Ht 6½ in. *c.* 1760

409 Wine glass; ogee bowl with basal flutes; centre-knopped MSOT. Ht 5½ in. *c.* 1760

410 Wine glass; RF bowl; centre-knopped MSOT. Ht 6 in. *c.* 1760. Portsmouth City Museums

411 Wine glass; RF bowl with vertical ribs; centre-knopped MSOT. Ht 6 in. *c.* 1760. Smith Collection. Harvey's Wine Museum, Bristol

412 Ale glass; hammered ogee bowl; centre-knopped MSOT. Ht 7½ in. *c.* 1760

413 Wine glass; large RF bowl; MSOT with shoulder and basal knops. Ht 6½ in. *c.* 1760

414 Cordial glass; RF bowl, basal flutes; MSOT with shoulder and central knops. Ht 6½ in. *c.* 1760

415 Sweetmeat glass; lipped double-ogee bowl with honeycomb moulding; shoulder-knopped SSOT – 20-ply spiral band, between collars; D & FF to match. Ht 6¾ in. *c.* 1760

416 Wine glass; stepped RF ('Lynn') bowl; DSOT – 12-ply spiral band outside pair of spiral tapes. Ht 5½ in. *c.* 1765. Hartshorne Collection

417 Wine glass; stepped RF ('Lynn') bowl; DSOT – 12-ply spiral band outside pair of spiral tapes. Ht 6¼ in. *c.* 1765

418 Wine glass; stepped RF ('Lynn') bowl; DSOT – 12-ply spiral band outside pair of spiral tapes. Ht 6 in. *c.* 1765

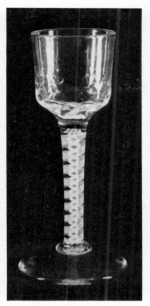

419 Wine glass; octagonal ogee bowl; DSOT – 12-ply spiral band outside pair of spiral tapes. Ht 6 in. c. 1765

420 Wine glass; lipped ogee bowl; DSOT – 12-ply spiral band outside pair of spiral tapes. Ht 5½ in. c. 1765. Worthing Museum

421 Wine glass; ogee bowl, hammered base; DSOT – 12-ply spiral band outside pair of spiral tapes. Ht 6 in. c. 1765

422 Wine glass; large ogee bowl, engraved fruiting vine and bird in flight; DSOT – 11-ply spiral band outside pair of spiral tapes. Ht 7 in. c. 1765. Hartshorne Collection

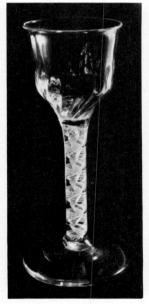

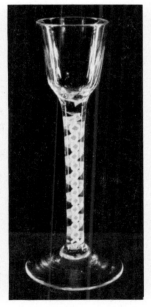

423 Wine glass; ogee bowl with wrythen-moulded base and everted rim; DSOT – 8-ply spiral band outside wide and narrow spiral tapes. Ht 6 in. c. 1765

424 Cordial glass; RF bowl with basal flutes; DSOT – 18-ply spiral band outside pair of spiral tapes. Ht 6½ in. c. 1765. Worthing Museum

425 Cordial glass; ogee bowl with faint vertical fluting; DSOT – 12-ply spiral band outside pair of spiral tapes. Ht 7 in. c. 1765

426 Cordial glass; slightly hammered RF bowl, engraved fruiting vine; DSOT – 12-ply spiral band outside pair of spiral tapes. Ht 6⅞ in. c. 1765

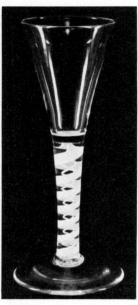

427 Wine glass; RF bowl with basal flutes; DSOT – solid spiral band outside pair of spiral tapes. Ht 6 in. *c.* 1765

428 Wine glass; trumpet bowl; DSOT – solid spiral band outside pair of spiral tapes. Ht 7 in. *c.* 1765

429 Wine glass; pan-topped trumpet bowl; DSOT – solid spiral band outside pair of spiral tapes. Ht 6 in. *c.* 1765

430 Ale glass; RF bowl; DSOT – solid spiral band outside pair of spiral tapes. Ht 7½ in. *c.* 1765. Worthing Museum

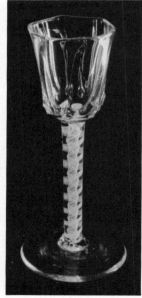

431 Ale glass; RF bowl, hammered base; DSOT – solid spiral band outside pair of spiral tapes. Ht 7½ in. *c.* 1765

432 Ratafia glass; RF bowl with basal flutes; DSOT – solid spiral band outside pair of spiral tapes. Ht 7 in. *c.* 1765

433 Wine glass; bucket bowl with engraved 'flowered' border below rim; DSOT – 12-ply spiral band outside gauze. Ht 6 in. *c.* 1765

434 Wine glass; hexagonal, panel-moulded bowl; DSOT – 8-ply spiral band outside gauze. Ht 6 in. *c.* 1765

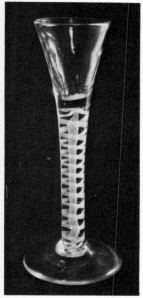

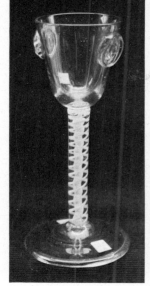

435 Cordial glass; trumpet bowl with faint basal fluting; DSOT – pair of 7-ply spiral bands outside gauze. Ht 7 in. *c*. 1765

436 Wine glass; RF bowl with a seal on each side embodying the arms 'a fesse between three garbs, in an arabesque border'; DSOT – pair of spiral tapes outside gauze; FF. Ht 6 in. *c*. 1765. The seals are an extremely rare feature on a wine glass. Hartshorne Collection (Fig. 219)

437 Wine glass; RF bowl; DSOT – pair of spiral tapes outside gauze. Ht 6 in. *c*. 1765. Worthing Museum

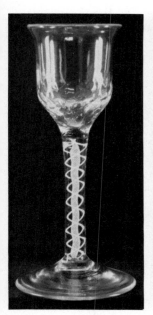

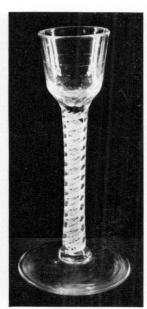

438 Wine glass; lipped ogee bowl; DSOT – pair of heavy spiral threads outside gauze. Ht 5¾ in. *c*. 1765. Hartshorne Collection

439 Wine glass; waisted bucket bowl; DSOT – pair of spiral threads outside gauze. Ht 6¼ in. *c*. 1765. Hartshorne Collection

440 Ale glass; long bell bowl; DSOT – pair of spiral tapes outside gauze. Ht 7¾ in. *c*. 1765

441 Cordial glass; ogee bowl, hammered base; DSOT – pair of spiral tapes outside gauze. Ht 6½ in. *c*. 1765

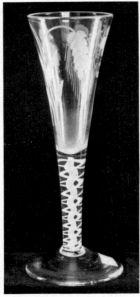

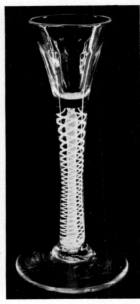

442 Ale glass; trumpet bowl, engraved hops and barley; DSOT – corkscrew and spiral thread alternating outside spiral gauze. Ht 7¾ in. *c.* 1765. Hartshorne Collection

443 Wine glass; ogee bowl with vertically moulded base; DSOT – three spiral threads outside spiral gauze. Ht 7 in. *c.* 1765

444 Wine glass; ogee bowl, gilt rim; DSOT – four heavy spiral threads outside gauze. Ht 5¾ in. *c.* 1770

445 Cordial glass; trumpet bowl, basal flutes; DSOT – four spiral threads outside gauze. Ht 6½ in. *c.* 1770

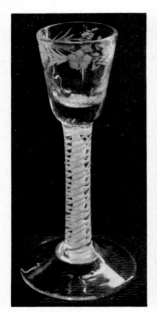

446 Cordial glass; RF bowl, basal flutes, engraved floral band below rim; DSOT – four heavy spiral threads outside gauze. Ht 6¼ in. *c.* 1770

447 Mead glass; cup bowl, gadrooned base; DSOT – four heavy spiral threads outside gauze; FF. Ht 6¼ in. *c.* 1770

448 Dram glass; trumpet bowl; DSOT – four heavy spiral threads outside spiral gauze; firing foot. Ht 4½ in. *c.* 1770

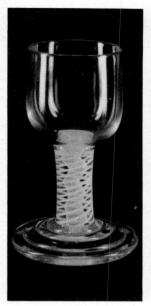

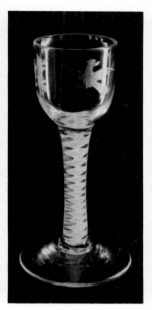

449 Firing glass; cup bowl; DSOT – four heavy spiral threads outside spiral gauze; terraced foot. Ht 4¾ in. *c.* 1770

450 Wine glass; cup bowl, engraved flowers and bird in flight; DSOT – 4-ply spiral band outside corkscrew. Ht 5½ in. *c.* 1770

451 Wine glass; pointed RF bowl decorated with festoons in white enamel; DSOT – 12-ply spiral band outside corkscrew. Ht 6 in. *c.* 1770. Attributed to Beilby

452 Wine glass; ogee bowl; DSOT – 5-ply spiral band outside multi-ply corkscrew. Ht 5¾ in. *c.* 1770

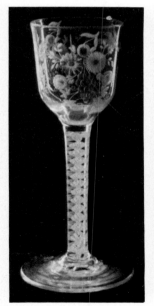

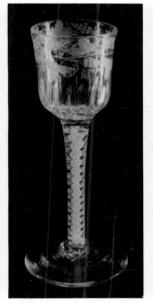

453 Wine glass; ogee bowl, engraved fruiting vine and bird in flight; DSOT – 4-ply spiral band outside lace twist. Ht 6 in. *c.* 1770

454 Wine glass; ogee bowl with basal flutes; DSOT – pair of 6-ply spiral bands outside lace twist. Ht 5½ in. *c.* 1770. Hartshorne Collection (Fig. 240)

455 Wine glass; ogee bowl with engraved border of fruiting vine and basal flutes; DSOT – pair of 6-ply spiral bands outside lace twist. Ht 6 in. *c.* 1770

456 Wine glass; ogee bowl with basal flutes; DSOT – 8-ply spiral band outside lace twist. Ht 6½ in. *c.* 1770

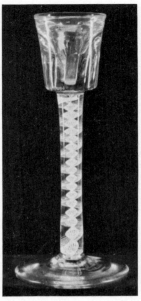

457 Toastmaster's glass; deceptive bucket bowl with basal flutes; DSOT – 11-ply spiral band outside lace twist. Ht 7 in. *c.* 1770. Hartshorne Collection (Plate 52/2)

458 Toastmaster's glass; deceptive RF bowl with basal flutes; DSOT – 12-ply spiral band outside lace twist; 'helmet' domed foot. Ht 6½ in. *c.* 1770

459 Firing glass; ogee bowl; DSOT – pair of 6-ply spiral bands outside lace twist; terraced foot. Ht 3¾ in. *c.* 1770. Worthing Museum

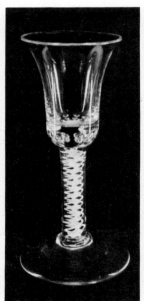

460 Firing glass; ovoid bowl with basal flutes; DSOT – pair of 9-ply spiral bands outside lace twist; terraced foot. Ht 4 in. *c.* 1770. Hartshorne Collection

461 Wine glass; bell bowl with solid teared base; DSOT – pair of heavy spiral threads outside corkscrew. Ht 6⅛ in. *c.* 1770

462 Wine glass; ovoid bowl with basal flutes; DSOT – pair of spiral tapes outside a multiply corkscrew. Ht 5¾ in. *c.* 1770

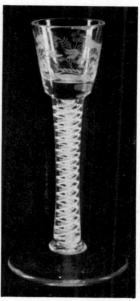

463 Wine glass; ogee bowl decorated with pastoral scene in white enamel ('Beilby'); DSOT – pair of heavy spiral threads outside lace twist. Ht 5¾ in. *c.* 1770

464 Sweetmeat; honeycomb-moulded double-ogee bowl with everted rim; collar; DSOT – pair of spiral tapes outside lace twist; D & FF to match. Ht 6½ in. *c.* 1770

465 Cordial glass; bucket bowl, engraved flowers and bird in flight, solid base; DSOT – pair of heavy spiral threads outside lace twist. Ht 6½ in. *c.* 1770. Hartshorne Collection (Fig. 299)

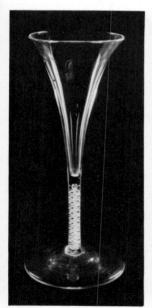

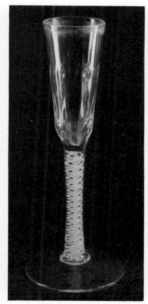

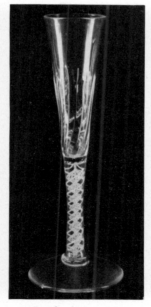

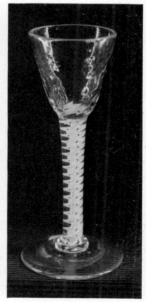

466 Wine flute; trumpet bowl; DSOT – pair of heavy spiral threads outside lace twist. Ht 7½ in. *c.* 1770

467 Ratafia glass; ogee bowl with basal flutes; DSOT – pair of heavy spiral threads outside lace twist. Ht 7¼ in. *c.* 1770

468 Ratafia glass; trumpet bowl with basal flutes; DSOT – pair of heavy spiral threads outside lace twist. Ht 8 in. *c.* 1770

469 Wine glass; pointed RF bowl, hammered; DSOT – pair of corkscrews outside spiral cable. Ht 6 in. *c.* 1770

469A Wine glass; ogee bowl engraved in Jacobite manner; DSOT – pair of multi-ply corkscrews outside pair of spiral threads. Ht 6 in. c. 1770

470 Short ale glass; ogee bowl; DSOT – pair of corkscrews outside pair of heavy spiral threads. Ht 6½ in. c. 1770. Hartshorne Collection (Fig. 278)

471 Small goblet; ogee bowl with slightly everted rim; DSOT – pair of heavy spiral threads outside vertical cable. Ht 7¼ in. c. 1770

472 Ale glass; pointed RF bowl, engraved hops and barley; DSOT – pair of spiral threads outside spiral cable. Ht 8¼ in. c. 1770

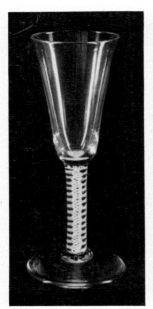

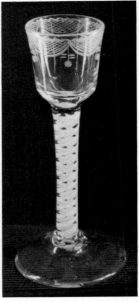

473 Ale glass; pointed RF bowl; DSOT – pair of 4-ply spiral bands outside four heavy spiral threads. Ht 7 in. c. 1770

474 Wine glass; lipped ogee bowl, engraved floral band; DSOT – 12-ply spiral band outside four spiral threads. Ht 5¾ in. c. 1770

475 Wine glass; RF bowl, hammered and fluted; DSOT – pair of heavy spiral threads outside four heavy spiral threads. Ht 6 in. c. 1770

476 Cordial glass; ogee bowl, engraved festoons below rim; DSOT – pair of solid spiral bands outside corkscrew. Ht 6¼ in. c. 1770. Hartshorne Collection (Fig. 301)

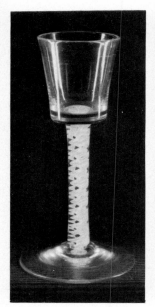

477 Wine glass; bucket bowl; DSOT – pair of spiral tapes outside corkscrew. Ht 6 in. *c.* 1770

478 Wine glass; ogee bowl with basal flutes; DSOT – pair of spiral gauzes outside pair of spiral tapes. Ht 5¾ in. *c.* 1770. Worthing Museum

479 Firing glass; stepped RF ('Lynn') bowl; DSOT – pair of 2-ply spiral bands outside pair of multi-ply spiral tapes. Ht 6 in. *c.* 1770

480 Wine glass; bucket bowl; DSOT – two pairs of spiral threads outside pair of spiral tapes. Ht 6 in. *c.* 1770

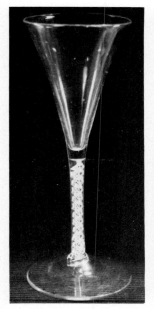

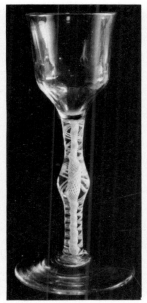

481 Wine flute; trumpet bowl; DSOT – pair of 5-ply spiral bands outside four spiral threads. Ht 7 in. *c.* 1770

482 Wine glass; lipped ogee bowl; central-knopped DSOT – pair of spiral threads outside gauze. Ht 6 in. *c.* 1770. Hartshorne Collection (Fig. 231)

482A Wine glass; ogee bowl, moulded base; DSOT – pair of 3-ply spiral bands outside gauze; central swelled knop. Ht 6 in. *c.* 1770

483 Wine glass; bell bowl; DSOT with two knops – pair of spiral tapes outside lace twist. Ht 6¾ in. *c.* 1770

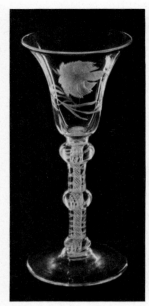

484 Wine glass; bell bowl,
engraved carnation (?Jacobite);
DSOT with three knops – pair
of 3-ply spiral bands outside
gauze. Ht 6½ in. c. 1770

485 Wine glass; bell bowl,
engraved fruiting vine and
bird in flight; DSOT with
four knops – pair of spiral
tapes outside gauze. Ht 6¾ in.
c. 1770

486 Wine glass; bell bowl,
engraved floral band below
rim; DSOT with four knops –
pair of spiral tapes outside
gauze. Ht 6¾ in. c. 1770

XI
Mixed and
Colour-Twist
Stems

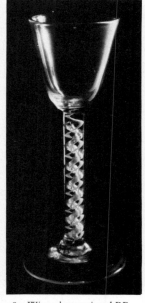

487 Wine glass; pointed RF
bowl; single-series mixed twist
– spiral air cable alternating
with opaque corkscrew.
Ht 6¼ in. c. 1760

488 Wine glass; pointed RF
bowl; single-series mixed twist
– spiral air cable alternating
with heavy opaque spiral
thread. Ht 6 in. c. 1760.
Hartshorne Collection (Fig.
183)

489 Wine glass; RF bowl;
double-series mixed twist –
pair of spiral air threads
outside loose multi-ply opaque
corkscrew. Ht 5¾ in. c. 1760

490 Wine glass; waisted ogee
bowl with basal flutes and
engraved formal border below
rim; double-series mixed twist
– spiral air cable alternating
with heavy spiral thread
outside slightly spiral opaque
rod. Ht 6¼ in. c. 1760

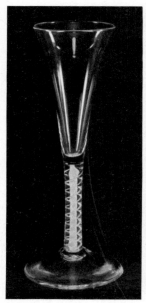

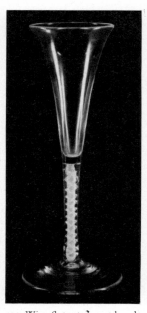

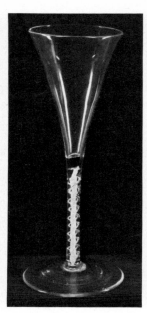

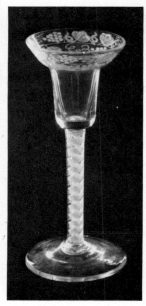

491 Wine flute; trumpet bowl; double-series mixed twist – pair of air spirals outside opaque gauze. Ht 7¼ in. *c.* 1760

492 Wine flute; trumpet bowl; double-series mixed twist – pair of air spirals outside opaque gauze. Ht 7½ in. *c.* 1760

493 Wine flute; trumpet bowl; double-series mixed twist – pair of air spirals outside opaque gauze. Ht 7⅜ in. *c.* 1760

494 Wine glass; saucer-topped bucket bowl, engraved fruiting vine below rim; double-series mixed twist – MSAT outside multi-ply opaque corkscrew. Ht 6½ in. *c.* 1760

495 Wine glass; pointed RF bowl; double-series mixed twist – pair of heavy opaque spiral threads outside air cable. Ht 6½ in. *c.* 1760

496 Wine glass; bell bowl; double-series mixed twist – four opaque spiral threads outside air cable. Ht 7 in. *c.* 1760

497 Wine glass; tulip bowl; double-series mixed twist – pair of opaque corkscrews outside pair of air corkscrews. Ht 6 in. *c.* 1760

498 Wine glass; RF bowl; colour-twist stem – pair of brown heavy spiral threads only. Ht 6 in. *c.* 1770

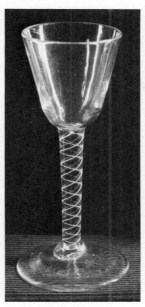

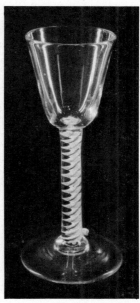

499 Wine glass; bell bowl;
single-series colour twist –
spiral air gauze alternating with
spiral red thread. Ht 7 in.
c. 1760

500 Wine glass; RF bowl;
single-series colour twist –
opaque corkscrew edged red
and green alternating with
opaque spiral gauze. Ht 5¾ in.
c. 1770

501 Wine glass; RF bowl;
'tartan' twist, comprising
threads of blue, red, green and
opaque white. Ht 5¾ in. c. 1770

502 Wine glass; RF bowl;
double-series colour twist –
pair of red and blue heavy
spiral threads alternating
outside OW corkscrew.
Ht 6 in. c. 1770

503 Goblet; RF bowl; double-
series colour twist – pair of
blue heavy spiral threads
outside OW lace twist.
Ht 7½ in. c. 1770

504 Firing glass; trumpet bowl; double-series colour twist – pair
of green and white heavy spiral threads outside OW gauze. Ht
4½ in. c. 1770

505 Firing glass; trumpet
bowl; double-series colour
twist – pair of green and white
spiral threads outside OW
gauze. Ht 4⅜ in. c. 1770

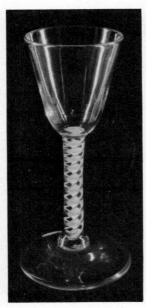

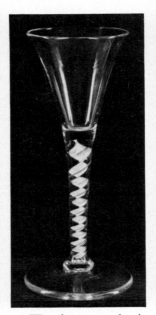

506 Ale glass; ogee bowl; double-series colour twist – pair of mixed OW and blue corkscrews outside pair of heavy spiral OW threads. Ht 7⅛ in. c. 1770

507 Wine glass; pointed RF bowl; double-series colour twist – pair of heavy spiral OW threads outside OW corkscrew edged with pink. Ht 6 in. c. 1770

508 Wine glass; trumpet bowl; double-series colour twist – pair of alternating red and green spiral threads outside OW corkscrew edged with blue and green. Ht 6½ in. c. 1770. Hartshorne Collection

509 Wine glass; bell bowl, solid base; double-series colour twist – pair of heavy OW spiral threads outside OW corkscrew edged alternately with green and maroon. Ht 6¼ in. c. 1770. Hartshorne Collection

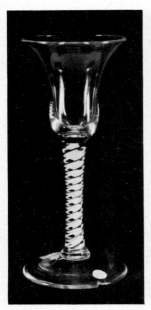

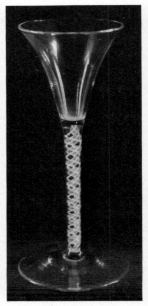

510 Wine glass; waisted bell bowl; double-series colour twist; pair of heavy OW spiral threads outside OW corkscrew edged with green and maroon. Ht 6¾ in. c. 1770

511 Wine glass; bell bowl; double-series colour twist – pair of OW spiral tapes outside OW corkscrew edged with red and green. Ht 6¼ in. c. 1770

512 Wine glass; ogee bowl; double-series colour twist – pair of OW spiral tapes outside OW edged with blue. Ht 6 in. c. 1770

513 Wine glass; trumpet bowl; double-series colour twist – pair of OW heavy threads outside OW loose multi-ply corkscrew edged with red and turquoise. Ht 6¾ in. c. 1770

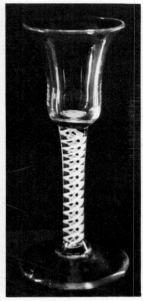

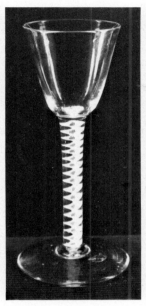

514 Wine glass; bell bowl; double-series colour twist – pair of OW spiral gauzes outside yellow lace twist edged with white. Ht 5⅞ in. c. 1770. Cecil Higgins Museum, Bedford

515 Wine glass; RF bowl; double-series colour twist – 12-ply OW spiral band outside pair of pale blue heavy spiral threads. Ht. 5¾ in. c. 1770

516 Wine glass; RF bowl; double-series colour twist – OW corkscrew outside column of six yellow threads. Ht 5⅞ in. c. 1770. Cecil Higgins Museum, Bedford

517 Wine glass; honeycomb-moulded RF bowl; double-series colour twist – pair of spiral OW gauzes outside vertical yellow thread. Ht 6 in. c. 1770

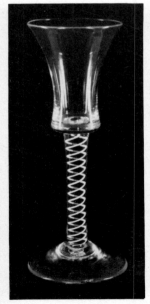

518 Wine glass; waisted bucket bowl; double-series colour twist – pair of pink spiral heavy threads outside mauve gauze. Ht 7 in. c. 1770

519 Wine glass; waisted bucket bowl; double-series colour twist – pair of OW spiral heavy threads outside column of four yellow spiral threads. Ht 6⅛ in. c. 1770

520 Wine glass; ogee bowl; double-series colour twist – four OW spiral heavy threads outside vertical blue thread. Ht 6½ in. c. 1770

521 Wine glass; ogee bowl with engraved festoons below rim and basal flutes; double-series colour twist – 2-ply OW spiral band outside pale blue spiral gauze. Ht 5⅝ in. c. 1770

XII
Faceted Stems

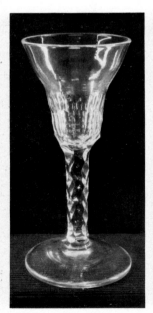

522 Wine glass; bell bowl; diamond-faceted stem. Ht 6½ in. *c.* 1785

523 Wine glass; pan-topped ogee bowl; diamond-faceted stem. Ht 6 in. *c.* 1785. Hartshorne Collection

524 Wine glass; pan-topped RF bowl, faceted base; diamond-faceted stem. Ht 7¼ in. *c.* 1785

525 Wine glass; ogee bowl with basal flutes; scalloped, diamond-faceted stem; scalloped, faceted foot. Ht 6 in. *c.* 1785

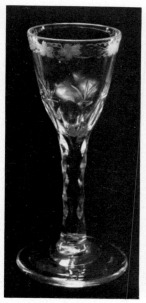

526 Wine glass; RF bowl with engraved border of fruiting vine below rim and basal fluting and cutting; diamond-faceted stem. Ht 6 in. *c.* 1785

527 Ale glass; RF bowl; diamond-faceted stem. Ht 8¼ in. *c.* 1785

528 Goblet; RF bowl; border of engraved stars below rim; diamond-faceted stem. Ht 6¼ in. *c.* 1800

529 Wine glass; RF bowl, engraved flowers and birds in flight below formal border; hexagonal-faceted stem; engraved foot. Ht 5½ in. *c.* 1785

530 Wine glass; RF bowl, engraved rose, two buds and butterfly (Jacobite type); hexagonal-faceted stem. Ht 5½ in. *c.* 1785

531 Wine glass; pointed RF bowl, engraved and polished formal border below rim, faceted base; hexagonal-faceted stem. Ht 6 in. *c.* 1785

532 Wine glass; ovoid bowl, engraved bee and flowers with polished petals; hexagonal-faceted stem; ground-out pontil-mark. Ht 4⅝ in. *c.* 1790

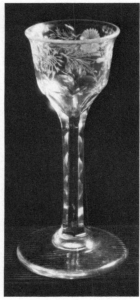

533 Wine glass; honeycomb-moulded ovoid bowl; hexagonal-faceted stem. Ht 6¾ in. *c.* 1785

534 Ratafia glass; RF bowl, engraved and polished festoons; hexagonal-faceted stem. Ht 6¼ in. *c.* 1785. Harvey's Wine Museum, Bristol

535 Goblet; ovoid bowl, engraved rose and bud (Jacobite type); hexagonal-faceted stem. Ht 7 in. *c.* 1790. Hartshorne Collection (Fig. 250)

536 Wine glass; lipped ogee bowl, engraved floral design; stem comprising alternate flutes and facets. Ht 6 in. *c.* 1785

537 Wine glass; ovoid bowl, engraved flowers with polished petals and scale-cut base; notched stem. Ht 5 in. *c.* 1790

538 Wine glass; ovoid bowl; notched stem. Ht 5½ in. *c.* 1790

539 Sweetmeat glass; double-ogee cut bowl with scalloped rim; hexagonal columnar stem; domed foot with scalloped edge. Ht 6⅛ in. *c.* 1760

540 Dram glass; RF bowl, engraved hops and barley (!); scale-cut base; hexagonal-fluted stem; faceted foot. Ht 4¼ in. *c.* 1790. Hartshorne Collection (Fig. 281)

541 Goblet; straight-sided bowl, engraved initials J M in a decorative border; fluted, incurved stem. Ht 7 in. *c.* 1800

542 Christening glass (?); ovoid bowl engraved A T P and, on other side, I H S, within shields flanked by floral engraving; fluted, incurved stem. Ht 4¾ in. *c.* 1800

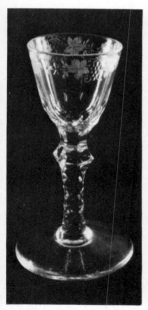

543 Wine glass; RF bowl, engraved band of fruiting vine with polished fruits; scale-cut base; diamond-faceted stem with single knop. Ht 5¼ in. *c.* 1785

544 Sweetmeat glass; faceted double-ogee bowl with band of engraved stars below the rim; diamond-faceted stem with two knops; faceted DF. Ht 7 in. *c.* 1790

545 Wine glass; hexagonally cut ogee bowl; diamond-faceted stem with shoulder knop; faceted foot. Ht 5½ in. *c.* 1785

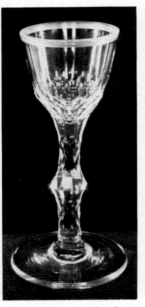

546 Wine glass; waisted ogee bowl, scale–cut base; diamond–faceted stem with central knop. Ht 5⅞ in. c. 1785

547 Wine glass; ogee bowl with gilt rim and scale–cut base; diamond–faceted stem with central knop. Ht 5½ in. c. 1785

548 Sweetmeat glass; double-ogee cut bowl with scalloped rim; diamond-faceted stem with central IB knop; faceted DF with scalloped edge. Ht 7 in. c. 1785

549 Ale glass; RF bowl, engraved hops and barley; two faceted knops in a fluted stem. Ht 8¾ in. c. 1785

XIII
Rudimentary
Stems

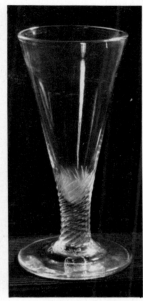

550 Dwarf ale glass; wrythen bowl; no stem. Ht 4¼ in. 18th century. Smith Collection. Harvey's Wine Museum, Bristol

551 Dwarf ale glass; trumpet bowl; short wrythen stem. Ht 5¼ in. Late 18th century. Hartshorne Collection

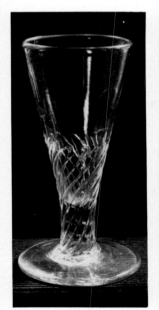

552 Dwarf ale glass; trumpet bowl; wrythen base and short wrythen stem. Ht 5 in. Late 18th century

553 Dwarf ale glass; wrythen trumpet bowl; collar; winged knop; FF. Ht 6 in. Early 18th century

554 Dwarf ale glass; wrythen-funnel bowl; wrythen knop; FF. Ht 4½ in. Early 18th century

555 Dwarf ale glass; wrythen-funnel bowl; two wrythen knops; FF. Ht 5¼ in. Early 18th century

556 Short ale glass; wrythen-funnel bowl with flammiform fringe; short plain stem between two knops; FF. Ht 6 in. Mid 18th century

557 Short ale glass; wrythen-funnel bowl with flammiform fringe; short plain stem between wrythen knop and basal knop; FF. Ht 6¼ in. Mid 18th century

558 Short ale glass; wrythen-funnel bowl; two flattened knops. Ht 5¼ in. Mid 18th century

559 Dwarf ale glass; wrythen-funnel bowl with flammiform fringe; wrythen knop. Ht 4½ in. Mid 18th century. Smith Collection. Harvey's Wine Museum, Bristol

560 Short ale glass; panel-moulded funnel bowl, engraved hops and barley; collar above true baluster. Ht 7 in. c. 1800

561 Short ale glass; lipped RF bowl with gadrooned base; two wrythen knops above short wrythen stem; FF. Ht 5¾ in. Early 18th century

562 Short ale glass; pointed RF bowl, engraved hops and barley; knop above short plain stem. Ht 4¾ in. Late 18th century. Hartshorne Collection

563 Jelly glass; wrythen-hexagonal bowl; wrythen knop as stem; wrythen DF. Ht 4 in. Early 18th century

564 Jelly glass; bell bowl; flattened knop as stem. Ht 3¾ in. Late 18th century

565 Jelly glass; honeycomb–moulded flared bowl; collar; moulded FF. Ht 2¼ in. Mid 18th century

566 Jelly glass; flared bowl with folded rim and gadrooned base; FF with high dome. Ht 2 in. Mid 18th century

567 Jelly glass; lipped RF bowl with 'nipt diamond waies'; ball knop; moulded DF. Ht 3½ in. Early 18th century

568 Jelly glass; panel-moulded pan-topped bowl; collar; panel-moulded DF. Ht 4 in. Early 18th century

569 Jelly glass; pan-topped, honeycomb-moulded bowl; DF moulded to match. Ht 4½ in. c. 1750

570 Jelly glass; wrythen pan-topped bowl; collar; panel-moulded D & FF. Ht 3½ in. Early 18th century

571 Jelly glass; pan-topped bowl with moulded fluting; bladed collar; D & FF. Ht 5 in. c. 1750

572 Jelly glass; pan-topped bowl; collar; flat foot. Ht 4½ in. c. 1780

573 Jelly glass; straight-sided bowl; pair of B-handles; DF. Ht 3¾ in. *c.* 1750

574 Jelly glass; cup bowl; pair of B-handles; beaded knop; DF. Ht 4¼ in. *c.* 1750

575 Jelly glass; vertically moulded funnel bowl; pair of B-handles. Ht 4¼ in. *c.* 1750

576 Monteith (or 'bonnet' glass); double-ogee honeycomb-moulded bowl; flattened knop; scalloped foot. Ht 3 in. *c.* 1750

577 Monteith; double-ogee honeycomb-moulded bowl with blue rim. Ht 3 in. *c.* 1750

578 Monteith; ogee bowl with notched rim and notched ribs; collar above rudimentary stem; stepped square-moulded 'lemon-squeezer' base. Ht 3½ in. *c.* 1800

579 Monteith; diamond-cut cup bowl; faceted collar and rudimentary stem; lozenge-shaped foot. Ht 3¾ in. *c.* 1800

580 Monteith; cut double-ogee bowl with scalloped rim; collar above short plain stem; square solid base. Ht 3½ in. *c.* 1800

581 Monteith; cut double-ogee bowl with scalloped rim; set directly upon a circular faceted foot. Ht 3 in. *c.* 1800

582 Posset pot; vertically moulded cylindrical body; pair of single-looped handles; swan-neck spout with raven's head seal; high-kick base. Pale blue, slightly crizzled metal. Ht $3\frac{5}{16}$ in. *c.* 1677. The seal indicates that this pot was made by George Ravenscroft of the Henley-on-Thames and Savoy Glasshouses. It originated, with two others, also sealed, from Wentworth Woodhouse and was probably made for William Wentworth, Earl of Stafford (1626–95). Pilkington Glass Museum St. Helens

583 Dram glass; funnel bowl; short plain stem; FF. Ht $3\frac{1}{2}$ in. *c.* 1740

584 Firing glass; funnel bowl engraved THE FRIENDLY SOCIETY; firing foot. Ht $3\frac{5}{8}$ in. *c.* 1740. Harvey's Wine Museum, Bristol

585 Dram glass; deceptive conical bowl; collar; short plain stem bisected by flattened knop. Ht 4½ in. c. 1800

586 Dram glass; bell bowl; beaded knop as stem; DF. Ht 4 in. c. 1750. Hartshorne Collection

587 Firing glass; funnel bowl, engraved rose, two buds, oak leaf and REDEAT (Jacobite); set directly upon a firing foot. Ht 3½ in. c. 1745

588 Firing glass; waisted bell bowl, solid base; set directly upon a firing foot. Ht 4½ in. c. 1740. Hartshorne Collection (Fig. 307)

589 Dram glass; bell bowl; foot a similar but smaller bowl; (single and double measure). Ht 4 in. *c.* 1750

590 Rummer; conical bowl; annulated knop over short plain stem; flat foot. Ht 6 in. *c.* 1790

591 Rummer; ogee bowl with engraved formal border below rim; large flat facets at base of bowl; collar above short plain stem; flat foot. Ht 5½ in. *c.* 1800

592 Rummer; bucket bowl, fluted base; bladed knop. Ht 5 in. Early 19th century. Portsmouth City Museums

593 Rummer; square bucket bowl engraved T J G and agricultural arms above SPEED THE PLOUGH (*see also* 705); square-moulded 'lemon-squeezer' base. Ht 5¼ in. Early 19th century

594 Rummer; incurved bowl, engraved with ballooning scene (*see also* 691); collar above rudimentary stem; square-moulded 'lemon-squeezer' base. Ht 5¼ in. *c.* 1800. King's Lynn Museum

595 Tankard; band of eight threads below rim; gadrooned base containing Maundy penny (?1767); single-loop handle. Ht 6 in. *c.* 1770

596 Tankard; band of three threads below rim; gadrooned base; single-loop handle. Ht 6 in. *c.* 1770

597 Tankard; band of eight threads below rim; gadrooned base; single-loop handle. Ht 4¼ in. *c.* 1770

598 Tankard; band of multiple threads below rim; coin dated 1762 in base; single-loop handle. Ht 4½ in. *c.* 1765

599 Tumbler; barrel shaped. Ht 5¼ in. *c.* 1800

600 Tumbler; stepped cylindrical bowl with seven corrugations ('Lynn'); low kick. Ht 4¾ in. *c.* 1775. King's Lynn Museum

601 Tumbler; stepped cylindrical bowl with six narrow and three broad corrugations ('Lynn'); low kick. Ht 3⅞ in. *c.* 1775. King's Lynn Museum

602 Tumbler; stepped cylindrical bowl with four corrugations ('Lynn'); low kick. Ht 4¾ in. *c.* 1775. King's Lynn Museum

XIV
Decoration:
Diamond-point
Engraving

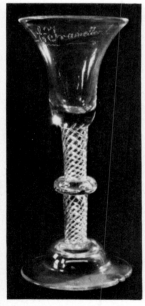

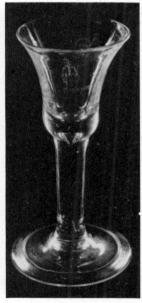

603 Wine glass; bell bowl, solid base engraved in diamond-point E. TRAVELLER; MSAT with beaded collar; DF. Ht 6¾ in. *c.* 1750. Ipswich Museum

604 Rummer; bucket bowl engraved in diamond-point H S within a garland of leaves; moulded base; short plain stem divided by bladed knop; flat foot. Ht 5½ in. *c.* 1800

605 Wine glass; bell bowl, solid base with tear, engraved in diamond-point COOPER below cello on one side, GILES inside a French horn on the other and dated 1757; plain stem; FF. Ht 6⅛ in. *c.* 1740 (engraved later?)

606 Wine glass; drawn trumpet bowl, engraved in diamond-point with cypher of James VIII in monogram below a crown, flanked by verses of Jacobite hymn ending with AMEN; tear in plain stem; FF engraved TO THE PROSPERITY OF THE FAMILY OF LOCHIELL. Ht 6½ in. *c.* 1750. Royal Scottish Museum, Edinburgh

607 Goblet; drawn trumpet bowl, engraved in diamond-point with a blackbird on a rose bough looking behind at a dragon-fly on a spray of carnation, the inscription THE GLORIOUS MEMORY undulating below the rim; plain stem with tear; FF. (Disguised Jacobite, i.e. pretending to be a Williamite but with the Jacobite emblems.) Ht 8¾ in. *c.* 1740. Cecil Higgins Museum, Bedford

608 Reverse of 607 showing engraving of dragon-fly

609 Wine glass; trumpet bowl, engraved in diamond-point with Welsh dragon, scale-cut base; six-sided fluted stem. Ht 5⅜ in. *c.* 1785

610 Goblet; RF bowl engraved in diamond-point THE NOBLE NAVIGATION ANNE 1771; DSOT – pair of heavy spiral threads outside lace twist. Ht 8 in. *c.* 1771. Pilkington Glass Museum, St Helens

611 Goblet; trumpet bowl, engraved in diamond-point with trees in leaf; plain stem; FF. Ht 9¼ in. *c.* 1745

XV

Decoration: Wheel-Engraving and Stippling

612 Goblet; thistle bowl, solid faceted base, engraved with crown above monogram F P and on the reverse the Prince of Wales's feathers. The monogram refers to Frederick, father of George III and the glass was probably engraved to commemorate his creation as Prince of Wales in 1729; diamond-faceted teared swelled knop and faceted basal knop; D & FF. Ht 10¼ in. *c.* 1730. NOTE: F. B. Haynes suggests that this may be a Lauenstein glass (op. cit., p. 284); if English it is either an extraordinarily early example of faceting, or, more probably, was faceted later. Hartshorne Collection (Plate 47)

613 Reverse of 612 showing Prince of Wales's feathers

614 Goblet; RF bowl engraved with Royal coat of arms and signed on foot by Jacob Sang; stem comprising two faceted ball knops above faceted IB knop and basal knop; stepped foot with scalloped rim. Ht. 7¼ in. *c.* 1760. Jacob Sang was working *c.* 1752–62. Hartshorne Collection

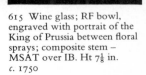

615 Wine glass; RF bowl, engraved with portrait of the King of Prussia between floral sprays; composite stem – MSAT over IB. Ht 7⅛ in. *c.* 1750

616 Wine glass; pointed RF bowl, engraved with the arms of the House of Orange below legend VIVAT DE PRINS VAN ORANIE: 'Newcastle' light baluster stem including teared IB. Ht 7½ in. c. 1750. Smith Collection. Harvey's Wine Museum, Bristol

617 Wine glass; ovoid bowl, engraved THE ROYAL DOZEN. THE KING QUEEN AND : TEN : CHILDREN!; plain stem. Ht 4⅜ in. c. 1774. Cecil Higgins Museum, Bedford

618 Wine glass; trumpet bowl, engraved equestrian portrait of William III within a ribbon lettered THE GLORIOUS MEMORY OF KING WILLIAM and on the reverse BOYNE 1ST JULY 1690; plain stem between collars; FF. (Williamite.) Ht 6½ in. c. 1740

619 Reverse of 618

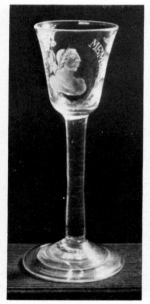

620 Wine glass; RF bowl, engraved band of fruiting vine above THE IMMORTAL MEMORY; centre-knopped MSAT. (Williamite.) Ht 7½ in. c. 1750. Hartshorne Collection (Plate 67)

621 Reverse of 620 showing engraving of rose and single bud

622 Wine glass; RF bowl, engraved with portrait of William III within the inscription GLORIOUS MEMORY; plain stem; FF. (Williamite.) Ht 6¼ in. c. 1740

623 Reverse of 622 showing engraving of an Irish harp below a crown

624 Cordial glass; bucket bowl, engraved with portrait of William III within the inscription THE IMMORTAL MEMORY and on the reverse an Irish harp below a crown; plain stem. (Williamite.) Ht 6½ in. *c.* 1740. Cecil Higgins Museum, Bedford

625 Wine glass; drawn trumpet bowl engraved with five-petalled flower (?buttercup) and butterfly; plain stem with tear. (Jacobite.) Ht 6½ in. *c.* 1740

626 Wine glass; RF bowl, engraved rose and single bud; plain stem; FF. (Jacobite.) Ht 6¾ in. *c.* 1740

627 Wine glass; bucket bowl, engraved rose, single bud and butterfly; plain stem; FF. (Jacobite.) Ht 6½ in. *c.* 1740

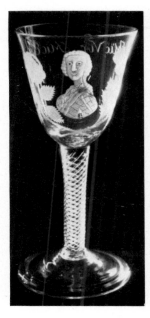

629 Wine glass; pointed RF bowl, engraved full-face portrait of Prince Charles Edward in Highland costume between thistle spray on his left and rose with single bud on his right with, on the reverse, the motto HIC VIR HIC EST (the portrait after an engraving by Sir Robert Strange); MSAT; FF. (Jacobite.) Ht 7⅜ in. *c.* 1760 Cecil Higgins Museum, Bedford

628 Wine glass; trumpet bowl, engraved portrait of Charles II in the Boscobel oak beneath three crowns; IB Kit-Kat stem. (Jacobite.) Ht 7 in. *c.* 1740

630 Reverse of 629 showing the engraved motto HIC VIR HIC EST

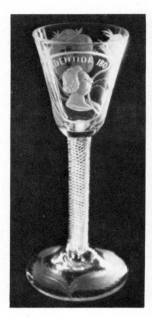

631 Wine glass; pointed RF bowl, engraved on one side with profile portrait of Prince Charles Edward or James Francis Edward below the motto AUDENTIOR IBO and on the reverse a six-petalled rose with two buds; MSAT; foot engraved with thistle leaves. (Jacobite.) Ht 6 in. *c.* 1750. Cecil Higgins Museum, Bedford

632 Wine glass; pan-topped bucket bowl, engraved round the rim with band of rose, oak leaves and other Jacobite symbols; MSAT. (Jacobite.) Ht 6¾ in. *c.* 1750

633 Goblet; bucket bowl, engraved rose and two buds below motto TURNO TEMPUS ERIT and on the reverse the motto FIAT; MSAT with vermiform collar; foot engraved with the motto REDEAT. (Jacobite.) Ht 8½ in. *c.* 1750

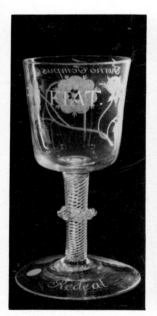

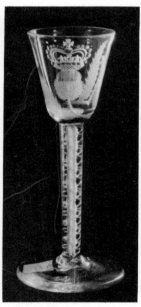

634 Reverse of 633 showing engraved motto FIAT

635 Wine glass; RF bowl, engraved with crowned thistle; DSAT – pair of spiral threads outside cable. (Jacobite.) Ht 6¼ in. *c.* 1750

636 Wine glass; drawn trumpet bowl, engraved rose and two buds, oak leaf and motto FIAT; MSAT. (Jacobite.) Ht 6 in. *c.* 1750

637 Wine glass; pan-topped RF bowl, engraved band of apple, pear, rose, carnation, vines and honeysuckle; MSAT with central swelled knop. (Jacobite.) Ht 6¼ in. *c.* 1750

638 Wine glass; pan-topped RF bowl, engraved band of crowned thistle, rose with two buds and oak leaf; MSAT with central swelled knop. (Jacobite.) Ht 5⅝ in. *c.* 1750

639 Wine glass; pointed RF bowl, engraved rose, two buds and motto FIAT; MSAT with shoulder knop. (Jacobite.) Ht 6¼ in. *c.* 1750

640 Wine glass; pointed RF bowl, engraved carnation and moth; shoulder-knopped MSAT. (Jacobite.) Ht 5¾ in. *c.* 1750

641 Wine glass; bucket bowl, engraved moth, fruiting vine and wine glass within the motto BIEN VENU; double-knopped MSAT; foot engraved with border of roses. (Jacobite.) Ht 5⅞ in. *c.* 1750

642 Wine glass; pointed RF bowl, engraved with full-face portrait of Prince Charles Edward in Highland costume below the motto AUDENTIOR IBO and on the reverse a rose and two buds; double-knopped MSAT. (Jacobite.) Ht 6¼ in. *c.* 1750

643 Reverse of 642 showing engraved rose

644 Goblet; pointed RF bowl, engraved rose, two buds, oak leaf and motto FIAT; double-knopped MSAT; foot engraved with Prince of Wales's feathers. (Jacobite.) Ht 8¼ in. *c.* 1750. Smith Collection. Harvey's Wine Museum, Bristol

645 Goblet; RF bowl, engraved rose and single bud; double-knopped MSAT. (Jacobite.) Ht 9½ in. *c.* 1760. (Haynes places single-bud Jacobites before 1741 or after 1766.)

646 Wine glass; RF bowl, engraved rose, single bud, oak leaf and star; double-knopped MSAT. (Jacobite.) Ht 6 in. *c.* 1760. (*See* note to 645)

647 Goblet; RF bowl, engraved sunflower, bees, butterflies, dragon-fly and beetles; incised-twist stem. (Jacobite.) Ht 7⅝ in. *c.* 1760. Cecil Higgins Museum, Bedford

648 Reverse of 647 showing engraving of dragon-fly and other insects

649 Wine glass; trumpet bowl, engraved rose, two buds, oak leaf and star; incised-twist stem. (Jacobite.) Ht 6¼ in. *c.* 1760. Cecil Higgins Museum, Bedford

650 Decanter; globular body, engraved on one side with eight-petalled rose and two buds and on the other with a pair of compasses pointing towards a double oak-leaf spray and star. (Jacobite.) Ht 9¾ in. (without stopper). *c.* 1750. Cecil Higgins Museum, Bedford

651 Reverse of 650 showing engraved compass and oak-leaf spray

652 Wine glass; square bucket bowl, engraved rose and single bud; SSOT – pair of spiral gauzes. (Jacobite.) Ht 6 in. *c.* 1770. (*See* note to 645.) Hartshorne Collection

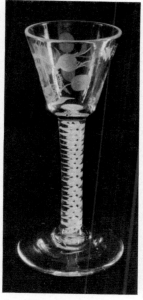

653 Wine glass; ogee bowl, engraved crown, the motto FIAT, rose with two buds, the dexter bud detached; DSOT – pair of heavy spiral threads outside gauze. (Jacobite.) Ht 6 in. c. 1766 (the year in which James Francis Edward died)

654 Wine glass; ogee bowl, engraved rose, single bud and thistle; DSOT – pair of spiral threads outside cable. (Jacobite.) Ht 5⅞ in. c. 1770

655 Wine glass; pointed RF bowl, engraved rose, single bud and initials W N; DSOT – pair of corkscrews outside tight corkscrew. (Jacobite.) Ht 5¾ in. c. 1770

656 Wine flute; trumpet bowl, engraved rose, two buds and moth; DSOT – pair of spiral threads outside cable. (Jacobite.) Ht 7 in. c. 1765

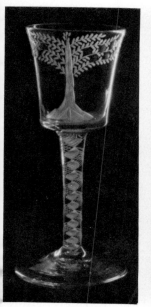

657 Wine glass; bucket bowl, engraved tree in leaf and butterfly; DSOT – 6-ply spiral band outside corkscrew. (? Jacobite.) Ht 6½ in. c. 1765. Hartshorne Collection (Fig. 287)

658 Wine glass; bell bowl, engraved rose, two buds and moth; DSOT – pair of heavy spiral threads outside corkscrew edged with blue and green. (Jacobite.) Ht 6½ in. c. 1765. Cecil Higgins Museum, Bedford

659 Firing glass; bowl with everted rim, engraved rose, two buds, thistle, oak leaf, star and the motto FIAT; firing foot. (Jacobite.) Ht 3⅛ in. c. 1750

660 Firing glass; flared bowl, engraved rose, two buds, oak leaf and the motto REDEAT; firing foot. (Jacobite.) Ht 3½ in. c. 1750

661 Wine glass; bell bowl, solid base, engraved profile portrait within a medallion lettered HIS ROYAL HIGHNESS WILLIAM DUKE OF CUMBERLAND; plain stem over heavy knop. Ht 6½ in. c. 1730

662 Wine glass; drawn trumpet bowl, engraved profile portrait below the inscription PROSPERITY TO THE DUKE OF CUMBERLAND; plain stem. (Anti-Jacobite.) Ht 6½ in. c. 1745. Cecil Higgins Museum, Bedford

663 Goblet; drawn trumpet bowl, engraved three eagles with wings outspread below the inscription SIR WATKIN WILLIAMS WYNNE; plain stem with tear; FF. Ht 8½ in. c. 1745. Cecil Higgins Museum, Bedford

664 Wine glass; RF bowl, engraved with the arms of the Clitheroe family; 'Newcastle' light baluster including a drop knop and a beaded knop; DF. Ht 7 in. c. 1750

665 Engraved bowl bearing arms comprising crossed daggers quartered with ship's wheels (on a 'Newcastle' light baluster stem including teared knop). Ht 11½ in. c. 1750. Smith Collection. Harvey's Wine Museum, Bristol

666 Goblet; lipped RF bowl, engraved with the arms of King's Lynn and the Blencowe and Everard families above bands of fine and coarse diamond cutting; stem containing large faceted knop; square, radially cut foot. Ht 9½ in. c. 1800. King's Lynn Museum

667 Reverse of 666 showing the arms of King's Lynn

668 Tankard; band of three threads below rim; engraved EDMUND MORRIS LYNN REGIS 1771. Ht 7⅛ in. c. 1771. King's Lynn Museum

669 Tumbler; engraved festooned border below rim, WM FLETCHER 1776 and on reverse a bird in flight, bee, acorn and flowers. Ht 3¾ in. c. 1776

670 Tumbler; engraved fluted border below rim, monogram WB and on reverse a dove with olive branch in beak. Ht 5½ in. Late 18th century

671 Ale jug; bulbous body, engraved hops and barley below inscription ANN FOWLER [!]. Ht 5½ in. Late 18th century

672 Rummer; cup bowl, engraved initials W F N above ear of barley; square-domed 'lemon-squeezer' base. Ht 4¾ in. c. 1800. Worthing Museum

673 Rummer; square bucket bowl, engraved W G/1801 within a shield and on reverse a floral spray; flattened knop. Ht 5 in. c. 1801. Worthing Museum

674 Wine glass; RF bowl, engraved with full-face portrait of Sarah Siddons, in a medallion; DSOT stem – pair of 3-ply spiral bands outside gauze. Ht 6 in. *c.* 1780

675 Wine glass; bell bowl, engraved three-masted sailing-ship below motto SALUS PATRIAE; stem comprising knop between opposing balusters. Ht 6⅞ in. *c.* 1740

676 Wine glass; bucket bowl, engraved with the legend SUCCESS TO CAPTAIN DIBDIN AND THE EAGLE FRIGATE above a three-masted sailing-ship; SSOT – pair of spiral gauzes. Ht 6⅜ in. *c.* 1757. The Eagle Frigate was a Bristol Privateer commanded by Captain Dibdin (*see London Chronicle*, April 12th 1757) and later by Captain Knill. Cecil Higgins Museum, Bedford

678 Wine glass; bucket bowl, engraved with the legend SUCCESS TO THE EAGLE FRIGATE above a three-masted sailing ship and on the reverse in diamond-point JOHN KNILL COMMDR. above a sword piercing a fleur-de-lys; below this is the signature JOHNS SCULPT. The initials (?) N FLY are linked to the bows of the ship; SSOT – pair of spiral gauzes. Ht 6 in. *c.* 1757. (*See* note to 676.) Cecil Higgins Museum, Bedford

677 Reverse of 676 showing engraved name of Captain Dibdin

678A Wine; RF bowl engraved SUCCESS TO THE DUKE OF CORNWALL PRIVATEER DAVID JENKINS: COMMANDER over a three-masted frigate; SSOT – single corkscrew. Ht 6 in. *c.* 1760. Sotheby & Co

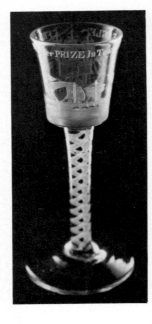

679 Wine glass; bucket bowl, engraved with three-masted sailing-ship towing another ship with masts shot away below the inscription THE EAGLE FRIGATE WITH HER PRIZE IN TOW; SSOT – pair of spiral gauzes. Ht 6 in. *c.* 1757. This is the only known example of a Privateer showing the prize in tow. Cecil Higgins Museum, Bedford

680 Wine glass; bucket bowl, engraved with two ships in full sail below the inscription SUCCESS TO THE EAGLE FRIGATE, A PRIZE; SSOT – pair of spiral gauzes. Ht 6⅜ in. *c.* 1757. Cecil Higgins Museum, Bedford

681 Goblet; RF bowl, engraved with three men-of-war in full sail within a rectangular panel below the legend SUCCESS TO THE BRITISH FLEET · 1749; plain stem. Ht 7¼ in. *c.* 1749. Cecil Higgins Museum, Bedford

682 Reverse of 681 showing engraved date

683 Goblet; pan-topped RF bowl, engraved with stars above a sailing-boat, two men and a dog on the shore and, below, the inscription HESPERUS UNUS LUCESSIT; 'Newcastle' light baluster stem with four knops; D & FF. Ht 7 in. *c.* 1750

684 Rummer; cup bowl, engraved HANNAH OF LYNN within a floral spray and on reverse a two-masted barque in full sail; square 'lemon-squeezer' base. Ht 7 in. *c.* 1800. King's Lynn Museum

685 Rummer; cup bowl, engraved TRAFALGAR above catafalque and NELSON'S VICTORY I E W, and LORD NELSON OCTR 21 1805 between ships-of-the-line; collar above rudimentary stem. Ht 6¼ in. *c.* 1805

686 Reverse of 685 showing the date of Nelson's victory and death

687 Rummer; bucket bowl, engraved TRAFALGAR above catafalque and LORD NELSON within laurel wreath. Ht 5¼ in. *c.* 1805

688 Rummer; bucket bowl, engraved LORD NELSON within a laurel wreath opposite the *Victory* in full sail. Ht 5½ in. *c.* 1805

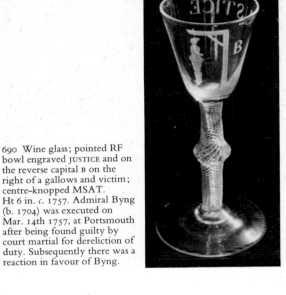

690 Wine glass; pointed RF bowl engraved JUSTICE and on the reverse capital B on the right of a gallows and victim; centre-knopped MSAT. Ht 6 in. c. 1757. Admiral Byng (b. 1704) was executed on Mar. 14th 1757, at Portsmouth after being found guilty by court martial for dereliction of duty. Subsequently there was a reaction in favour of Byng.

689 Rummer; ovoid bowl, engraved SUCCESS TO THE VOYAGE above a three-masted sailing-ship and a girl resting on an anchor beneath a tree; collar, stepped conical foot. Ht 5¾ in. Early 19th century

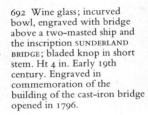

692 Wine glass; incurved bowl, engraved with bridge above a two-masted ship and the inscription SUNDERLAND BRIDGE; bladed knop in short stem. Ht 4 in. Early 19th century. Engraved in commemoration of the building of the cast-iron bridge opened in 1796.

691 Rummer; incurved bowl, engraved with near and distant balloons in landscape of tree, houses and birds in flight; collar above rudimentary stem; square-moulded 'lemon-squeezer' base. Ht 5¼ in. c. 1800. Possibly executed in commemoration of the first crossing of the English Channel by Blanchard and Jeffries on Jan 7th 1785. King's Lynn Museum

693 Wine glass; trumpet bowl, engraved FULLER AND BROWN THE 394; plain stem with large tear; FF. Ht 6½ in. c. 1740

694 Wine glass; pointed RF bowl, engraved OUR LIBERTY PRESERVED BY TAYLOR; plain stem; FF. Ht 6 in. c. 1740. Probably refers to Joseph Taylor elected for Ashburton in 1739

695 Wine glass; ogee bowl, engraved G. E. DURANT FOR EVER above fruiting vine; DSOT stem – 12-ply spiral band outside three spiral threads. Ht 5½ in. c. 1768. G. E. Durant was returned to Parliament in 1768 as the second Member for Evesham.

695A Goblet; bucket bowl engraved, within simple cartouche, SUCCESS TO SIR FRANCIS KNOLLYS; plain stem. Ht 7⅝ in. c. 1745 (In the Reading parliamentary election of 1761, two members were returned, John Dodd and Sir Francis Knollys) Sotheby & Co.

696 Wine glass; ogee bowl, engraved LOWTHER AND UPTON HUZZA; DSOT stem – pair of spiral tapes outside lace twist. Ht 6 in. c. 1761. Refers to the election of Sir James Lowther and John Upton in 1761: they stood jointly against a third candidate. There is a decanter in the Victoria and Albert Museum with the same inscription

697 Goblet; RF bowl, engraved MORTIMER AND FREEDOM between leaf borders; DSOT stem – four heavy spiral threads outside gauze. Ht 5⅝ in. c. 1774. Refers to Hans Winthrop Mortimer returned to Parliament in 1774 and 1780

698 Goblet; pointed RF bowl, engraved with a cherub placing wreaths on a newly-wed couple, an inscription in Dutch wishing them happiness and the date 18 APRIL, 1741; 'Newcastle' light baluster stem comprising three angular knops and a beaded IB. Ht 8⅞ in. c. 1740. Pilkington Glass Museum, St Helens

699 Tankard; coiled thread decoration round rim, engraved SUCCESS TO SARAH FINCH within a floral scroll; 'nipt diamond waies' decoration round base which contains silver coin of Queen Anne (?1709). Ht 7½ in. Mid 18th century

700 Wine glass; RF bowl, engraved VRIEND SCHAP (Friendship) above a festooned border and clasped hands within a sprigged medallion; composite stem – centre-knopped MSAT, teared knop, plain section and basal knop. Ht 7⅝ in. c. 1750. Engraved in Holland

699A Wine; RF bowl engraved with floral border above inscription in Dutch, translated 'The welfare of the new-born', below which is an engraving of a child lying on a rug; 'Newcastle' light baluster stem containing a beaded knop. One of a pair. Ht 9 in. c. 1740. Delomosne & Son Ltd

701 Goblet; RF bowl, engraved with Bacchus seated on a barrel between sprays of fruiting vines; knop over six-sided moulded pedestal stem; D & FF. Ht 11¼ in. c. 1740

702 Detail of engraving of 701

703 Cordial glass; funnel bowl, engraved TRADE AND NAVIGATION over fruiting vine; plain stem with basal knop; D & FF. Ht 6¾ in. c. 1740. Harvey's Wine Museum, Bristol

704 Wine glass; ovoid bowl engraved with plough; diamond-faceted stem. Ht 5¼ in. c. 1785

705 Rummer; square bucket bowl, engraved T J G between ears of barley and on reverse a shield containing agricultural implements above the inscription SPEED THE PLOUGH; collar above short plain stem; square-moulded 'lemon-squeezer' base. Ht 5¼ in. c. 1800

706 Tankard; engraved sprigged border below rim and between two bands of annulated rings a wildfowling scene, with the initials F J T within a garland of leaves on the reverse. Ht 6½ in. Mid 18th century. Worthing Museum

707 Goblet; square bucket bowl, engraved with monogram PT within a shield flanked by ears of barley and on reverse, within a medallion, the inscription SONS OF HARMONY over the sun shining on violin and music; collar; square-moulded 'lemon-squeezer' foot. Ht 5 in. c. 1800

708 Rummer; bowl engraved with hunting scene and monogram W D W; collar; short plain stem. Ht. 5 in. Early 19th century. King's Lynn Museum

708A Wine; thistle bowl engraved [later] R J GANN 1841; mushroom knop, basal knop; FF. Ht 8 in. c. 1710. Sotheby & Co

709 Wine glass; RF bowl, engraved with Cupid in a rustic landscape; hexagonal-faceted stem. Ht 6½ in. c. 1785

710 Firing glass; trumpet bowl, engraved with set square and dividers (Masonic emblems); firing foot. Ht 4 in. Mid 18th century. Hartshorne Collection (Fig. 316)

711 Tumbler; engraved beehive, crossed keys and other Masonic emblems; star-cut base. Ht 4 in. Early 19th century. One of a pair, with matching caraffe

712 Rummer; square bucket bowl, engraved with Masonic emblems; short plain stem. Ht 5½ in. Early 19th century

713 Reverse of 712

714 Rummer; incurved bucket bowl, engraved with Masonic emblems; short stem with bladed knop. Ht 5 in. Early 19th century

715 Wine glass; RF bowl, engraved with the arms of King's Lynn above the motto LOYALTY; SSAT – single spiral cable. Ht 5¼ in. c. 1750. King's Lynn Museum

716 Wine glass; pointed RF bowl, engraved with the arms of Utrecht; 'Newcastle' light baluster stem – ball knop between two angular knops; DF. Ht 8 in. c. 1745

717 Wine glass; RF bowl, engraved with floral border above diamond-engraved inscription DORDRECHTS WELVAREN; 'Newcastle' light baluster stem including angular knop; DF. Ht 7⅜ in. c. 1745. Pilkington Glass Museum, St Helens

718 Goblet; pointed RF bowl, engraved with Chinese figures and pagodas in four oval medallions; DSAT – pair of air spirals outside cable; foot engraved with floral border. Ht 7⅞ in. c. 1750. Cecil Higgins Museum, Bedford

719 Wine glass; lipped ogee bowl, engraved with Chinese pagoda scene; SSOT – loose multi-ply corkscrew outlined. Ht 6 in. c. 1765

720 Wine glass; waisted RF bowl, engraved with Chinese pagoda scene; hexagonal-faceted stem. Ht 5¾ in. c. 1790. Portsmouth City Museums

721 Wine glass; ogee bowl, engraved with Chinese figure and pagodas; diamond-faceted stem. Ht 6 in. c. 1785

722 Wine glass; ogee bowl, engraved with unidentified scene of buildings and trees (imaginary?); diamond-faceted centre-knopped stem. Ht 5¾ in. c. 1785. Harvey's Wine Museum, Bristol

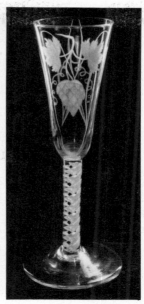

723 Wine glass; pointed RF bowl, engraved with deep floral border below rim; DSAT – spiral cable outside thin spiral. Ht 6 in. *c.* 1750

724 Wine glass; ogee bowl, engraved with deep floral border below rim; DSOT – pair of corkscrews outside tight corkscrew. Ht 5⅞ in. *c.* 1765

725 Ale glass; pointed RF bowl, engraved hops and barley; collar above double-knopped MSAT. Ht 7¾ in. *c.* 1750. Hartshorne Collection (Plate 50)

726 Ale glass; pointed RF bowl, engraved hops and barley; SSOT – four corkscrews. Ht 7½ in. *c.* 1765. Hartshorne Collection

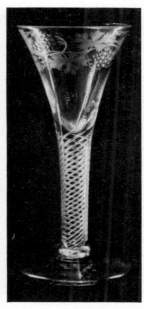

727A Wine glass; bell bowl, engraved fruiting vine below rim, solid base; IB at base of plain stem. Ht. 7¼ in. *c.* 1740. Portsmouth City Museums

727 Tankard; engraved festooned border below the rim and hops and barley on the body, gadrooned base; hollow knop containing George III shilling dated 1787. D & FF. Ht 8 in. Late 18th century

727B Wine glass; drawn trumpet bowl, engraved vine with polished fruit below rim; MSAT. Ht 6½ in. *c.* 1750

728 Cider glass; pointed RF
bowl, engraved fruiting apple;
DSOT – pair of heavy spiral
threads outside multi-ply
corkscrew. Ht 7¾ in. *c.* 1765

729 Water glass; pan-topped RF bowl, engraved with a border of
coronets below the rim; D & FF. Ht 4 in. *c.* 1740

730 Wine glass; ovoid bowl,
stipple-engraved with portrait
of William III of Holland by
David Wolff; diamond-faceted
stem. Ht 5¾ in. *c.* 1790. Wolff
was active from 1784 to 1795

XVI
Decoration:
Enamelling

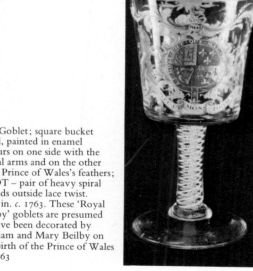

731 Goblet; square bucket bowl, painted in enamel colours on one side with the Royal arms and on the other with Prince of Wales's feathers; DSOT – pair of heavy spiral threads outside lace twist. Ht 9 in. *c.* 1763. These 'Royal Beilby' goblets are presumed to have been decorated by William and Mary Beilby on the birth of the Prince of Wales in 1763

732 Another view of 731 showing supporter and Prince of Wales's feathers

733 Goblet; square bucket bowl, painted in enamel colours on one side with the Royal arms and on the other with Prince of Wales's feathers; DSOT – pair of 6-ply spiral bands outside lace twist. Ht 8¾ in. *c.* 1763. Attributed to Beilby. See note to 731

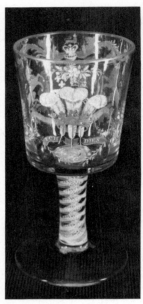

734 Reverse of 733 showing Prince of Wales's feathers

735 Goblet; RF bowl with gilt rim, painted in enamel colours with a coat of arms surmounted by a coronet; DSOT – pair of heavy spiral threads outside lace twist. Ht 9¼ in. *c.* 1765. Attributed to Beilby. Pilkington Glass Museum, St Helens

736 Goblet; bucket bowl painted in enamel colours with the arms and crest of Vaughan of Dorset above the name THOS. VAUGHAN: on the reverse is the inscription PLYMOUTH DOCK below the rim; DSOT – five heavy spiral threads outside pair of spiral tapes. Ht 7¼ in. *c.* 1770. Attributed to Beilby. Cecil Higgins Museum, Bedford

737 Goblet; square bucket bowl, painted in enamel colours with the arms of Buckmaster of Lincoln on one side and on the other with fruiting vine in white enamel; gilded rim; DSOT – four heavy spiral threads outside gauze. Ht 7¼ in. *c.* 1765. Attributed to Beilby. Cecil Higgins Museum, Bedford

738 Dram glass; waisted bowl, painted in enamel colours with the arms of the Lodge of Journeymen and Masons, No. 8, Edinburgh, and on the reverse with Masonic devices. Ht 3 in. *c.* 1770. Attributed to Beilby. See Thorpe, *English and Irish glass*, Plate iii

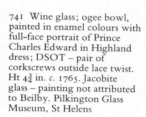

741 Wine glass; ogee bowl, painted in enamel colours with full-face portrait of Prince Charles Edward in Highland dress; DSOT – pair of corkscrews outside lace twist. Ht 4¾ in. *c.* 1765. Jacobite glass – painting not attributed to Beilby. Pilkington Glass Museum, St Helens

739 Wine glass; RF bowl with gilt rim, painted in enamel colours with a crest (probably fictitious) of a heart pierced by two arrows; 'Newcastle' light baluster stem including teared IB. Ht 7 in. *c.* 1760. Attributed to Beilby

740 Tumbler; painted in white enamel with initials T W A in a floral cartouche and with floral spray on reverse. Ht 4 in. *c.* 1770. Attributed to Beilby

742 Wine glass; ogee bowl, painted in enamel colours with a crest comprising a demi-man armed with sword between the motto PRO PATRIA; MSOT; FF. Ht 6 in. *c.* 1765. Could be attributed to Beilby. Cecil Higgins Museum, Bedford

743 Close-up of bowl of 742

744 Wine glass; ogee bowl, painted in white enamel with hunting scene; DSOT – pair of 8-ply spiral bands outside lace twist. Ht 6 in. *c.* 1770. Attributed to Beilby

745 Wine glass; ogee bowl, painted in white enamel with stag-hunting scene; DSOT – pair of 8-ply spiral bands outside pair of heavy spiral threads. Ht 5⅜ in. *c.* 1770. Attributed to Beilby

746 Wine glass; ogee bowl, painted in white enamel with wildfowling scene; DSOT – pair of 6-ply spiral bands outside lace twist. Ht 6 in. *c.* 1770. Attributed to Beilby

747 Wine glass; ogee bowl, painted in white enamel with wildfowling scene; DSOT – pair of heavy spiral threads outside multi-ply spiral band. Ht 5⅜ in. *c.* 1770. Attributed to Beilby

748 Wine glass; ogee bowl, painted in white enamel with skating scene; DSOT – pair of 6- to 8-ply spiral bands outside lace twist. Ht 5¾ in. *c.* 1770. Attributed to Beilby

749 Wine glass; ogee bowl, painted in white enamel with fishing scene; SSOT – pair of heavy spiral threads alternating with spiral gauze. Ht 5⅜ in. *c.* 1770. Attributed to Beilby

750 Goblet; square bucket bowl, painted in enamel colours with rural landscape; DSAT – 11-ply spiral band outside loose spiral. Ht 7 in. *c.* 1760. Attributed to Beilby

751 Wine glass; pointed RF bowl, painted in white enamel with rustic scene, shepherd and flock; DSOT – pair of 8-ply spiral bands outside pair of heavy spiral threads. Ht 6 in. *c.* 1770. Attributed to Beilby

752 Wine glass; pointed RF bowl, painted in white enamel with rustic scene, shepherdess and flock; DSOT – pair of 8-ply spiral bands outside pair of heavy spiral threads. Ht 6 in. *c.* 1770. Attributed to Beilby

753 Wine glass; pointed RF bowl, painted in white enamel with pair of goats in a rustic scene; DSOT – pair of heavy spiral threads outside lace twist. Ht 6 in. *c.* 1770. Attributed to Beilby

754 Wine glass; pointed RF bowl, painted in white enamel with sheep and goats in a rustic scene; DSOT – pair of 8-ply spiral bands outside pair of heavy spiral threads. Ht 6 in. *c.* 1770. Attributed to Beilby

755 Wine glass; pointed RF bowl, painted in white enamel with a pair of goats in a rustic scene; DSOT – pair of 8-ply spiral bands outside pair of heavy spiral threads. Ht 6 in. *c.* 1770. Attributed to Beilby

756 Wine glass; ogee bowl, painted in white enamel with shepherdess, dog and sheep in a rustic scene; DSOT – pair of heavy spiral threads outside lace twist. Ht 5¾ in. *c.* 1770. Attributed to Beilby

757 Wine glass; RF bowl, painted in white enamel with scene of Classical ruins; coarse incised-twist stem. Ht 4½ in. *c.* 1760. Attributed to Beilby. Ex-Horridge Collection

758 Wine glass; RF bowl, painted in white enamel with urn on pedestal flanked by trees and obelisk; SSOT – lace twist outlined. Ht 5⅞ in. *c.* 1770. Attributed to Beilby

759 Wine glass; RF bowl, painted in white enamel with pyramid flanked by trees; DSOT – 12- to 20-ply spiral band outside pair of heavy spiral threads. Ht 6 in. *c.* 1770. Attributed to Beilby

760 Wine glass; pointed RF bowl, painted in white enamel with obelisk flanked by trees; DSOT – pair of 6- and 7-ply spiral bands outside pair of heavy spiral threads. Ht 6 in. c. 1770. Attributed to Beilby

761 Wine glass; RF bowl, painted in white enamel with Classical ruins flanked by trees; DSOT – pair of 8-ply spiral bands outside pair of heavy spiral threads. Ht 6 in. c. 1770. Attributed to Beilby

762 Wine glass; RF bowl, painted in white enamel with tracery of windows of a ruined church; DSOT – pair of 8-ply spiral bands outside pair of spiral tapes. Ht 6 in. c. 1770. Attributed to Beilby

763 Wine glass; RF bowl, painted in white enamel with Classical ruins flanked by trees; DSOT – pair of 7-ply spiral bands outside pair of spiral tapes. Ht 6 in. c. 1770. Attributed to Beilby

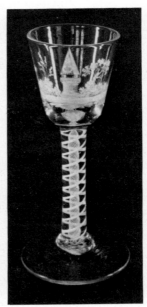

764 Wine glass; RF bowl, painted in white enamel with ruined arch flanked by trees, gilded rim; DSOT – four heavy spiral threads outside gauze. Ht 5¾ in. c. 1770. Attributed to Beilby

765 Wine glass; RF bowl, painted in white enamel with Classical ruins flanked by trees; DSOT – four heavy spiral threads outside gauze. Ht 5¾ in. c. 1770. Attributed to Beilby

766 Wine glass; RF bowl, painted in white enamel with obelisk on pedestal, flanked by trees; DSOT – pair of spiral tapes outside gauze. Ht 5¾ in. c. 1770. Attributed to Beilby

767 Wine glass; RF bowl, painted in white enamel with statue beneath canopy, flanked by trees; DSOT – pair of heavy spiral threads outside lace twist. Ht 5⅞ in. c. 1770. Attributed to Beilby

768 Goblet; square bucket bowl, painted in white enamel with obelisk flanked by trees; DSOT – pair of 7- and 8-ply spiral bands outside lace twist. Ht 7⅛ in. c. 1770. Attributed to Beilby

769 Wine glass; ogee bowl, painted in white enamel with exotic bird; DSOT – pair of 8-ply spiral bands outside lace twist. Ht 5¾ in. c. 1770. Attributed to Beilby

770 Wine glass; RF bowl, painted in white enamel with birds, fruit and trees; DSOT – alternate 4-ply and single-ply spirals outside lace twist. Ht 5⅝ in. c. 1770. Attributed to Beilby

771 Wine glass; ogee bowl, painted in white enamel with exotic bird, bee and trees; DSOT – pair of heavy spiral threads outside lace twist. Ht 5¾ in. c. 1770. Attributed to Beilby

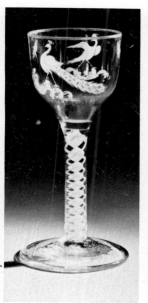

772 Tumbler; painted in white enamel with a bee and exotic bird on a balustrade. Ht 4 in. c. 1770. Attributed to Beilby

773 Wine glass; ogee bowl, painted in white and pale blue enamels with peacock, pea-hen and butterflies; DSOT – pair of heavy spiral threads outside multi-ply corkscrew. Ht 6⅜ in. c. 1770. Attributed to Beilby. Pilkington Glass Museum, St Helens

774 Ale glass; RF bowl with gilt rim, painted in white enamel with beehive, bees and flowering plants; DSOT – 20-ply spiral band outside pair of heavy spiral threads. Ht 7 in. c. 1770. Attributed to Beilby

775 Goblet; RF bowl, painted in green and red enamels with plant and bee design below diamond-point engraved inscription в 1769 *Xmafs* 1770; DSOT – pair of heavy spiral threads outside gauze. Ht 10 in. *c.* 1769/70. Believed by the owner to have been presented to William Beilby

776 Reverse of 775 showing diamond-point inscription

777 Goblet; RF bowl with gilt rim, painted in white enamel with fruiting vine, butterfly on reverse; DSOT – pair of heavy spiral threads outside lace twist. Ht 7½ in. *c.* 1770. Attributed to Beilby

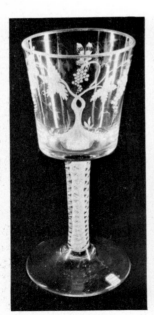

778 Goblet; bucket bowl with gilt rim, painted in white enamel with growing vine; DSOT – four 3-strand spiral bands outside gauze. Ht 7½ in. *c.* 1770. Attributed to Beilby

779 Dram glass; ogee bowl, painted in white enamel with growing vine; DSOT – 20-ply spiral band outside pair of spiral tapes; terraced foot. Ht 3¾ in. *c.* 1770. Attributed to Beilby. Hartshorne Collection

780 Tumbler; painted in white enamel with basket of fruit surmounted by exotic birds. Ht 4 in. *c.* 1770. Attributed to Beilby

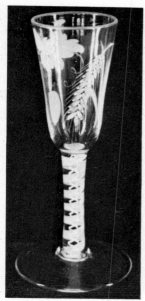

781 Ale glass; RF bowl, painted in white enamel with hops and barley; DSOT – solid multi-ply spiral band outside pair of spiral tapes. Ht 7¼ in. *c.* 1770. Attributed to Beilby

782 Ale glass; ogee bowl, painted in white enamel with hops and barley; DSOT – 18-ply spiral band outside pair of spiral tapes. Ht 7½ in. *c.* 1770. Attributed to Beilby

783 Sweetmeat; double-ogee bowl painted in white enamel with floral border; eight-sided moulded pedestal stem with diamonds on shoulders, between collars; D & FF. Ht 6½ in. *c.* 1750, but decorated later. Attributed to Beilby

784 Wine glass; cup bowl, painted in white and green enamel with vine border; balustroid stem with single central knop. Ht 6⅝ in. *c.* 1750, but decorated later. Attributed to Beilby

785 Wine glass; trumpet bowl, painted in white enamel with vine border; MSOT. Ht 6¾ in. *c.* 1760. Attributed to Beilby

786 Goblet; bucket bowl, painted in white enamel with scrolled festoons; DSOT – pair of heavy spiral threads outside multi-ply corkscrew. Ht 6⅞ in. *c.* 1770. Attributed to Beilby

787 Ale glass; ogee bowl, painted in white enamel with geometrical and scroll border; DSOT – solid multi-ply spiral band outside pair of spiral tapes. Ht 7¼ in. *c.* 1770. Attributed to Beilby. Cecil Higgins Museum, Bedford

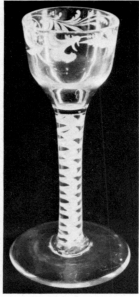

788 Ratafia; trumpet bowl with gilt rim, painted in white enamel with scroll border above drops in pale blue enamel; DSOT – 12-ply spiral band outside lace twist. Ht 7½ in. *c.* 1770. Attributed to Beilby

789 Wine glass; bell bowl, painted in white enamel with vine border; DSOT – solid multi-ply spiral band outside pair of heavy spiral threads. Ht 6⅜ in. *c.* 1770. Attributed to Beilby

790 Wine glass; RF bowl, painted in white enamel with floral border; DSOT – 16-ply spiral band outside pair of spiral tapes. Ht 5¾ in. *c.* 1770. Attributed to Beilby

791 Wine glass; ogee bowl, painted in white enamel with floral border; DSOT – pair of 6-ply spiral bands outside multi-ply corkscrew. Ht 5¾ in. *c.* 1770. Attributed to Beilby

792 Wine glass; ogee bowl, painted in white enamel with scroll and star border; DSOT – pair of 8-ply spiral bands outside lace twist. Ht 6 in. *c.* 1770. Attributed to Beilby

793 Wine glass; ogee bowl, painted in white enamel with vine border; DSOT – pair of heavy spiral threads outside lace twist. Ht 5¾ in. *c.* 1770. Attributed to Beilby

794 Dram glass; waisted bowl, painted in white, red and yellow enamels with a floral border above Masonic symbols. Ht 3 in. *c.* 1770. Attributed to Beilby

795 Reverse of 794

796 Toastmaster's glass; deceptive RF bowl, painted in white enamel with lilies-of-the-valley and the inscription TEMPERANCE; short MSAT stem; terraced foot. Ht 4 in. *c.* 1750, but decorated later. Attributed to Beilby

797 Decanter; mallet-shaped body, painted in white enamel with fruiting vine, butterfly and inscription PORT; conical-faceted stopper. Ht 12 in. (including stopper). *c.* 1770. Attributed to Beilby. Hartshorne Collection

798 Decanter; mallet-shaped body, painted in coloured enamels with armorial device and fruiting vines above inscription, in script, TRUTH AND LOYALTY: signed, above the crest *Beilby inv^t & pinx^t* (Beilby designed and painted); conical-faceted stopper. Ht 12 in. (including stopper). *c.* 1770

799 Close-up of 798 showing Beilby signature

XVII
Decoration:
Gilding

800 Wine glass in green metal; cup bowl with gilt rim, decorated in gilt with sprays of flowers; plain stem. Ht 6¼ in. c. 1765. Attributed to James Giles of Bristol. Smith Collection. Harvey's Wine Museum, Bristol

801 Small goblet; vertically ribbed cup bowl with gilt rim, decorated in gilt with insects and sprays of flowers; slightly wrythen plain stem; radially moulded foot. Ht 5 in. c. 1765

802 Goblet; pointed RF bowl, decorated in gilt with fruiting vine; DSOT – 12-ply spiral band outside lace twist. Ht 7½ in. c. 1770

803 Wine glass; ogee bowl with gilt rim, decorated in gilt with fruiting vine; DSOT – pair of corkscrews outside pair of heavy spiral threads. Ht 6 in. c. 1770

804 Wine glass; RF bowl with
gilt rim, decorated in gilt with
floral border above vertical
panels; DSOT – multi-ply
spiral band outside spiral of one
heavy and two light threads.
Ht 6 in. *c.* 1770

805 Wine glass; RF bowl with
gilt rim, decorated in gilt with
fruiting vine; DSOT – pair of
spiral tapes outside gauze.
Ht 5½ in. *c.* 1770. Smith
Collection. Harvey's Wine
Museum, Bristol

806 Wine glass; ogee bowl
with gilt rim, decorated in gilt
with bouquet of flowers;
diamond-faceted stem. Ht 6 in.
c. 1785

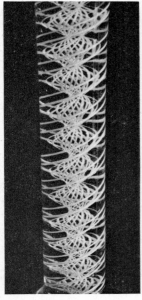

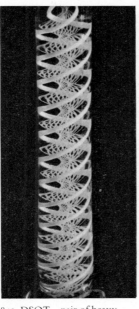

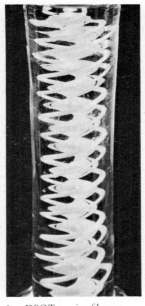

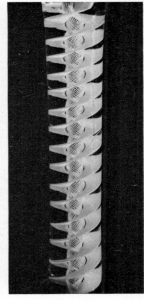

841 DSOT – two pairs of spiral threads outside lace twist

842 DSOT – pair of heavy spiral threads outside lace twist

843 DSOT – pair of heavy spiral threads outside multi-ply corkscrew

844 DSOT – pair of corkscrews outside gauze

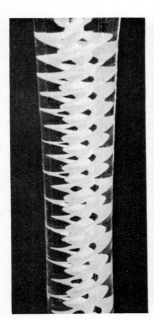

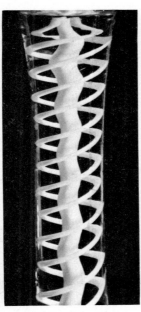

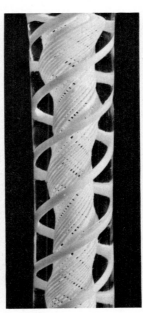

845 DSOT – pair of corkscrews outside single corkscrew

846 DSOT – pair of heavy spiral threads outside solid vertical cable

847 DSOT – pair of heavy spiral threads outside loose vertical cable

848 DSOT – pair of spiral threads outside spiral cable

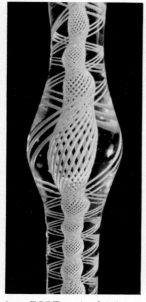

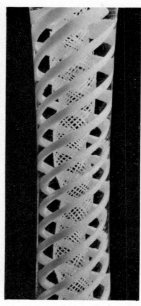

833A DSOT – pair of 3-ply spiral bands outside gauze

834 DSOT – pair of 7-ply spiral bands outside gauze

835 DSOT – 12-ply spiral band outside gauze

836 DSOT – four heavy spiral threads outside gauze

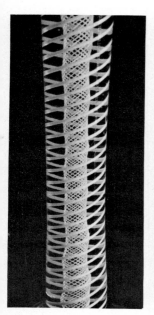

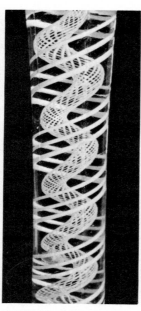

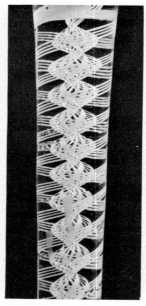

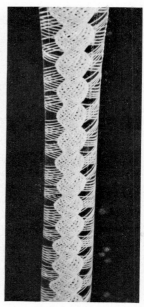

837 DSOT – four spiral threads outside gauze

838 DSOT – band of three spiral threads outside spiral gauze

839 DSOT – pair of 4-ply spiral bands outside lace twist

840 DSOT – pair of 5- and 6-ply spiral bands outside lace twist

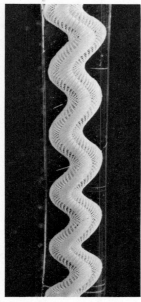

826 SSOT – spiral gauze with core

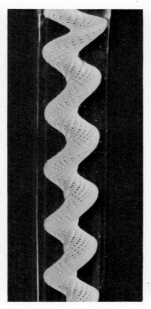

827 SSOT – spiral cable

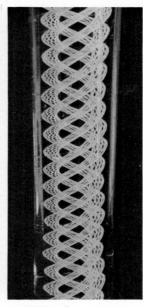

828 SSOT – four spiral gauzes

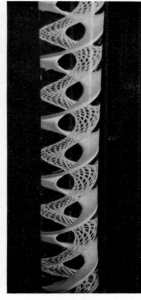

829 SSOT – spiral gauze alternating with single corkscrew

830 SSOT – four heavy spiral threads outside long tear

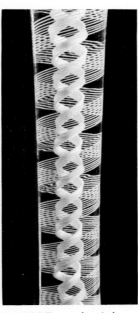

831 DSOT – 12-ply spiral band outside pair of spiral tapes

832 DSOT – solid multi-ply spiral band outside pair of heavy spiral threads

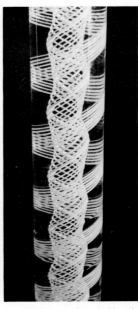

833 DSOT – 6-ply spiral band outside spiral gauze

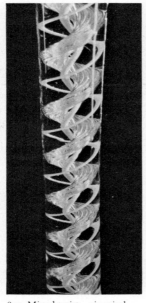

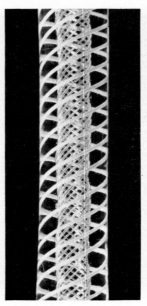

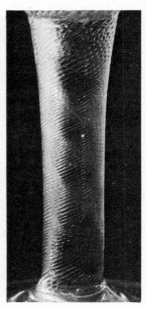

818 Mixed twist – pair of air spirals outside opaque gauze

819 Mixed twist – air spiral cable alternating with opaque spiral thread outside single opaque heavy spiral thread

820 Mixed twist – four opaque heavy spiral threads outside multiple-spiral air twist

821 Incised twist

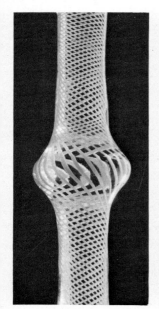

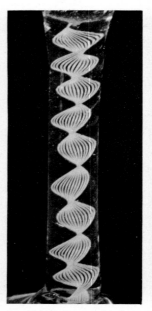

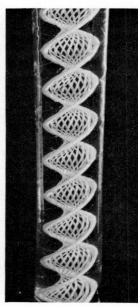

822 MSOT – multiple-spiral opaque twist

823 SSOT – multi-ply corkscrew outlined

824 SSOT – loose multi-ply corkscrew

825 SSOT – lace twist outlined

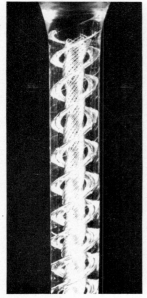

810 DSAT – pair of
corkscrews outside cable

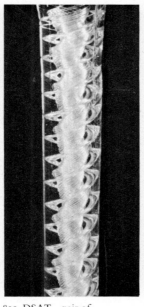

811 DSAT – pair of
corkscrews outside spiral cable

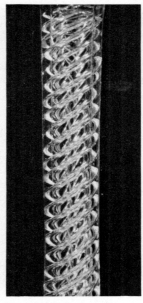

812 DSAT – four spirals
outside loose vertical cable

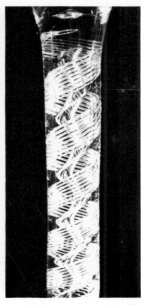

813 DSAT – 8-ply spiral band
outside loose spiral cable

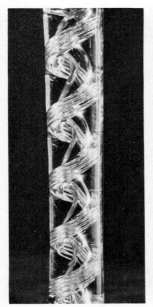

814 DSAT – 4-ply spiral band
outside loose spiral threads

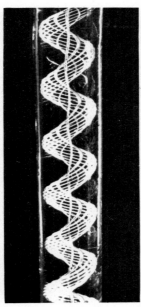

815 DSAT – spiral gauze
outside vertical thread

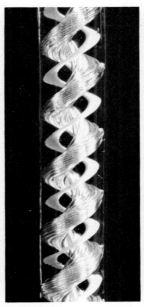

816 Mixed twist – spiral air
cable alternating with opaque
corkscrew

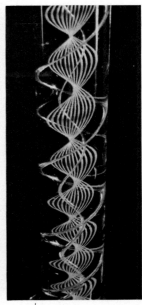

817 Mixed twist – pair of air
spiral threads outside opaque
loose corkscrew

XVIII
Details of Stems

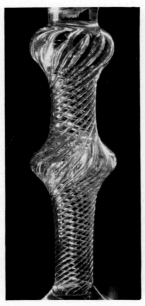

806A MSAT – Multiple-spiral air twist

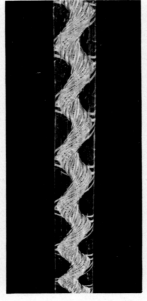

807 SSAT – single spiral cable

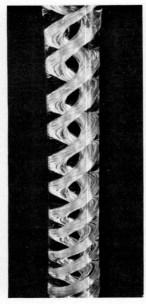

808 SSAT – pair of spiral cables

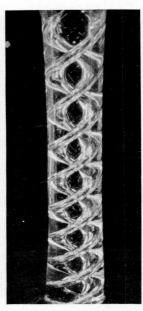

809 SSAT – pair of corkscrews ('mercury twist')

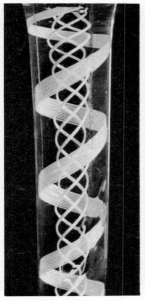

849 DSOT – 12-ply spiral band outside 4-ply column

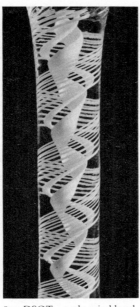

850 DSOT – 9-ply spiral band outside alternate wide and narrow spiral tapes

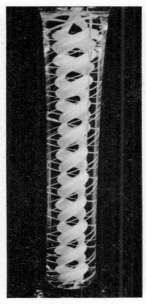

851 DSOT – two pairs of spiral threads outside pair of spiral tapes

852 DSOT – pair of loose multi-ply corkscrews outside pair of heavy spiral threads

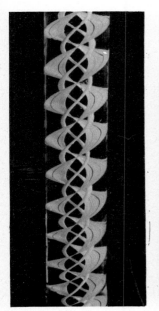

852A DSOT – pair of multi-ply corkscrews outside pair of spiral threads

853 Faceted stem – diamond facets

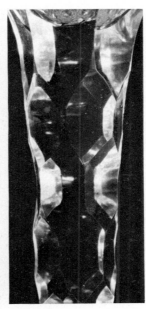

854 Faceted stem – hexagonal facets

Bibliography
of English Glass

Bibliographer's note

In this bibliography an attempt is made to cover the literature produced in the field of English glass studies during the last hundred years or so. The list excludes pure technology, book reviews, ancient glass and sale catalogues. The reader is reminded, however, that catalogues of important sales provide useful supplementary information on all types of glass.

For reasons of space the entries are not critical but explanatory annotations or notes have been added where it has seemed desirable to clarify the title or content of an item. As a large proportion of the material dealt with consists of articles, the Bibliography is to a considerable degree analytical in form. In order to increase the specific subject coverage the analytical principle has been extended in several cases to books where important subject content is not revealed by the title of the work. The most straightforward arrangement has been adopted, that is, alphabetically by author or title, with the general index providing the subject key; late entries, compiled while this book was in the press, are grouped together alphabetically at the end. The Bibliography as a whole will, it is hoped, complete the purpose of this volume, which is to supply a working guide for all interested in studying and collecting English glass.

Abbreviations of periodical titles most referred to

A	*Antiques*
AC	*Antique Collector*
ADCG	*Antique Dealer and Collector's Guide*
AP	*Apollo*
BUR	*Burlington Magazine*
CJGS	*Journal of Glass Studies* (Corning Museum of Glass, New York)
CL	*Country Life*
CONN	*Connoisseur*
GC	*Papers of the Circle of Glass Collectors* (Glass Circle). London (duplicated typescripts)
GN	*Glass Notes* (Arthur Churchill, Ltd – no longer issued)
ILN	*Illustrated London News*
JSGT ⎱ *TSGT* ⎰	*Journal and/or Transactions of the Society of Glass Technology* (Sheffield)

NOTE Readers are reminded that the volumes of the *British Union Catalogue of Periodicals* (which may be consulted at most public reference libraries) will provide locations for the periodicals referred to in the bibliography.

Other abbreviations

Assn.	Association	Jnl.	Journal
bibliog.	bibliography	Mag.	Magazine
Bull.	Bulletin	nd.	no date
col.	coloured	priv. print.	privately printed
comp.	compiler	Proc.	Proceedings
diags.	diagrams	p.	page(s)
ed.	edition, editor	ports.	portraits
facsims.	facsimiles	Rev.	Review
Gaz.	Gazette	Soc.	Society
illus.	illustration(s)	Trans.	Transactions
Inst.	Institute		

D. R. ELLERAY

1 'Adam and Eve engraved on a seventeenth-century goblet' [from the Marshall Collection, Ashmolean Museum]. In *CL*, Sept 1969, p. 569, *illus.*

2 ADAMSON, C. E. 'John Dagnia of South Shields, Glass-maker'. In *Proc. of the Society of Antiquaries of Newcastle-upon-Tyne*, v. 6, p. 163–8.

3 [AITKEN, William Costen]. *The glass manufacturers of Birmingham and Stourbridge*. Birmingham, J. F. Feeney, 1851, 18p. Reprinted for private distribution from the *Birmingham Journal*, May 31st 1851.

4 ALFIERI, Bernard. 'The beauty of glass'. In *British Jnl. of Photography*, Jan 1958, p. 58–60, *illus.*

5 'Ancient Irish glasses'. In *CONN*, Jan–Apr 1903, p. 282–3, *illus.*

6 ANGUS-BUTTERWORTH, Lionel Milner. *British Table and ornamental glass*. L. Hill, 1956, 123p., *illus.*
Contents include: Annals of glass in Britain, AD 1220–1953, p. 105–9; Apsley Pellatt (cameo incrustations), p. 26–8; Fred. Stuart and the Red House Glass-works, p. 41–3; Glossary of terms used in the glass industry, p. 110–19; The Hills and Webbs of Coalbournehill, p. 44–7; The Powell family (Whitefriars Glassworks), p. 29–32; Pressed glass – Sowerby of Tyneside, p. 59–62; The Richardsons of Wordsley Hall, p. 55–8; Stourbridge glass – Royal Brierley Crystal, Stevens and Williams Ltd, p. 33–6; Thomas Webb of Dennis Park, p. 37–40.

7 'Colouring agents in glass'. In *Glass*, 1930, p. 8–10 and 52–4.

8 'Glass' [manufacture, 1750–1850]. In Singer, Charles *and others, eds. History of Technology*, O.U.P., 1957, v. 4, p. 358–78, *illus., bibliog.*
see also MARSON, Percival.

9 'Annealed glass'. In *Art Jnl.*, 1875, p. 229–30. Deals especially with the annealed glass of M. de la Bastie.

10 'Antique cider glasses'. In *The Times*, Oct 28th 1961, p. 11, *illus.*

11 'Antique [glass] salvers'. In *The Times*, May 11th 1968, p. 23, *illus.*

12 'Apsley Pellatt'. In *Tableware*, June 1963, p. 459–60.

13 ARLOTT, John. 'Three wine glasses'. In *Adelphi*, v. 28, 1952, p. 601–4. Describes particular glasses for certain wines.

14 ARMSTRONG, E. F. 'Constituents of glass'. In *GC*, no. 46.

15 'Cordials and their glasses'. In *GC*, no. 20.

16 'Long forgotten drinks and their glasses'. In *GC*, no. 3.

17 ARMY AND NAVY STORES. *Yesterday's shopping: the Army and Navy Store's catalogue, 1907*. David and Charles, 1969. A reprint containing a section on domestic glassware, described and priced, p. 921–50, *illus.*

18 'Art of John Hutton' [glass engraver]. In *CL*, Feb 1969, p. 485, *illus.*

19 ART GALLERY OF NEW SOUTH WALES, SYDNEY. *G. Gordon Russell Collection of seventeenth- and eighteenth-century English drinking glasses* [Catalogue]. Sydney, 1964.

20 ASH, Douglas. 'English glass: a brief survey'. In *AC*, 1967, p. 131–7, *illus.*

21 'Flute glasses in England: a fashion for tall drinks deriving from Venice and the Netherlands'. In *AC*, 1968, p. 85–9, *illus.*

22 'Glasses that have no feet'. In *ADCG*, Jan 1968, p. 52–5, *illus.*

23 *How to identify English drinking glasses and decanters, 1680–1830*. Bell, 1962, 200p., *illus., bibliog.*

24 'Newcastle glass'. In *AC*, 1964, p. 191–5, *illus.*

25 'Attraction of English glass: the Times-Sotheby Index' [current prices]. In *The Times*, Apr 18th 1970, *Saturday Rev.* p. 1, *illus.*

26 BACON, John Maunsell. 'Acrostics in glass: a Jacobite puzzle' [acrostic on the name 'Charles']. In *CL*, Sept 1947, p. 523, *illus.*

27 'Ale glasses'. In *GC*, no. 47.

28 'Beilby enamel glasses'. In *GC*, nos. 9 and 82.

29 'Bottle-decanters and bottles'. In *GC*, no. 6.

30 'Bottle decanters and bottles'. In *AP*, Jly–Dec 1939, p. 13–15, *illus.*

31 'Criticism of . . . article in the *Connoisseur* [Jly–Dec 1942, p. 47–51] by W. Horridge and E. B. Haynes, on Amen glasses'. In *GC*, no. 33.

32 'Decanters, 1677–1750 *and* 1745–1800'. In *GC*, nos. 41 and 42.

33 'The elements of glass collecting'. In *GC*, no. 2.

34 *English glass collecting for beginners in a series of five letters to one of them*. Penrith, Reed, 1942, 16p.

35 'Extracts from Woburn Abbey glass-sellers' bills (Thorpe)'. In *GC*, no. 14.

36 'More Newcastle glass'. In *GC*, no. 40.

37 'A note on King's Lynn glass'. In *GC*, no. 29A.

38 'Privateer and other nautical glasses . . .'. In *GC*, nos. 50 and 53.

39 'Two Jacobite glasses'. In *GC*, no. 30.

39

joint author see WILLIAMS, Jane *and* BACON, John Maunsell.

40 BADDELEY, W. St C. 'The glass-house at Nailsworth (sixteenth and seventeenth centuries)'. In *Trans. of the Bristol Archaeological Soc.*, v. 42, 1920.

41 'BALUSTER' *pseud*. 'Ale and ale glasses'. In *GN*, 1946, p. 17–23, *illus*.

42 BAMFORD, Joan. 'Early crystal glass compotes. In *ADCG*, June 1967, p. 97–9, *illus*.

43 BANISTER, Judith. 'Bold John Barleycorn: a century of English ale-glasses'. In *ADCG*, Sept 1961, p. 27–9, *illus*.

44 'Relics of a gentlemanly vice: cut-glass decanters of the eighteenth and nineteenth centuries'. In *ADCG*, June 1961, p. 34–6, *illus*.

45 BANKFIELD MUSEUM, HALIFAX. *The H. P. Jackson loan collection of English glass* [Catalogue]. Halifax, 1948.

46 BARKER, T. C. *Pilkington Brothers and the glass industry*. Allen and Unwin, 1960, 296p., *illus*.

47 BARKER, Wilfred R. 'Notes on some old Yorkshire glasshouses'. In *TSGT*, 1925, p. 322–33, *illus., maps*.

48 BARRAUD, Ronald. 'John Davenport: a nineteenth-century glass decorator'. In *CONN*, Jan–Apr 1970, p. 186–8, *illus*.

49 BARRETT-LENNARD, T. 'Glassmaking at Knole, Kent'. In *The Antiquary*, v. 41, 1905, p. 127–9.

50 BATE, Percy. 'An eighteenth-century industry: Bristol enamel glass'. In *Mag. of Fine Arts*, v. 7, 1905, p. 151.

51 *English table glass*. Newnes, 1905, 130p., *illus*.

52 'Historic English drinking glasses'. In *Studio*, 1902, p. 106–12, *illus*.

53 'Old English glasses'. In *Studio*, 1902, p. 45–8, *illus*.

54 'Beakers'. In *GN*, 1946, p. 29–32, *illus*. A condensed version of E. B. Haynes's 'Common tumbler' in *AC*, 1946, p. 93–8.

55 BEARD, Geoffrey W. 'The documentation and variety of Stourbridge glass'. In *GC*, no. 135.

56 'English makers of cameo glass'. In *A*, 1954, p. 472–4, *illus*.

57 'George Woodall's cameo glass' [two articles]. In *CL*, Feb 1954, p. 347, *illus*. and *AC*, June 1956, p. 109–12, *illus*.

58 *Modern glass*. Studio Vista, 1968, 160p., *illus., bibliog*. Contents include: Modern English glass, p. 72–113, *illus*.

59 *Nineteenth-century cameo glass*. Foreword by E. Barrington Haynes. Monmouth, 1956, 149p., *illus. (some col.), bibliog*. Contents include: John Northwood (1836–1902) and the revival of cameo glass carving, p. 11–26; The Woodall brothers, p. 35–54, *illus*.

60 'Sparkling crystal'. In *AP*, Jly–Dec 1953, p. 151, *illus*.

61 BEATSON, CLARK AND CO. LTD. *The glass works, Rotherham, 1751–1951*. Rotherham, 1952, 52p., *illus., plans*.

62 BECK, A. M. L. 'Glass in Windsor Castle and Buckingham Palace'. In *BUR*, Jly–Dec 1925, p. 12–19, *illus*.

63 BECK, G. M. A. 'Ogniabene Luteri: a Surrey glass-maker'. In *TSGT (News and Reviews)*, 1953, p. 69–70.

64 BEDFORD, John. *Bristol and other coloured glass*. Cassell, 1964, 64p., *illus*. (Collectors' Pieces 2).

65 *English crystal glass*. Cassell, 1966, 64p., *illus*. (Collectors' Pieces 9).

66 *Paperweights*. Cassell, 1968, 64p., *illus*. (Collectors' Pieces 14).

67 'Beilby goblet' [unrecorded]. In *GN*, 1952, p. 21.

68 BELL, P. L. 'Airtwist glasses'. In *GC*, no. 141.

69 BENNETT, Raymond. *Collecting for pleasure*. Bodley Head, 1969. Contents include: Decanters, p. 68–71; Nailsea glass, p. 102–5; Tumblers and beakers, p. 110–14.

70 BERGSTROM, Evangeline H. *Old glass paperweights: their art, construction and distinguishing features*. Faber, 1947. First pub. Chicago, 1940. 132p., *illus*.

71 'Bergstrom paperweight collection'. In *A*, 1961, p. 486, *illus*.

72 BEWICK, Thomas. *Memoir of Thomas Bewick written by himself, 1822–1828*. Bodley Head, 1924, 274p., *illus*. Mention of the Beilby family. First pub. 1862.

73 BICKERTON, Leonard Marshall. 'Art of the English glass maker: the Alexander Collection'. In *CL*, Oct 1969, p. 1005–6, *illus*.

74 'English engraved glasses of the eighteenth century'. In *The Australasian Antique Collector*, no. 6, Jan–June 1969, p. 29–33, *illus*.

75 'Fascinations of the air-twist'. In *CL*, Jan 1970, p. 24–5, *illus*.

76 'A glass-lover's collection reunited: the Hartshorne Exhibition at Worthing' [1968]. In *CL*, Apr 1968, p. 911–12, *illus*.

77 'Glassmaking traditions in King's Lynn'. In *CL*, June 1969, p. 1514–15, *illus*. *comp. see* WORTHING MUSEUM AND ART GALLERY.

78 BIGNALL, R. G. 'Label decanters'. In *AC*, Apr 1957, p. 66–7, *illus.*

79 'Birmingham Exhibition of Manufactures and Art, 1849' [Descriptions and illustrations of glassware exhibited by George Bacchus and Sons, p. 314; Rice Harris (Islington), p. 307; Richardson (Stourbridge), p. 302, *etc.*]. In *Art Jnl.*, 1849.

80 BISHOP, John. 'Glass at the Antique Dealers' Fair' [two articles]. In *AP*, Jly–Dec 1936, p. 157–60, *and* p. 199–203, *illus.*

81 BLACKHAM, Robert J. *London's Livery Companies.* Sampson Low, 1932.
Contents include: Glass Sellers' and Glaziers' Companies, p. 285–90, *illus.*

82 BLES, Joseph. *Rare English glasses of the seventeenth and eighteenth centuries.* G. Bles, 1925, 269p., *illus.*
Contents include: 'Commemorative glass' by Sir J. S. Risley, p. 157–76.

83 BOARD OF TRADE. *Hand-blown domestic glassware* [Working party report]. H.M.S.O., 1947.

84 BOORE, J. P. 'Glossary of terms used by paperweight collectors'. In *Bull. of the National Early American Glass Club*, Dec 1960, p. 6–8.

85 'Old glass paperweights'. In *Hobbies*, June 1966, p. 98F–98G, *illus.*

86 'Old glass paperweights – a brief history of the art'. In *Hobbies*, June 1961, p. 90–1, *illus.*

87 'Old glass paperweights: some little-known English makers'. In *Hobbies*, Feb 1961, p. 80–1, *illus.*

88 BOULGER, G. S. 'Christopher Merret (1614–1695)'. In *Dictionary of National Biography*, v. 37, 1894, p. 288–9. Merret translated Neri's *Art of glass* in 1662.

89 BOWLES, William Henry. *History of the Vauxhall and Ratcliff glasshouses and their owners, 1670–1800.* London (priv. print.), 1926, 62p.

90 BRADDICK, Leonard E. 'Old Sussex glass'. In *Glass*, 1935, p. 509, *illus.*

91 BRADFORD, Ernle. *Antique collecting.* E.U.P., 1963. Teach Yourself Series.
Contents include: Glass, p. 60–75, *illus.*

92 BRENTON-ATKINS, G. T. 'A collector's résumé of English drinking glasses: the Hamilton Clements Collection recently auctioned'. In *The Antiquarian*, v. 16, May 1931, p. 21–4 and p. 62, *illus.*

93 BRIDGEWATER, N. P. 'Glasshouse Farm, St Weonards: a small glassworking site'. In *Trans. of the Woolhope Naturalists Field Club*, v. 37, 1963, p. 300–13.

94 'A small glassworking site at Glasshouse Farm, St Weonards'. In *GC*, no. 134.

95 BRIERLEY HILL PUBLIC LIBRARIES. *Check list of books and pamphlets on glass in the reference library special collection.* Brierley Hill Public Libraries and Arts Committee, 1962, 23p. Duplicated typescript.
see also THORPE, William Arnold.

96 'Bristol blue glass'. In *ADCG*, Aug 1958, p. 28–30, *illus.*

97 BRISTOL CITY ART GALLERY. *Treasures from West Country Collections* [exhibition catalogue including glass]. Bristol City Art Gallery, 1967, *illus.*

98 'Bristol opaque-white glass'. In *Glass.* 1958, p. 260, *illus.*

99 BRITISH MUSEUM. *Masterpieces of glass: a selection* [from the 1968 Exhibition at the British Museum] *compiled by* D. B. Harden, K. S. Painter, R. H. Pinder-Wilson, Hugh Tait. British Museum, 1968, 199p., *illus.* (some col.), *bibliog.*
Contents include: European glass, Middle Ages to 1862, by Hugh Tait, p. 127–85.

100 *The Portland Vase* by D. E. L. Haynes. British Museum, 1964, 48p., *illus.*, *bibliog.*

101 BRITISH STANDARDS INSTITUTION. *Glossary of terms used in the glass industry.* B.S.I., 1962, 56p.

102 BROOKS, Oscar. 'Jacobite glasses, usual and unusual'. In *AC*, Oct 1961, p. 206–8, *illus.*

103 'The scarcity of coin glasses'. In *CL*, May 1962, p. 1021, *illus.*

104 BROTHERS, J. Stanley. 'The miracle of enclosed ornamentation' [paperweights, marbles]. In *CJGS*, 1962, p. 116–26, *illus.*, *diagrs.*

105 BROWN, F. Harmar. 'Bristol Venetian glass'. In *CONN*, Jan–June 1934, p. 25–7, *illus.* In 1788 Venetian glass craftsmen settled near Bristol and Nailsea.

106 BROWNE, R. C. 'Sir Jerome Bowes (d. 1616)'. In *Dictionary of National Biography*, v. 6, 1886, p. 57–8. Bowes was granted a special licence to make drinking glasses in 1592.

107 BUCKLEY, Francis. *Alphabetical list of glass sellers, chinamen or vendors of earthenware of London, recorded in the newspapers and other records . . . 1660–1800. Collected by F.B. c. 1935.* Guildhall MS. 3384. A photocopy of this MS. is in the National Art Library, Victoria and Albert Museum.

108 'Art and politics: the Jacobite iconography'. In *Fine Arts* (U.S.A.), v. 19, Nov 1932, p. 16–18, *illus.*

109 'The Birmingham glass trade, 1740–1833'. In *TSGT*, 1927, p. 374–86.

110 'Bottles'. In *Glass*, 1925, p. 618. Mainly medicine phials.

111 'Cruet bottles of the eighteenth century'. In *Glass*, 1924, p. 489.

112 'Cumberland glasshouses'. In *TSGT*, 1926, p. 384–6.

113 'The Cycle Club and Jacobite Hunts and some commemorative glasses'. In *CONN*, Jan–June 1940, p. 57–62, *illus*. The 'Cycle Club' was the principal Jacobite club in the north of England.

114 'The development of English cut glass in the eighteenth century'. In *BUR*, Jly–Dec 1924, p. 299–304, *illus*.

115 'Development of the wine glass in the nineteenth century'. In *Glass*, 1924, p. 441.

116 'The dove as a Jacobite emblem'. In *AC*, 1936, p. 262–4, *illus*.

117 'Earlier cut drinking glasses'. In *AC*, 1937, p. 78–80, *illus*.

118 'The early glasshouses of Bristol' [area]. In *TSGT*, 1925, p. 36–61, *map*.

119 *English baluster-stemmed glasses of the seventeenth and eighteenth centuries*. Edinburgh (priv. print.), Ballantyne Press, 1912, 36p., *illus*.

120 'A fine glass collection: some outstanding pieces in the possession of Mr T Scholes of Manchester'. In *AC*, 1937, p. 5–7, *illus*.

121 'Fine old English glasses'. In *Glass*, 1930. Contents: Bonnet glasses, tea caddies and ink-pots, p. 490–2; Candlesticks, p. 356–8; Decanters, p. 396–8; Drinking glasses (cut), p. 274–6; Drinking glasses (plain stem), p. 241–3; Earlier and twisted stems, p. 184–6; Jugs and jelly glasses, p. 318–20; Glass salts, p. 344–5; Tankards, p. 450–2, *all illus*.

122 'Glasshouses of Dudley and Worcester'. In *TSGT*, 1927, p. 287–93.

123 'Glasshouses on the Tyne in the eighteenth century'. In *TSGT*, 1926, p. 26–51.

124 'Glasshouses on the Wear in the eighteenth century'. In *TSGT*, 1925, p. 105–11.

125 *The glass trade in England in the seventeenth century*. Stevens (priv. print.), 1914, 64p.

126 'Great names in the history of English glass'. In *Glass*, 1928. Contents: Cassilari, p. 103–4, *illus*.; John Bellingham, p. 150; Sir Robert Mansell, p. 199–200, *illus*.; John Akerman [glass-cutter], p. 247–8, *illus*.; Thomas Betts [eighteenth-century glass-cutter and engraver], p. 299–300, *illus*.; Duke of Buckingham [owned glasshouses at Green-wich and Vauxhall], p. 341–2 and 366, *illus*.; Jerom Johnson [cutter and engraver, *c.* 1750], p. 392–3, *illus*.; Jackson [and Co.], p. 488–9, *illus*.; John Bowles, p. 540, 548, *illus*.

127 *A history of old English glass*. Foreword by Bernard Rackham. Benn, 1925, 155p., *illus*. Contents include: lists of contemporary references in books, newspapers, etc., to the following: Glass wares other than cut glass, p. 142–51; The cut-glass trade and English eighteenth-century flint glasshouses, p. 9–16; Specialists in cut glass, p. 139–41.

128 'The jelly glass and its relations'. In *AC*, 1938, p. 298–300, *illus*.

129 'Lancashire glasshouses of the eighteenth century'. In *Glass*, 1924, p. 489.

130 'The London glass sellers'. In *AC*, 1938, p. 112–14, *illus*.

131 '[Mrs Petrocochino's] collection of old English and Irish glasses'. In *CL*, Nov 1930, p. 33–6, *illus*.

132 'Note on the glasshouses of the Leeds district in the seventeenth, eighteenth and early nineteenth centuries'. In *TSGT*, 1924, p. 268–77.

133 'Notes on the glasshouses of Stourbridge, 1700–1830'. In *TSGT*, 1927, p. 106–23.

134 'Notes on various old glasshouses'. In *TSGT*, 1930, p. 30–6. Includes Scotland and Wales.

135 'Old cut-glass chandeliers: the development of "lustre" making from George I to the Regency'. In *AC*, 1936, p. 178–81, *illus*.

136 'Old decanters'. In *CL*, Dec 1928, p. 94–8, *illus*.

137 'Old English glass at Wilbury Park'. In *CL*, Dec 1929, p. 845–6, *illus*.

138 'Old English glasses'. In *Glass*, 1931. Contents: Bottles, p. 322–4; Bowls, p. 102–3; Cruet bottles, plates, rummers and carafes, p. 65–6; Chandeliers, p. 230–2; Enamel glass, p. 278–80; Hogarth glasses, p. 498–9; Lamps, p. 230–2; Ravenscroft sealed glasses, p. 461–2; Tumblers, p. 186–8; Two-handled glasses and punch and toddy lifters, p. 146–8; Sweetmeat glasses, p. 15–16; Witch balls and pocket flasks, p. 364–6; Worcestershire glass [drinking glasses of that area], p. 415–17, *all illus*.

139 'Old English glasses'. In *Glass*, 1934. Contents: Amateur engraving [signatures, initials scratched on glasses], p. 66–7; Birmingham glass pinchers [seals, buttons, etc.], p. 187–8; British glassmakers abroad, p. 266–7; Curious pieces of glass, p. 12–13;

Famous London glasshouse [Whitefriars], p. 308–11; Glass salts, p. 344–5; Old flower vases and glasses, p. 474, 476; Remarkable table set [Anglo-Venetian], p. 388, 391; The war tax on glass 1695, p. 100–1. All except the article on Whitefriars are *illus*.

140 'Old English glasses'. In *Glass*, 1935.
Contents: An account of glassmaking [1754], p. 74; Ink horns and ink pots, p. 155–6; Water glasses and mugs, p. 205–6, *all illus*.

141 'Old English glass salts'. In *AC*, 1939, p. 44–6, *illus*.

142 'Old glass lamps and candlesticks'. In *CL*, Apr 1929, p. 492–4, *and* May 1929, p. 710–12, *illus*.

143 'Old Lancashire glasshouses'. In *TSGT*, 1929, p. 229–42.

144 *Old London drinking glasses*. Edinburgh (priv. print.), Ballantyne Press, 1913, 37p., *illus*. Deals with sixteenth- and seventeenth-century styles.

145 *Old London glasshouses*. Stevens (priv. print.), 1915, 42p.

146 'Old London glasshouses: Southwark'. In *TSGT*, 1930, p. 137–49, *illus*.

147 'Old Nottingham glasshouses'. In *TSGT*, 1926, p. 270–3.

148 'A rare Jacobite glass'. In *CONN*, Jly–Dec 1931, p. 36–7, *illus*.

149 'The sequence of drinking glasses in the eighteenth century'. In *Arundel Soc. of Manchester Minutes*, 1927–8.

150 'Seventeenth-century English table glass from pre-Ravenscroft fragments to early flint glass'. In *AC*, 1936, p. 150–2, *illus*.

151 'Seventeenth- and eighteenth-century ribbed glasses: some examples of English "rib twisting"'. In *AC*, 1939, p. 138–40, *illus*.

152 'Some Jacobite relics: a newly discovered glass inscription' [on a water glass]. In *AC*, 1935, p. 56–8, *illus*.

153 *The taxation of English glass in the seventeenth century*. Stevens (priv. print.), 1914, 74p.

154 'Thomas Betts's accounts'. In *Glass*, 1928, p. 300.

155 'Unusual old English glass . . .'. In *AC*, 1939, p. 249–51, *illus*.

156 'West country glasshouses'. In *TSGT*, 1929, p. 124–9.

157 BUCKLEY, Wilfred. 'Anglo-Dutch glasses of the eighteenth century'. In *Old Furniture*, 1928, p. 151.

158 'Anglo-Dutch stem glasses of the eighteenth century'. In *Arts and Decoration*, Sept 1939, p. 10–11, *illus*.

159 *The art of glass, illustrated from the Wilfred Buckley Collection at the Victoria and Albert Museum . . .* Allen and Unwin, 1939, 286p., *illus*.
Contents include: English glass, p. 75–86, and catalogue of the English items (nos. 465–595).

160 *The celebrated Horridge Collection of drinking glasses . . . illustrated catalogue*. Jackson-Stops and Staff, 1959.

161 *Diamond-engraved glasses of the sixteenth century with particular reference to five attributed to Giacomo Verzelini*. Benn, 1929, 24p., *illus*. A limited ed. Appendix reprints two articles from *BUR* by Bernard Rackham and Wilfred Buckley, both entitled 'An early diamond-engraved glass at South Kensington'.

162 *European glass*. Benn, 1926, 96p., *illus*. A limited ed. The glass discussed is from the Buckley Collection; English glass, p. 81–93; also included is an 'Essay on Dutch glass engravers' by F. Hudig.

163 *Notes on Frans Greenwood and the glasses that he engraved*. Benn, 1930, 15p., *illus*.

164 *D. Wolff and the glasses that he engraved. With a supplementary note on a glass engraved by Frans Greenwood*. Methuen, 1935, 41p., *illus*. A limited ed. Appendix D is a 'Report on signatures' by C. J. Van Ledden Hulseboch.

165 BUECHNER, Thomas S. 'Glass: ancient times to the nineteenth century'. In *Encyclopedia Britannica*, 1970 ed., v. 10, p. 456–63, *illus*.

166 'Glass drinking vessels in the collection of Jerome Strauss'. In *Connoisseur Year Book*, 1957, p. 42–7, *illus*.

167 BUNT, Cyril G. E. 'Wonderful Waterford – Ireland's debt to English craftsmen'. In *ADCG*, Oct 1959, p. 20–2, *illus*.

168 BURGESS, Frederick W. *Chats on household curios*. Fisher Unwin, 1914.
Contents include: Glass and enamels, p. 175–81.

169 BURING, L. 'The service of glass in the serving of wine'. In *Wine Trade Rev.*, Nov 15th and 22nd 1929.

170 BURTON, John. *Glass: philosophy and method, hand-blown, sculptured, coloured*. Pitman, 1969, 278p., *illus*. (some col.), bibliog.
see also 'Survey of contemporary glass'.

171 BUTLER, Joseph T. 'The Connoisseur in America – three landmarks in early English glass'. In *CONN*, Sept–Dec 1967, p. 134–5, *illus*. Includes a Verzelini glass.

172 BUTLER, R. F. 'Glass' [-making in Gloucester-

shire]. In *Victoria County History of Gloucestershire*, v. 2, 1907, p. 213.

173 BUTTERWORTH, Walter. 'Glass: cut and engraved'. In *TSGT*, 1929, p. 183–94, *illus.*

174 CAMPBELL, Alister. 'Beauty in glass candlesticks'. In *ADCG*, Aug 1954, p. 29–31, *illus.*

175 'Bottles of great charm'. In *ADCG*, Sept 1954, p. 23–5, *illus.*

176 'Early English drinking glasses'. In *ADCG*, Apr 1954, p. 29–31, *illus.*

177 'Early English glass makers'. In *ADCG*, Mar 1954, p. 20–2, *illus.*

178 'For and against cut glass'. In *ADCG*, Jly 1954, p. 26–8, *illus.*

179 'Fragile perfection: seventeenth-century drinking glasses'. In *ADCG*, Feb 1955, p. 26–8, *illus.*

180 'Glass, the domestic art'. In *ADCG*, June 1954, p. 34–6, *illus.* English and continental.

181 'The glass engraver's art'. In *ADCG*, May 1954, p. 20–2, *illus.*

182 'Glass, mould of fashion'. In *ADCG*, Nov 1954, p. 26–8.

183 'Glass toys and animals'. In *ADCG*, Oct 1954, p. 26–8, *illus.*

184 'History in glass: symbolic Jacobite table ware'. In *ADCG*, Mar 1955, p. 26–8, *illus.*

185 'How glass came to England'. In *ADCG*, Feb 1954, p. 24–6, *illus.*

186 'More beautiful than china: opaque-white glass'. In *ADCG*, Jly 1955, p. 22–4, *illus.*

187 'A new approach to glass collecting – tomorrow's antiques'. In *ADCG*, Jan 1955, p. 21–33, *illus.*

188 CARNEY, Clive. *Furnishing art and practice.* O.U.P., 1950, Contents include: Glass styles, old and modern, p. 173–86, *illus.*

189 CARVEL, John Lees. *The Alloa Glass Works.* An account of its development since 1750. Edinburgh (priv. print.), 1953, 102p., *illus.*

190 'Catalogue of the collection of Sir Harrison Hughes'. In *GC*, no. 8.

191 CECIL HIGGINS ART GALLERY. *Glass in the Cecil Higgins Art Gallery.* Bedford, Borough. Council, 1969, 16p., *illus.*

192 'Cecil Higgins Collection'. In *GN*, 1949, p. 25–7.

193 CHAFFERS, William. *Catalogue of the collection formed by Felix Slade, etc. (drawn up . . . and nearly rewritten by W. A. Nicholls). With notes on the history of glass making by A. Nesbitt . . . Edited by A. W. Franks.* London, 1871.

194 'Champagne decanter'. In *CL*, Jly–Dec 1957, p. 294, *illus.*

195 'Champagne glasses'. In *The Times*, Aug 9th 1963, p. 9, *illus.*

196 'Champagnes with cut bottoms'. In *The Times*, Aug 10th 1963, p. 9, *illus.*

CHAMPION, R. *see* OWEN, Hugh.

197 CHANCE, Sir Hugh. 'The Donnington Wood glasshouses'. In *GC*, no. 140.

198 'Nailsea glass'. In *GC*, no. 128.

199 'The Nailsea glassworks'. In *Pottery Gaz. and Glass Trade Rev.*, 1958, p. 111–13, *illus.*, *plan.*

200 'Records of the Nailsea glassworks'. In *CONN*, May–Aug 1967, p. 168–72, *illus.*

201 CHANCE, J. F. *History of the Firm of Chance Brothers and Company, glass and alkali manufacturers.* Priv. print., 1919.

202 'Chance Brothers Ltd tableware in moulded glass'. In *Art and Industry*, Dec 1952, p. 190–5, *illus.*

203 CHARLESTON, Robert Jesse. 'Ancient glass-making methods' [and abrasive decoration]. In *GC*, nos. 124 *and* 129.

204 'Apropos of tea-caddies in cut glass'. In *AC*, Aug 1966, p. 151–5, *illus.*

205 'Apropos of tea-caddies in cut glass'. In *GC*, no. 148.

206 'Cut and engraved glass'. In *Pottery and Glass*, Oct–Nov 1950, *illus.*

207 'A decorator of porcelain and glass – James Giles in a new light'. In *Trans. of the English Ceramic Circle*, 1967, pt. 3, *illus.*

208 'Decorators of glass and porcelain'. In *GC*, no. 114.

209 'A documentary Beilby glass' [tumbler]. In *CONN*, May–Aug 1964, p. 81–3, *illus.*

210 'Dutch decoration of English glass'. In *TSGT*, 1957, p. 229–43, *illus.*, *bibliog.* and also In *GC*, no. 104.

211 'English glass'. In *Encyclopedia Britannica*, 1970 ed., v. 10, p. 460–2, *illus.*

212 [English] 'Glass' [1500–1810]. In *Connoisseur Complete Period Guides*, 1968. Contents: Tudor, p. 122–6; Stuart, p. 417–20; Early Georgian, p. 658–64; Late Georgian, p. 981–8, *all illus.*

213 'English glass – an exhibition at the Victoria and Albert Museum'. In *A*, 1968, p. 541–7, *illus.*

214 [CHARLESTON, R. J.] 'English glass in the Collection of Mr Donald H. Beves, Cambridge connoisseur'. In *CONN*, June 1960, p. 32–7, *illus.*

215 CHARLESTON, R. J. 'English glass in the reserve collection at the Rijksmuseum'. In *CONN*, Jly–Dec 1965, p. 236–8, *illus.*

216 'English glass-making and its spread from the seventeenth to the middle of the nineteenth century'. In *Annales du Ier Congrès des*

Journées Internationales du Verre. Liège, 1960, p. 155–72, *illus.*

217 'English opaque-white glass. In *GC*, no. 111.

218 'George Ravenscroft: new light on the development of his crystalline glasses'. In *CJGS*, 1968, p. 156–67, *illus.*

219 'Glass'. In *The Queen*, Oct 26th 1960, p. 123, *illus.*

220 'Glass' [Pts I–V]. In Singer, Charles *and others*, eds. *History of Technology*, O.U.P., 1957, v. 3, p. 206–29, *illus., diags.*

221 'The Glass Circle Commemorative Exhibition of 1962'. Pt 1: 'Some important early English glasses'. Pt 2: 'The Beilby glasses'. In *A*, Jan 1963, p. 92–4, and Mar 1963, p. 320–3, *illus.*

222 'The import of Western glass into Turkey'. In *GC*, no. 146.

223 'The import of Western glass into Turkey, sixteenth–eighteenth centuries'. In *CONN*, May–Aug 1966, p. 18–26, *illus., bibliog.*

224 'James Giles as a decorator of glass'. In *CONN*, May–Aug 1966, p. 96–101, and p. 176–81, *illus., bibliog.*

225 'James Giles as a decorator of glass'. In *GC*, no. 147.

226 'Lead in glass'. In *Archaeometry*, 1960, p. 1–4.

227 'Medieval and later glass'. In Cunliffe, Barry, *Winchester excavations, 1949–1960.* Winchester, 1964. v. 1, p. 145–51, *illus.*

228 'Michael Edkins and the problem of English enamelled glass'. In *TSGT*, 1954, p. 3–16, *illus.*

229 'A notable London collection of glass' [Hamilton Clements Collection]. In *CONN* Jly–Dec 1958, p. 238–41, *illus.*

230 'A painter of opaque-white glass'. In *GN*, 1953, p. 13–20, *illus.*

231 'A panoply of English glass: loan exhibition at the Victoria and Albert Museum'. In *CL*, Jly 1968, p. 38–9, *illus.* An exhibition arranged to coincide with the eighth International Commission on Glass, London, 1968.

232 'The pleasures of collecting glass'. In *The Listener*, Jan 9th 1958, p. 61–3, *illus.*

233 'The Richard Weoley glass'. In *GC*, no. 132.

234 'Some notable glass on public view in England'. In *GC*, no. 107.

235 'Some tools of the glassmaker in Medieval and Renaissance times, with special reference to the glassmaker's chair'. In *Glass Technology*, 1962, p. 107–11, *illus.*

236 'The transport of glass: seventeenth–eighteenth centuries'. In *GC*, no. 152.

237 'Twenty-five years of glass collecting: a commemorative exhibition, "The Art of Glass", at the Victoria and Albert Museum'. In *CONN*, May–Aug 1962, p. 121–4, *illus.* An exhibition marking the twenty-fifth Anniversary of the Glass Circle.

238 'Le verre blanc opaque anglais du 18e siècle à décor polychrome'. In *Cahiers de la Céramique, du Verre and des arts du feu*, 1962, no. 28, p. 260–77, *illus.* English summary.

239 'Waterford glass'. In *A*, 1956, p. 522–5, *illus.*

240 'Wheel engraving and cutting: some early equipment: (1) Engraving; (2) Water-power and cutting'. In *CJGS*, 1964, p. 83–100, *and* 1965, p. 41–54, *illus.*
   comp. see
   (1) GUILDHALL MUSEUM
   (2) CIRCLE OF GLASS COLLECTORS
   (3) LEEDS CITY ART GALLERY
   (4) VICTORIA AND ALBERT MUSEUM

241 CHARLESWORTH, Dorothy. 'The English glossary of glass terms'. In *Annales du 3e Congrès des Journées Internationales du Verre*, Liège, 1966, p. 210–11.

242 CHOPE, R. Pease. 'Inscribed drinking glass' [1764]. In *Devon and Cornwall Notes and Queries*, Apr 1921, p. 211–12, *illus.*

243 CHURCH, A. H. *Josiah Wedgwood, master potter.* Seeley, 1903.
   Contents include: The Barberini or Portland Vase, p. 30–3, *illus.*

244 CHURCHILL, ARTHUR, LTD. *Catalogue of old English glass. 2nd ed. . . . with articles by Grant R. Francis, D. B. Harden, G. F. Laurence, W. A. Thorpe, etc.* A. Churchill Ltd, 1937. 122p., *illus., bibliog.* Prices given.

245 'Check lists of drinking glasses'. In *GN*.
   Contents: Air-twist glasses, 1947, p. 32–40; Balustroid stems, 1953, p. 35–48; Plain stems, 1955, p. 42–7; Hollow and incised stems, 1956, p. 45–50; *all illus.* Prices given.

246 *Exhibition of engraved glass* [Catalogue]. A. Churchill Ltd, 1957, 128p., *illus.*

247 *A Coronation Exhibition of royal, historical, political and social glasses commemorating eighteenth- and nineteenth-century events in English history . . . Apl–May 1937.* A. Churchill Ltd, 1937. 42p., *illus.* A catalogue: cover-title: 'History in Glass'.

248 *P. B. List of old English and Irish glass. For the use of owners of 'English table glass', by Percy Bate.* A. Churchill Ltd, 1939, 24p. Cover-title: 'A list of Old English and Irish glass offered for sale . . .'.

249 CIRCLE OF GLASS COLLECTORS. *Catalogue of the Circle of Glass Collectors' Commemorative Exhibition, 1937–1962, at the*

Victoria and Albert Museum. Introduction and notes by R. J. Charleston. London, 1962. 72p., *illus.*

250 'Paper devoted to John M. Bacon [founder of the Circle], died April 1948 – a sketch of his family and writings'. In *GC*, no. 88.

251 CLAIR, Colin, *ed. Glass.* Bruce and Gawthorn, n.d. 64p., *illus.* (Things we need.)

252 CLARK, George Thomas. *Some account of Sir Robert Mansell, Kt, Vice-admiral of England . . .* Dowlais, 1883, 110p.

253 CLEPHAN, James. 'The manufacture of glass in England. Rise of the art on the Tyne'. In *Archaeologia Aeliana* (Newcastle), *New Series*, v. 8, 1880, p. 108–26, *illus.*

254 CLOAK, Evelyn Campbell. *Glass paperweights. The complete collection of glass paperweights and related items . . . of the Bergstrom Art Centre and Museum.* Studio Vista, 1969, 196p., *illus.* (col.), *bibliog.*
Contents include: British and continental weights, p. 97–115, and a bibliography of some 300 items.

255 COCKRAM, A. J. 'William Parker and his chandeliers'. In *The Bath Critic*, v. 3, no. 8 [1953?].

256 COKE, Desmond. *Confessions of an incurable collector.* Chapman and Hall, 1928.
Contents include: So-called Bristol blue glass, p. 205–8.

257 'College glassworks'. In *Tableware*, 1963, p. 558–9, *illus.* The Royal College of Art Glassworks.

258 'Coloured [glass] bottles'. In *The Times*, Mar 18th 1959, p. 9, *illus.*

259 'Colourful Victorian art glass'. In *The Times*, Nov 7th 1964, p. 11, *illus.*

260 COMMISSION OF ENQUIRY INTO THE EXCISE ESTABLISHMENT. [Report on the] *Glass* [trade]. London, 1835.
An important document in the history of the glass trade. Reproduces relevant documents and lists contemporary glass manufacturers.

261 'Competitive friggers – encouraging the glass craftsman'. In *Pottery Gazette and Glass Trade Rev.*, 1963, p. 552–3, *illus.*

262 COMSTOCK, Helen. 'Beilby glass in America including some recent discoveries'. In *CONN*, Jan–June 1951, p. 106–11, *illus.*

263 'An engraved English glass water jug'. In *CONN*, Jan–June 1946, p. 109–10, *illus.*

264 'Exhibition of English and Irish glass'. In *CONN*, Jan–June 1942, p. 65–6, *illus.* An Exhibition held at the Steuben Glass Shop, New York.

265 'Sequence of English chandeliers'. In *A*, Jly 1944, p. 36–8, *illus.*

266 CONNOISSEUR. *Connoisseur Complete Encyclopedia of Antiques, ed.* by L. G. G. Ramsey. Connoisseur, 1962.
Contents include: English glass, p. 418–21; Irish glass, p. 423–5; General glossary of glass, p. 432–72, *all illus.*

267 COOK, Jean M. 'A fragment of early medieval glass from London'. In *Medieval Archaeology*, 1958, p. 173–7, *illus.*

268 COOK, N. C. 'Medieval glass from the City of London'. In *Antiquaries Journal*, v. 47, Pt 2, 1967, p. 287.

269 COOK, W. E. *The Art and craft of glassmaking.* Stourbridge, Stuart and Sons, Ltd, 1934, 25p., *illus.*

270 COPE, E. E. 'Some notes on the Warrington glassworks'. In *CONN*, Sept–Dec 1923, p. 40.

271 'Cordial glasses and decanters'. In *ADCG*, Nov 1958, p. 23–5, *illus.*

272 CORNING MUSEUM OF GLASS. *English nineteenth-century cameo glass. Introduction by A. C. Revi; preface and catalogue by P. N. Perrot.* New York, Corning, 1963, 43p., *illus.*

273 'Coronation glass and vase [1952]'. In *AP*, Jan–June 1953, p. 134, *illus.* By Royal Brierley Crystal and Stuart and Sons, Ltd, respectively.

274 COXSON, A. O. 'Enchantment in Bristol coloured glass'. In *ADCG*, Sept 1966, p. 71–4, *illus.*

275 COYSH, A. W. and KING, J. *Buying antiques reference book.* David and Charles, 1970.
Contents include: Glass collections open to the public, p. 27–9; Glass prices at auction, 1967–9, p. 202–7 *and* 248–52.

276 *Buying antiques general guide.* David and Charles, 1968.
Contents include: Glass, p. 108–24, *illus.*

CRAIG, Algernon *see* FREEMASONS UNITED GRAND LODGE OF ENGLAND.

277 CROMPTON, Sidney. 'Collecting English eighteenth-century glass'. In *ADCG*, June 1966, p. 83–5, *illus.*

278 'Mainly about rummers'. In *ADCG*, Nov 1966, p. 62–4, *illus.* Includes a 'classified list of unengraved rummers by stem forms'.

279 *ed. English glass. Edited by Sidney Crompton, contributors E. M. Elville and E. Ross.* Ward, Lock, 1967. 254p., *illus.*
Contents: 'Traditions of English glass' by Euan Ross; 'Techniques of the glassmaker'

by E. M. Elville; 'Collections and collecting' and 'Fakes and forgeries' by Sidney Crompton.

280 *History in glass.* Fontwell (Sussex), Centaur Press, *illus.* Publication expected in 1971.

281 CROSSLEY, D. W. 'Glassmaking in Bagot's Park, Staffordshire, in the sixteenth century'. In *Post-Medieval Archaeology*, v. 1, 1967, p. 44–83, *illus.*

282 'Cupping or bleeding glasses'. In *CL*, Jly–Dec 1954, p. 291, *illus.*, 502; 819; 994; 1079; 1497; 2111; 2324. A series of letters.

283 'Cut-glass fruit bowls'. In *ADCG*, Oct 1958, p. 28–30, *illus.*

284 DANIEL, Dorothy. *Cut and engraved glass, 1771–1905.* 6th ed. New York, Barrows, 1965, 441p., *illus.*

285 DANIELS, John Stuart. *The Woodchester Glass House: a record of the Huguenot glass workers with a description of the glass produced at the Woodchester site.* Gloucester, Bellows, 1950, 42p., *illus.*, *map, bibliog.*

286 DAVENPORT, Cyril J. H. *Cameos.* Seeley, 1900, 66p., *illus.*

287 DAVIDSON, Ruth. English cameo glass. In *A*, 1963, p. 694, *illus.*

288 DAVIS, Cecil. 'Old glass for export'. In *CONN*, Jly–Dec 1941, p. 108–11, *illus.* Export of English and Irish glass to America about 1800.

289 'Story of English glass: some lecture notes'. In *AC*, p. 202–7, *illus.*

290 DAVIS, Derek C. *English and Irish antique glass.* A. Barker, 1964, 152p., *illus.*, *bibliog.*
Contents include: Special types of glasses attributed to specific drinks, p. 47–60.

291 'Five phases in eighteenth-century glass'. In *AC*, Dec 1961, p. 252–6, *illus.*

292 'John Wilkes and political glasses'. In *AC*, Feb 1961, p. 14–16, *illus.*

293 and MIDDLEMAS, Keith. *Coloured glass. Photographs by Michael Plomer.* H. Jenkins, 1968, 119p., *illus.* (*col.*).

294 DAVIS, Frank. 'Butcher Cumberland and Prince Charlie'. In *CL*, Nov 1960, p. 1096–7, *illus.*

295 'The Butler Buggin bowls'. In *CL*, Jly 1963, p. 88–9, *illus.*

296 'The conservative English'. In *ILN*, Dec 1954, p. 1020, *illus.* Engraved glasses.

297 *The Country Life book of glass.* Country Life, 1966. Contents include: English and Irish glass, p. 39–58, *illus.*

298 'Decanter and enamelled wine glasses by William Beilby of Newcastle'. In *CL*, Feb 1960, p. 264, *illus.*

299 'The embellishment of glass'. In *The Times*, Oct 5th 1968, p. 23, *illus.* Dutch decoration of 'Newcastle' glass.

300 'English eighteenth-century glass'. In *ILN*, Jly 1929, p. 138, *illus.*

301 'English enamelled glass'. In *CL*, May 1958, p. 1072–3, *illus.*

302 'An engraved glass bowl, about 1760, with drinking scenes and mottos of the Walpole and Fitzwilliam families'. In *CL*, Jly 1964, p. 106, *illus.*

303 'English history in glass'. In *ILU*, June 1937, p. 1056, *illus.*

304 'The Francis Collection at Christies'. In *ILN*, Jly 1934, p. 32, *illus.*

305 'Glass decanters'. In *ILN*, Nov 1930, p. 984, *illus.*

306 'Glass exports westwards in the eighteenth century'. In *ILN*, Oct 1955, p. 700.

307 'Inscribed English glasses'. In *ILN*, Nov 1929, p. 778, *illus.*

308 'Jacobite glasses' [from the collection of W. Horridge]. In *ILN*, Feb 1960, p. 258, *illus.*

309 'Kneller portrait illustrates fashions in eighteenth-century glass'. In *ILN*, Jan 1966, p. 27, *illus.*

310 'Old English glass at Christies'. In *ILN*, Oct 1934, p. 578, *illus.*

311 'Old glass at the Marlborough and Queen Anne Exhibition'. In *ILN*, Feb 1934, p. 216, *illus.*

312 'Ravenscroft decanter jug'. [Engraved in the Low Countries or Germany *c.* 1676]. In *CL*, Sept 1964, p. 556–7, *illus.*

313 'Richness of a National Collection: glass at the British Museum'. In *CL*, Jly 1968, p. 101–2, *illus.*

314 'Sixteenth–eighteenth-century bottles'. In *ILN*, Dec 1932, p. 902, *illus.*

315 'Some eighteenth-century glass'. In *ILN*, Oct 1932, p. 586, *illus.*

316 'Success to aerostation'. In *ILN*, Jly 1954, p. 148, *illus.* A late eighteenth-century glass engraved with a ballooning scene.

317 'Two enamelled decanters, etc. by the Beilby family'. In *CL*, Jly 1960, p. 194, *illus.*

318 DAWSON, Charles. 'Old Sussex glass: its origin and decline'. In *The Antiquary*, v. 41, 1905, p. 8–11.

319 DEANE, Ethel. *Byways of collecting.* Cassell, 1908, 200p., *illus.*
Contents include: Old glass, Chapter 13.

320 DEAR, Herbert R. 'Why not collect old drinking glasses'. In *AC*, 1935, p. 291–4, *illus.*

321 *'Decorative Art in Modern Interiors* (formerly *Studio Year Book*). Published annually.

Contents include: Illustrated surveys of contemporary glassware (since 1906).

322 'Decorative brilliance – English cut glass'. In *ADCG*, Sept 1958, p. 33–5, *illus.*

323 DENNIS, Richard. 'The Butler Buggin bowls'. In *The Ivory Hammer: the year at Sotheby's*, Longmans, 1963, p. 198–9, *illus.*

324 'Changing tastes in English [eighteenth-century] drinking glasses'. In *Art at auction, 1967–8*, New York, Viking Press, 1968, p. 48–51, *illus.*

325 [Description and illustration of glassware designed by Harry J. Powell.] In *Art Jnl.*, 1905, p. 61–5, and 1906, p. 88, *illus.*

326 'Design Exhibition explained to the glass industry'. In *Pottery Gazette*, 1946, p. 161–8, *illus.* Illustrated survey of contemporary glass.

327 'Design in the glass industry'. In *Pottery Gazette*, 1946, p. 328–30, *illus.*

328 'Designed for sparkling wines: English champagne glasses'. In *ADCG*, Jly 1958, p. 29–31, *illus.*

329 'Diamond-point engraved drinking glass dated 1577' [attributed to Verzelini]. In *AP*, Jly–Dec 1939, p. 86, *illus.*, and In *CONN*, Jly–Dec 1939, p. 42, *illus.*

330 DICK, *Mrs.* 'Glass speaks to me, with instances from my collection'. In *GC*, no. 79.

331 DILLON, Edward. *Glass*. Methuen, 1907, 374p., *illus.* (some col.), bibliog. (Connoisseur's Library).
Contents include: English glass of sixteenth to seventeenth centuries, p. 299–336; English medieval glass, p. 139–40.
DIMBLEBY, Violet, *ed. see* DUNCAN, George Sang.

332 DON, Robin. 'Harvey's Wine Museum, Bristol'. In *Museum Jnl.*, v. 66, June 1966, p. 24–9, *illus.*

333 DORMER, Ernest W. 'Fine glass'. In *Antiques Rev.*, 1952, Pt. 12, p. 37–8, *illus.*

334 DOSSIE, Robert. *Handmaid to the arts. New ed.* 2v., London, 1796. First pub. 1758.
Contents include: On the nature and composition of glass, etc., v. 2, p. 158–238.

335 DOUGLAS, Jane. *Collectable glass*. Longacre Press, 1961, 64p., *illus.*
Contents include: Slagware, p. 47–50 (with list of registry marks).

336 DOUGLAS, R. W. 'Glass technology' [1850–1900]. *In* Singer, Charles *and others, eds. History of Technology*, O.U.P., 1957, v. 5, p. 671–82, *illus.*, bibliog.

337 'W. E. S. Turner, applied scientist'. In *Glass Technology*, 1967, p. 19–28, *illus.*, *ports.* The first W. E. S. Turner Memorial Lecture.

338 'William Ernest Stephen Turner'. In *Biographical Memoirs of the Fellows of the Royal Society*, v. 10, 1964, p. 325–55, *illus.*

339 DOVER, Clare. 'Unearthing an Elizabethan glass works' [at Bickerstaffe, Lancs.]. In *The Daily Telegraph*, June 2nd 1969, p. 12, *illus.*

340 'Drinking glass apparently used by Queen Anne at Cambridge in 1705'. In *CL*, Apr 1967, p. 786, *illus.* Letter and editorial comment.

341 'Drinking vessels at the Antique Dealers' Fair...'. In *Wine and Spirit Trade Record*, 1960, p. 998; 1000; 1002, *illus.*

342 'Dublin Exhibition of Industrial Art, 1853'. [Exhibits by Harris and Sons of Birmingham, and Richardson of Stourbridge.] In *Art Jnl.*, 1853, p. 30; 35 (in supplement preceding main text).

343 DUBLIN SCIENCE AND ART MUSEUM. *General guide to the art collections: Pt. 9: Glass* [compiled by J. Day]. Dublin, H.M.S.O., 1906, 38p., *illus.*

344 *General guide to the art collections: Pt. 9, Glass* [compiled by M. S. D. Westropp]. Dublin, H.M.S.O., 1912, 74p., *illus.*

345 DUFFY, E. Mary. 'Philip Pargeter and John Northwood I: cameo glass pioneers'. In *A*, 1962, p. 639–41, *illus.*

346 DUNCAN, George Sang. *A bibliography of glass (from the earliest records to 1940) . . . edited [with supplement] by Violet Dimbleby. Subject index by Frank Newby.* Dawsons, for the Society of Glass Technology, 1960, 552p. An annotated list of 15,752 items covering the whole field of glass.

347 DUTHIE, Arthur L. *Decorative glass processes.* Constable, 1908, 267p., *illus.* (Westminster Series).

348 DYER, Walter A. *The lure of the antique.* New York, Century, 1910.
Contents include: English and American glassware, p. 309–35, *illus.*

349 'Earliest recorded glassmaker in England'. In *Glass Technology*, 1960, p. 137.

350 'Early coloured glass at Heaton Hall' [Manchester]. In *AC*, 1938, p. 326, *illus.* The Applewhaite-Abbot Collection.

351 'Early English drinking glasses'. In *The Times*, Apr 14th 1956, p. 9, *illus.*

352 'Early Orange glass from Ireland. A note by a collector'. In *CONN*, Jan–June 1946, p. 38–41, *illus.*

353 EDINBURGH MUSEUM OF SCIENCE AND ART. *List of books, etc. relating to*

glass in the library of the Museum. Edinburgh, 1893, 40p.

354 EDWARD, Robert. *On collecting engravings, pottery, porcelain, glass and silver.* Edward Arnold, 1904, 90p. (Wallet Series).

355 'Electioneering goblet' [inscribed LASCELLES FOR EVER]. In *AC*, 1936, p. 325, *illus.* A Yorkshire election of 1807.

356 ELMHURST, Sheila. 'The aesthetic and practical applications of diamond-point engraving'. In *International Congress on Glass, comptes rendus, Bruxelles, 1965.* Paper 215, p. 1–3, *illus.*

357 ELPHINSTONE, N. 'Recent museum acquisitions. The Harvey Collection of fine glasses'. In *BUR*, Jan–June 1969, p. 88, *illus.* Harvey's Wine Museum was founded in Bristol in 1965.

358 ELVILLE, Ernest Michael. *Collectors dictionary of glass.* Country Life, 1961, 194p., *illus., bibliog.*
Contents include: Candelabra, p. 34–8; Carafes, p. 40; Chandeliers, p. 42–9; Doorstops, p. 73–4; Frauds and reproductions, p. 96–9; James and William Tassie, 178–9; Lynn, or Norwich glass, p. 125–6; Michael Edkins, p. 77–8; Posset and caudle glasses, p. 157–8; Sand glasses, p. 163; Scottish glass, p. 164–5; Witch balls, p. 190–1.

359 'The colour of Waterford glass'. In *Apollo Annual*, 1948, p. 88–90.

360 'Comparison of some eighteenth-century tableware in metal and glass'. In *Apollo Miscellany*, 1950, p. 27–34, *illus.*

361 'Cut glass of the eighteenth century'. In *AP*, Jan–June 1950, p. 166–7, 171, *illus.*

362 'Cut wine glasses of the eighteenth century'. In *CL*, Dec 1948, p. 1382–3 and Jan 1949, p. 34–5, *illus.*

363 'Early drinking vessels' [wines, ales, rummers]. In *AP*, Jan–June 1950, p. 28–9, *illus.*

364 'Early engraved glass'. In *AP*, Jan–June 1947, p. 92–4 and 116–18, *illus.*

365 'Early glass chandeliers'. In *AP*, Jly–Dec 1948, p. 14–15, 17, *illus.*

366 'Eighteenth-century glass fakes'. In *CL*, Jan–June 1952, p. 28–9, *illus.*

367 'English glass in the seventeenth century'. In *CL*, Sept 1962, p. 516–17, *illus.* and in *Glass*, p. 599–602, *illus.*

368 *English and Irish cut glass, 1750–1950.* Country Life, 1953, 95p., *illus.*

369 *English tableglass.* Country Life, 1951, 275p., *illus., bibliog.*
Contents include: Methods of distinguish-

ing the genuine from the imitation, p. 247–55; Scientific investigation of old glass, p. 256–66.

370 'English table and ornamental glass: one hundred years' retrospect'. In *Apollo Annual*, 1951, p. 55–60, *illus.* Includes cameos.

371 'Famous English glasses [Five articles]. In *AP*.
(1) 'The Verzelini goblets'. Jan–June 1947, p. 154–5.
(2) 'The Beilby glasses'. Jly–Dec 1947, p. 40–1.
(3) 'Bristol glasses decorated by Michael Edkins'. Jly–Dec 1947, p. 73.
(4) 'Jacobite glasses'. Jan–June 1948, p. 18–19.
(5) 'The early balusters'. Jan–June 1948, p. 35. *All illus.*

372 'Fashions in Victorian glass'. In *CL*, June 1960, p. 1312–13. *illus.*

373 'The glass cameo work of James and William Tassie'. In *Glass*, 1962, p. 121–4, *illus.*

374 'Glass at the Great Exhibition'. In *CL*, Apl 1951, p. 1294–9, *illus.*

375 'Glass engraved with a diamond'. In *Country Life Annual*, 1963, p. 8–10, *illus.*

376 'Glass paperweights'. In *AP*, Jan–June 1948, p. 93–4 *and* 115–16, *illus.*

377 'Glass in borrowed forms: early English tableware'. In *Country Life Annual*, 1964, p. 114–17, p. 119 *illus.*

378 'Glasses with air-twist stems'. In *CL*, Mar 1949, p. 492–3, *illus.*

379 'Glasses with opaque-twist stems and folded feet'. In *CL*, Jan 1948, p. 232–3, *illus.*

380 'Glasses with Silesian stems'. In *CL*, Sept 1963, p. 765–6, *illus.*

381 'History of the glass chandelier'. In *Country Life Annual*, 1949, p. 200–4, *illus.*

382 'Irish glass of the eighteenth and nineteenth centuries'. In *CL*, June 1958, p. 1290–1, *illus.*

383 'Old English champagne glasses'. In *AP*, Jly–Dec 1946, p. 99–100, *illus.*

384 'Opaque-white glass of the eighteenth and nineteenth centuries'. In *CL*, Oct 1949, p. 1297–8, *illus.*

385 *Paperweights and other glass curiosities.* Country Life, 1954. 116p., *illus., bibliog.*
Contents include: Illuminating glassware, p. 63–72; Commemorative glasses, p. 95–103.

386 'The Portland vase and its copies'. In *ADCG*, Sept 1964, p. 50–1, *illus.*

387 'Portraits in powdered glass: cameo work of James and William Tassie'. In *CL*, June 1961, p. 351–2, *illus.*

388 'The quality and style of cut glass'. In *CL*, May and June 1947, p. 1008–9 and 1064–5, *illus*.

389 'Some features of early cut wine glasses'. In *AP*, Jan–June 1949, p. 130–1, *illus*.

390 'Some rarities in glasses with opaque-twist stems'. In *AP*, Jly–Dec 1949, p. 134–5, *illus*.

391 'Starting a collection of glass: English styles of the eighteenth century'. In *CL*, June 1959, p. 1329–30, *illus*.

392 'Techniques of the glassmaker'. In Crompton, Sidney, *ed. English glass*, 1967, p. 39–58, *illus*.

393 'Today's trends in table glass'. In *Country Life Annual*, 1962, p. 12–13, *illus*.

394 'Vogue of the baluster glass'. In *CL*, June 1963, p. 1417–19, *illus*.
   ELVILLE, Ernest Michael. *See also* CROMPTON, Sydney, *ed.*

395 'The empty bud' [Newcastle Jacobite glasses]. In *GN*, 1951, p. 18–21, *illus*.

396 *Encyclopedia of World Art*. McGraw Hill, 1962. [Article on] glass. In v. 6, p. 367–98, *illus.*, *bibliog*.

397 'English and continental glassmaking'. In *The Times*, Dec 5th 1902, p. 15.

398 'English Cameo glass: nineteenth-century collection of Mr and Mrs Albert Christian Revi'. In *Antiques Journal*, Jly 1963, p. 24–6, p. 33, *illus*.

399 'English export glass'. In *GN*, 1946, p. 23–4.

400 'English glass: a chronology for collectors' [1226–1851]. In *GN*, 1948, p. 19–21.

401 'English seventeenth-century glass'. In *GN*, 1946, p. 26–8, *illus*. Discusses differences between true Venetian and façon de Venise.

402 'Engraved commemorative glass'. In *The Times*, Sept 16th 1961, p. 11, *illus*.

403 'Engraving on glass'. In *The Times*, Jly 30th 1960, p. 9, *illus*.

404 EVANS, Wendy. 'Background to glass – history from early days'. In *Pottery Gazette and Glass Trade Review*, 1965, p. 952–5, *illus*.

405 EVANS, Wendy *and* WEEDEN, Cyril. *Making glass*. Glass Manufacturers' Federation, *c.* 1969. 40p., *illus*.

406 'Fair goods' [silvered glass]. In *GN*, 1952, p. 28–31, *illus*.

407 'Fairy cup of Ballafletcher'. In *CONN*, Jly–Dec 1936, p. 330, *illus*. Copy of the original glass tumbler made at the end of the eighteenth century now in the Manx Museum, Douglas, I.O.M.

408 'Falcon Glass Works: Messrs Apsley Pellatt & Co.'. In *Art Union*, 1847, p. 321–4, *illus*.

409 FARR, Michael. *Design in British industry: a mid-century survey*. C.U.P., 1955. Glass, p. 105–14, *illus*.

410 FELL, H. Granville. 'An old English blue vase by Ravenscroft' [and two jugs]. In *CONN*, Jly–Dec 1938, p. 78, *illus*.

411 FERLAY, John. 'Market favours glass wine bottles' [recent prices]. In *ADCG*, Feb 1969, p. 89, *illus*.

412 FFOOKS, Oliver. 'Opaque-twist soda glasses: are they of English or continental provenance?' In *AC*, 1969, p. 27–30, *illus*.

413 'Finger bowls once banned from royal banquets'. In *The Times*, Aug 11th 1962, *illus*.

414 FLEMING, Arnold. *Scottish and Jacobite glass*. Glasgow, Jackson, 1938. 196p., *illus*.
   Includes stained glass. Describes main Scottish glasshouses: Perth, Alloa, Dundee, Edinburgh, Leith, etc.

415 'Select bibliography' [of glass]. In G. Janneau, *Modern glass*, 1931, p. 54–6. About 320 items.

416 'Flint glass epergnes for the Georgian dessert table'. In *The Times*, Feb 29th 1964, p. 11, *illus*.

417 FLINT GLASS MAKERS . . . *Rules and regulations of the Flint Glass Makers' Friendly Society of Great Britain and Ireland revised at the conference held in London . . . . 1858*. Birmingham, T. J. Wilkinson [1858]. 22p.

418 'Fly-catcher, Victorian hand-blown' [Letter]. In *CL*, May 1961, p. 1037, *illus*.

419 FORBES, R. J. 'Glass through the ages'. In *Phillips Technical Review*, Jly 22nd 1961, p. 282–99, *illus*.

420 FORD, John. *John Ford, flint glass manufacturer . . . Holyrood Flint Glass Works, Edinburgh. c.* 1870, 77p., *illus*. There is a photocopy of this work in the National Art Library, Victoria and Albert Museum.

421 'Ford cameo glass decanter'. In *CONN*, May–Aug 1925, p. 97–8, *illus*. Refers to John Ford & Co., Edinburgh.

422 FOSS, C. John. 'Bells of the Bristol glasshouses. In *CL*, Oct 1961, p. 920–2, *illus*.

423 FOSTER, Kate. *Scent bottles*. Connoisseur and M. Joseph, 1966. (Connoisseur monograph). Glass, p. 33–44, *illus*.

424 FOWLER, James. 'On the process of decay in glass . . . and the composition and texture of glass at different periods and the history of its manufacture'. In *Archaeologia*, v. 46, 1880, p. 65–162, *illus*.

425 FRANCIS, Grant Richardson. 'Disguised Jacobite glasses'. In *BUR*, Jly–Dec 1936, p. 175–6, *illus*.

426 'Jacobite drinking glasses and their relation to

the Jacobite medals'. In *British Numismatic Jnl.*, 1921–2, p. 247–83, *illus.*

427 *Old English drinking glasses, their chronology and sequence, etc.* H. Jenkins, 1926, 222p., *illus.*

428 'Propaganda glasses' [Jacobite and Williamite]. In *Arthur Churchill Ltd. Catalogue of old English glass, 2nd ed.*, 1937, p. 3–6.

429 FREEMASONS UNITED GRAND LODGE OF ENGLAND. *Catalogue of the Museum of the Freemasons' Hall* [London]. Compiled by Algernon Craig. 1939, 41p., *illus.* Includes Masonic glass.

430 FRESCO-CORBU, Roger. 'How to smoke an economical cigar: some nineteenth-century holders'. In *CL*, Apr 1965, p. 747–8, *illus.* Includes glass examples.

431 'Galaxy of glass. The British and the Victoria and Albert Museums display Nation's finest glass treasures for International Glass Congress' 1968. In *AC*, 1968, p. 167–71, *illus.*

432 GANDY, Walter. *The romance of glass-making: a sketch of the history of ornamental glass.* Patridge, 1898, 160p., *illus.*

433 GARDINER, C. I. 'An eighteenth century flagon from Arlingham'. In *Trans. of the Bristol and Gloucestershire Archaeological Soc.*, v. 60, 1940, p. 190–3, *illus.*

434 'Georgian decanters'. In *ADCG*, Apr 1958, p. 24–6, *illus.*

435 'Georgian table glass: finger bowls and wine glass coolers'. In *ADCG*, May 1958, p. 31–3, *illus.*

436 GILBY, W. and GILBY, A. *The complete imbiber. A Centenary Exhibition* [Catalogue]. Gilby, 1958, 36p., *illus.*

437 GILL, Ann. 'English glasses' [eighteenth century]. In *Bulletin of the Royal Ontario Museum*, no. 25, June 1957, p. 19, *illus.*

438 GILL, William H. 'It's a favourite collector's glass' [opaque twists]. In *ADCG*, Dec 1965, p. 40–1, *illus.*

439 'On rare baluster glasses'. In *AC*, 1965, p. 216–22, *illus.*

440 'Plain and air twist'. In *ADCG*, Nov 1963, p. 32–4, *illus.*

441 'Some aspects of English glass'. In *AC*, Apr 1965, p. 84–9, *illus.*

442 'Some later glasses'. In *ADCG*, Jan 1964, p. 39–40, *illus.*

443 GILLINDER, William. *Treatise on the art of glass making . . . etc.* Birmingham, 1851, 127p.

444 'Girandole candlesticks'. In *ADCG*, Dec 1958, p. 36–8, *illus.*

445 GIUSEPPI, Montague S. 'Glass' [making in Surrey]. In *The Victoria County History of Surrey*, v. 2, 1905, p. 295–305.

446 'Glass in the Stourbridge Festival of Britain Exhibition'. In *JSGT* (*News and Reviews*), 1951, p. 61–5, *illus.*

447 'Glass collecting: another side of the picture'. From a correspondent. In *AP*, Jan–June 1943, p. 102.

448 'Glass flower pots'. In *CL*, Dec 1962, p. 1394, *illus.*

449 'Glass from the Victorian age' [Burmese glass]. In *The Times*, Feb 12th 1966, p. 11, *illus.*

450 'Glass blowers of Whitefriars'. In *Arts & Decoration* (U.S.A.), Nov 1938, p. 9–10, *illus.*

GLASS CIRCLE *see* CIRCLE OF GLASS COLLECTORS

451 'Glass craftsmen of today'. In *ADCG*, Oct 1946, p. 22–3, *illus.*

452 'Glass fountain by Messrs Osler'. In *Art Journal*, 1874, p. 272, *illus.* F. & C. Osler of Oxford Street, London. The fountain was exported to India for the Maharajah of Puttiala.

453 'Glass globes'. In *The Times*, June 22nd 1963, p. 11.

454 GLASS MANUFACTURERS FEDERATION [Hand-made crystal section]. *British crystal glass* [List of manufacturers]. G.M.F., 1957. Typescript.

455 'Glass paperweights'. In *The Times*, May 14th 1963, p. 14.

456 GLASS SELLERS' COMPANY. *Essays on the glass trade in England.* 1883.

457 *Papers relating to the Glass Sellers.* Sloane MS. no. 857 (British Museum).

458 'Glass Sellers' Company tercentenary'. In *The Times*, June 12th 1964, p. 14.

459 'The Glass Six of Stourbridge'. In *The Times*, Feb 18th 1965, p. 18, *illus.*

460 'Glasses to dress out the dessert'. In *ADCG*, Mar 1958, p. 27–9, *illus.*

461 'Goblets for Trinity College, Oxford' [by Laurence Whistler]. In *The Times*, Oct 23rd 1956, p. 7, *illus.*

462 GODDEN, Geoffrey A. *Antique china and glass under £5.* A. Barker, 1966.
Contents include: Victorian glass, fairy lights and paperweights, p. 83–116, *illus.*

463 'Fairy lamps for collectors'. In *ADCG*, Dec 1965, p. 55–7, *illus.*

464 'Makers' marks on nineteenth-century glass'. In *CL*, June 1962, p. 1452, 1455, *illus.*

465 'Victorian pressed glass'. In *ADCG*, Feb 1965, p. 51–2, *illus.*

466 GODFREY, Eleanor S. *The development of English glassmaking, 1560–1640.* Ph.D. Thesis (unpublished), Chicago University, 1957.

467 GOLDSMID, Beatrice. 'English glass'. In

ADCG, Apr 1950, p. 15–17 and May 1950, p. 25–7, *illus.*

468 'Glass in the Ashmolean Museum'. In *ADCG*, Feb 1951, p. 22–4, *illus.*

469 'Glass in the British Museum'. In *ADCG*, Jly 1950, p. 37–9, *illus.*

470 'Glass in the Fitzwilliam Museum. In *ADCG*, Mar 1951, p. 24–5, *illus.*

471 'Glass in the Victoria and Albert Museum'. In *ADCG*, Sept 1950, p. 31–3, *illus.* and Nov 1950, p. 28–30, *illus.*

GOODING, E. J. *ed. see* INTERNATIONAL COMMISSION ON GLASS, 1968.
joint ed. see SOCIETY ON GLASS TECHNOLOGY, SHEFFIELD.

472 GOODWIN, Michael. *Country Life pocket dictionary of collectors' terms.* Country Life, 1967. Glass terms, p. 91–121, *illus.*

473 GORDON, Hampden. *Antiques – the amateur's questions.* J. Murray, 1951. Glass, p. 1–29, *illus.*

474 *The lure of antiques – looking and learning today.* J. Murray, 1961. Variety in old glass, p. 49–66, *illus.*

475 'Trends of design in the crafts'. In *GC*, no. 94.

476 'Artist in glass: John Topham'. In *Scotland's Mag.*, Oct 1961, p. 7–8. *illus.*

477 GRAHAM, Andrew. 'Recent examples of the work of Laurence Whistler'. In *CONN*, May–Aug 1965, p. 92–7, *illus.*

478 GRAHAM, Fergus. 'The Antique Dealers' Fair' [1938]. In *AP*, Jly–Dec 1938, p. 187–9, *illus.* On collecting glass.

479 'Glass at the Antique Dealers' Fair' [1937]. In *AP*, Jly–Dec 1937, p. 155–7 and 214–16, *illus.*

480 'The glass collection of John M. Bacon, Esq.'. In *AP*, Jly–Dec 1936, p. 336–41 and Jan–June 1937, p. 140–7, *illus.*

481 'Glasses of the seventeenth century (1660–1685)'. In *GC*, no. 4.

482 'More early glass'. In *AP*, Jan–June 1938, p. 86–90, *illus.* Seventeenth-century examples showing Venetian influence.

483 'Early British glass'. In *AP*, Jly–Dec 1945, p. 184–7, *illus.*, p. 211 and p. 235–7, *illus.*

484 'Some English glass primitives'. In *AP*, Jly–Dec 1938, p. 296–8, *illus.* Early seventeenth-century glass.

485 'Some glass problems'. In *GC*, no. 70.

486 'Thoughts on early British glass'. In *Apollo Annual*, 1948, p. 79–82, *illus.*

487 'Twenty years: some aspects of English glass, 1665–1685' [Lead and soda glass]. In *AP*, Jly–Dec 1937, p. 9–15 and p. 316–20, *illus.*

488 'Wealden glass'. In *GC*, no. 81.

489 'Wrythen glass'. In *GC*, no. 1.

490 GRAY, H. St George. 'Nailsea glass'. In *CONN*, May–Aug 1911, p. 85–98, *illus.* (some col.).

491 'Notes on Nailsea glass'. In *Proc. Somerset Archaeological Soc.*, v. 52, Pt 2, p. 166.

492 'Notes on the Nailsea glassworks'. In *CONN*, Jan–June 1923, p. 127–33, *illus., port.*

493 *and* LAVINGTON, Margaret. 'Nailsea and other glass in the collection of Mr John Lane'. In *CONN*, May–Aug 1920, p. 67–76, *illus.*

494 GRAY, I. 'New factory, new glass'. In *Design*, Apr 1968, p. 48–9, *illus.* Ronald Stennett-Wilson's glass factory at King's Lynn.

495 GRAY, John Miller. *James and William Tassie: a biographical sketch with a catalogue of their [opaque-white glass paste] medallions . . . .* Edinburgh, W. G. Patterson, 1894, 174p.

496 GREAT EXHIBITION, LONDON, 1851. 'British glass'. In *Art Journal. Illustrated catalogue of the Exhibition (Supplementary Vol., 1851).* Contains numerous references to the main English glass manufacturers with illustrations.

497 'Great Exhibition of 1851: a review of the pottery and glass exhibits'. In *Pottery Gazette*, 1950, p. 523–7, *illus.*

498 GREEN, Mary. 'Glass of fashion and mould of form'. In *CL*, Aug 1963, p. 378–9, *illus.* Modern design in English and continental glass.

499 GREENHILL, B. J. 'The story of Nailsea glassworks'. In *The Clevedon Mercury*, Jan 21st 1961.

500 GREENSHIELDS, Margaret. 'Georgian elegance in glass'. In *ADCG*, Sept 1957, p. 30–2, *illus.*

501 'Seventeenth-century English glass'. In *ADCG*, Aug 1957, p. 25–7, *illus.*

502 'Greenwood, The art of'. In *GN*, 1947, p. 12–13, *illus.*

503 GRIFFENHAGEN, George. 'The evolution of the medicine glass'. In *Hobbies*, Jan 1964, p. 72, 84, *illus.*

504 GRIMWADE, A. G. 'Silver and glass cups: a comparison of sixteenth-century examples'. In *CONN*, Jan–June 1953, p. 86–7, *illus.*

505 GROS-GALLINER, Gabriella. *Glass: a guide for collectors.* Muller, 1970, 176p., *illus.* (some col.), bibliog. British glass, p. 95–116.

506 GROVER, Roy *and* GROVER, Lee. *Art glass nouveau.* Rutland, Vermont, Tuttle, 1967, 231p., *illus. (col.)*, bibliog. Covers American, English and continental coloured glass of the period.

507 'Guide to glasses'. In *Pottery and Glass*, 1958.

Feb, p. 51–8; Apr, p. 108–13; May, p. 127–33; June, p. 172–5; Jly, p. 194–8; Sept, p. 264–8; Oct, p. 284–6; Nov, p. 321–4, all illus.

508 GUILDFORD PUBLIC LIBRARY. *Glass subject specialisation list.* Guildford P.L., 1965, 14p. Duplicated typescript.

509 GUILDHALL MUSEUM. *Catalogue of the collection of London antiquities in the Guildhall Museum.* Guildhall Museum, 1908.

510 *Finds of glass in the City of London.* Exhibition catalogue compiled by R. J. Charleston. Guildhall Museum, 1968, 44p. Typescript.

511 GUTTERY, D. R. *From Broad-glass to cut crystal: a history of the Stourbridge glass industry.* L. Hill, 1956, 161p., illus., bibliog. Contents include: George Ensell and the Wordsley glasshouses, p. 96–104; The Henzey family, p. 12–31, 45–66; Paul Tyzack, the first Stourbridge glass-maker, p. I–II.

512 'These are glassmakers'. In *TSGT (News and Reviews)*, 1956, p. 21–32. A general article on English glassmakers, their history and conditions of work.

513 GWENNET, G. 'Anciennes verreries anglaises'. In *Clarté*, 11e année, no. 9 (Sept 1939).

514 'Ravenscroft et ses cristaux'. In *Clarté*, 12e année, no. 5 (Mai 1939).

515 HADEN, H. Jack. *Notes on the Stourbridge glass trade.* Brierley Hill Libraries and Arts Committee, 1949, 37p., illus.

516 'The problem of the origin of the Stourbridge glass trade'. In *Bull. of the Paperweight Collectors Assn.*, June 1964, p. 47–50, illus.

517 'The Richardson bequest of Stourbridge glass'. In *GN*, 1953, p. 24–6, illus.

518 'The Stourbridge glass collection'. In *Connoisseur Year Book*, 1956, p. 111–16, illus.

519 'Tumble-up'. In *Notes and Queries*, May 1959, p. 193. A letter commenting on the term 'tumble-up' – a glass resting on the shoulders of a carafe.

520 HADFIELD, Anna *and* HADFIELD, John. 'Vintage glasses'. In Ray, Cyril, *ed. The complete imbiber*, 4. Vista, 1961, p. 130–45, illus.

521 HADFIELD, John. 'Landscapes on glass: some recent goblets by Laurence Whistler'. In *CL*, Jly 1963, p. 198–9, illus.

522 'Some new examples of Laurence Whistler's engraved glass'. In *CONN*, Jly–Dec 1954, p. 96–100, illus.

523 'The Queen's homes in glass'. In *CL*, Nov 1953, p. 1483–4, illus. A set of engraved glasses by Laurence Whistler.

524 HAGGAR, Reginald George. *Glass and glass makers*, illustrated by the author. Methuen, 1961, 80p., illus. (Methuen's Outlines).

525 HALAHAN, Brenda C. *Chiddingfold glass and its makers in the Middle Ages.* A paper read to the Newcomen Society (London), Apr 21st 1925.

526 'The Frome Copse glass-house, Chiddingfold discovered September 1921'. In *Surrey Archaeological Collections*, 1921, p. 24–31, map.

527 HALL, William Douglas. 'The collection of glass in the City Art Galleries, Manchester'. In *CJGS*, 1961, p. 131–3, illus.

528 HALLEN, Arthur W. C. *French gentlemen glassmakers: their work in England and Scotland.* Edinburgh, 1893, 16p. Reprinted from *The Scottish Antiquary*.

529 'Glass-making in Sussex, Newcastle and Scotland'. In *The Scottish Antiquary (Northern Notes and Queries)*, v. 7, 1893, p. 145–56, illus.

530 'Scottish glass'. In *The Scottish Antiquary (Northern Notes and Queries)*, v. 4, 1890, p. 88, and v. 5, 1891, p. 88.

531 HANNAH, E. T. 'Glass of distinction'. In *GC*, no. 49A.

532 HARDEN, Donald Benjamin. 'Glass beakers [probably medieval] from Colchester Castle'. In *Antiquaries Jnl.*, 1950, p. 70–2, illus.

533 'Saxon glass from Sussex'. In *Sussex County Mag.*, 1951, p. 260–8, illus.
   see also BRITISH MUSEUM.

534 HARDING, Walter. *Old Irish glass: the Walter Harding Collection, including English and other pieces* [Catalogue]. Liverpool, 1930, 108p., illus.

535 HARRIS MUSEUM, PRESTON. *A nineteenth-century miscellany.* Preston (Lancs.), Harris Museum, 1952. (Picture Book no. 1). Includes section on lustres and coloured glass.

536 HARTSHORNE, Albert. *Old English glasses: an account of glass drinking vessels in England, from early times to the end of the eighteenth century. With introductory notices, original documents, etc.* Edward Arnold, 1897, 490p., illus. This book marks the beginning of glass literature (excluding technology) in England.
   Contents include: transcripts of State Papers, Patent Rolls, Ravenscroft's Patent (1674), p. 454–6.

537 *Antique drinking glasses. A pictorial history of glass drinking vessels.* New York, Brussel &

Brussel, 1967, 490p., *illus*. A facsimile reprint of *Old English glasses* with new title-page.

HAYNES, D. E. L. *see* BRITISH MUSEUM.

538 HAYNES, E. Barrington. 'The airtwist glasses: a study in comparative rarity'. In *AC*, 1940, p. 117–20, *illus*. and 1941, p. 18–20, *illus*.

539 'The air-twists re-examined'. In *AC*, 1948, p. 90–4 and 166–9, *illus*.

540 'An Anglo-Netherlandish baluster goblet'. In *CONN*, Jly–Dec 1940, p. 64–5, *illus*.

541 'An Anglo-Venetian vase'. In *CONN*, Jly–Dec 1939, p. 187–9, *illus*.

542 'Balustroid glasses'. In *AC*, 1946, p. 187–92 and 225–8, *illus*.

543 'The common tumbler'. In *AC*, 1946, p. 93–8, *illus*. Ancient, European and English.

544 'The common drinking glasses of the eighteenth century'. In *AP*, Jan–June 1954. Balusters, p. 31; Moulded and composite stems, p. 60; Balustroids, p. 91; Plain unknopped stems, p. 155; *all illus*.

545 'The composite stem in eighteenth century glasses'. In *AC*, 1943, p. 77–80, *illus*.

546 'A diversity of glasses [English and some continental]. In *AC*, 1950, p. 234–40 (continental); 1951, p. 233–8; 1952, p. 140–3 and 259–63; *all illus*.

547 'Eighteenth-century glass of Britain'. In *A*, Aug–Sept 1941, p. 157–61 and 297–9, *illus*.

548 'Faceted-stem glasses'. In *AC*, 1944, p. 56–60, *illus*.

549 'Fringed and looped sweetmeats'. In *AP*, Jly–Dec 1941, p. 75–7, *illus*.

550 'Glass for a specialist' [multiple-spiral stems]. In *AP*, Jan–June 1942, p. 118–19, *illus*.

551 'Glass from Ireland'. In *A*, 1950, p. 197–200, *illus*.

552 *Glass through the ages*. 2nd ed. Penguin Books, 1959, 310p., *illus*. First published 1948. Contents include: Glassmaking in England, p. 142–63; English glasses of the eighteenth century classified by stem formation, p. 193–299.

553 'The glorious memory' [Williamite]. In *AC*, p. 112–18, *illus*.

554 'The Greenwood glasses'. In *CONN*, Jan–June 1944, p. 34–7, *illus*.

555 'Historic relic: Amen glass from Dunvegan Castle'. In *A*, Mar 1944, p. 142–3, *illus*.

556 'Monteiths'. In *AP*, Jan–June 1941, p. 47–9, *illus*. Discusses salts, jelly glasses, bonnet glasses and sweetmeats.

557 'National impressionism in English glass'. In *AP*, Jly–Dec 1942, p. 8–11, *illus*. Evolution of drinking-glass design.

558 'A naval array'. In *AP*, Jan–June 1940, p. 74–7 and 125–7, *illus*.

559 'Old glass as an investment: some pertinent points for collectors in war-time'. In *AC*, Feb 1940, p. 17–20, *illus*.

560 'On baluster glasses: a classification for collectors'. In *AC*, 1942, p. 144–7, *illus*.

561 'The opaque-twist glasses'. In *AC*, 1941, p. 95–8 and 115–18, *illus*. Describes the varieties of twist and their chronological sequence.

562 'Perry and cider glasses'. In *A*, 1944, p. 204, *illus*.

563 'Plain stemmed glasses'. In *AC*, 1942, p. 65–8, *illus*.

564 'Post-war glass collecting'. In *AC*, 1943, p. 181–4, *illus*.

565 'Rummers'. In *AP*, Jly–Dec 1942, p. 165–6, *illus*.

566 'Some notes on Beilby's glass'. In *AC*, 1945, p. 65–6, *illus*.

567 'Some peace-treaty glasses'. In *AC*, 1944, p. 146–9, *illus*.

568 'Some pre-Ravenscroft glasses'. In *CONN*, Jan–June 1950, p. 88–93, *illus*. Includes a list of sealed glasses.

569 'Some Ravenscroft jugs' [decanter jugs and pitchers]. In *CONN*, Jly–Dec 1941, p. 175–9, *illus*. Includes a chart of styles and locations.

570 'Specialisation in old glass'. In *AC*, 1945, p. 198–201, *illus*.

571 'The trumpet bowl'. In *AP*, Dec 1940, p. 81–5, *illus*.

joint author see HORRIDGE, W. *and* HAYNES, E. Barrington.

joint author see W. H. P. *and* E. B. H. [E. Barrington Haynes].

572 HAYWARD, Helena. 'English decorated glass – William and Mary Beilby'. In *ADCG*, 1959, p. 26–8, *illus*.

573 'The English glass industry – George Ravenscroft'. In *ADCG*, 1959, p. 31–3, *illus*.

574 'Giacomo Verzelini – an Italian glasshouse in London'. In *ADCG*, 1959, p. 31–3, *illus*.

575 'Glass in disguise – English coloured wares'. In *ADCG*, 1960, p. 38–40, *illus*.

576 HEDDLE, G. M. *A manual on etching and engraving glass*. Tiranti, 1961, 66p., *illus*.

577 HENNESSY, F. 'Our humble servant, the bottle'. In *Chambers Jnl.*, Apr 1937, p. 283–4.

578 HERMAN, Felix. *Painting on glass and porcelain*. Scott Greenwood & Co., 1897.

579 HERRAGHTY, E. A. 'A discovery at Dunvegan' [An 'Amen' glass]. *In Scotland's Mag.*, Dec 1942, p. 23–5, *illus*.

580 HEWITT, Ethel M. 'Glass-making' [in Kent]. In *The Victoria County History of Kent*, v. 3, 1932, p. 400–2.

581 HEWLETT, S. G. 'Some eighteenth century glass'. In *CONN*, Sept–Dec 1919, p. 81–4, *illus*.

582 HIGNETT, H. N. 'Old English wine glasses'. In *CONN*, May–Aug 1909, p. 93–8, *illus*.

583 'Hiram Codd's bottles' [Letters discussing early aerated liquid bottles]. In *CL*, 1964; Jly, p. 247, *illus*.; Sept, p. 579; Oct, p. 845; Dec, p. 1718, *illus*. Bottles of this type were patented by Codd in 1875.

584 'Historic Pargeter-Northwood Vase'. In *Pottery Gazette and Glass Trade Rev.*, 1960, p. 752–5, *illus*. Describes the Pargeter-Northwood replica of the Portland Vase.

585 HLAVA, Pavel. 'Glass and ceramics at the British Design Centre'. In *The Czechoslovak Glass Rev.*, v. 22, no. 9, 1967, p. 279–83, *illus*.

586 HODGSON, J. C. 'Family of Williams of Newcastle, glass manufacturers'. In *Proc. of the Soc. of Antiquaries of Newcastle-upon-Tyne, (3rd series)*, v. 7, p. 207.

587 HODGSON, *Mrs* Willoughby. 'Frauds in old glass'. In *AP*, Jan–June 1943, p. 72–3.

588 'Old London and the glass trade'. In *AP*, Jly–Dec 1943, p. 3–6, *illus*.

589 *The quest of the antique.* H. Jenkins, 1924, *illus.* (*some col.*).
Contents include: Cut-glass, p. 159–62; Frauds in old glass, p. 243–7.

590 'Some glass from Mrs Reynolds-Peyton's collection' [English, Irish and continental items]. In *CONN*, Sept–Dec 1917, p. 195–204, *illus*.

591 HODKIN, F. W. 'The contribution of Yorkshire to glass'. In *TSGT (News and Reviews)*, 1953, p. 21–36.

592 HOGAN, D. E. 'The Pilkington Glass Museum'. In *Museum*, 1967, p. 220–1, *illus*.

593 HOGAN, James Humphries. 'Artistic table glass' [contemporary trends]. In *TSGT*, 1934, p. 96–105, *illus*.

594 'Design and form as applied to the manufacture of glassware'. In *Jnl. of the Royal Soc. of Arts*, 1933, p. 364–83, *illus*.

595 'Development in the design of English glassware during the last hundred years'. In *TSGT*, 1936, p. 735–40, *illus*.

596 'English design in glassware'. In *Jnl. of the Royal Soc. of Arts*, 1935, p. 426–38.

597 'Glass at the Exhibition of British Art and Industry'. In *TSGT*, 1935, p. 167–70, *illus*.

598 'Glassware in the modern home'. In *TSGT*, 1938, p. 12–15.

599 HOLDEN, E. W. 'Objects of glass found during the excavations at the medieval village of Hangleton, Sussex'. In *Sussex Archaeological Collections*, 1963, p. 162–5, *illus*.

HOLLAND, A. J. *joint author see* PRESTON, Eric, HOLLAND, A. J. *and* TURNER, William E. S.

600 HOLLAND, Margaret. 'Puzzles of Irish glass'. In *ADCG*, Nov 1964, p. 35–6, 38, *illus*.

601 HOLLISTER, Paul. 'Bacchus and other English weights'. In *Bergstrom Paperweight Symposium (USA)*, 1967, p. 17–29.

602 *The encyclopedia of glass paperweights.* W. H. Allen, 1970, 312p., *illus.* (*some col.*), *bibliog.* A comprehensive study originally published in America, 1969.

603 HOLLOWOOD, Albert Bernard. *Pottery and glass.* Penguin, 1947, 63p., *illus.* (The Things We See Series, no. 4.)

604 HONEY, William Bowyer. *English glass.* Collins, 1946, 48p., *illus.* (*some col.*). (Britain in Pictures Series). This book also appears as part of *British craftsmanship*, ed. by W. J. Turner, Collins, 1948, p. 107–56.

605 'English or Irish? Cut glass in the Francis T. Carter Collection'. In *CONN*, Jan–June 1935, p. 77–80, *illus*.

606 'The work of James Giles' [decorator of porcelain and glass]. In *Trans. of the English Ceramic Circle*, v. 1, no. 5, 1937, p. 7–22.
see also VICTORIA AND ALBERT MUSEUM.

607 HORRIDGE, W. 'Documents relating to the Lorraine glassmakers in North Staffordshire, with some notes thereon'. In *GN*, 1955, p. 26–35, *facsim*.

608 'The eighteenth-century champagne glass – a speculation'. In *GC*, no. 85.

609 'The emblems on Jacobite drinking glasses'. In *Apollo Annual*, 1948, p. 85–8, *illus*.

610 'The Lorraine glassmakers in Staffordshire'. In *GC*, no. 72.

611 'The rare emblems on Jacobite drinking glasses'. In *GC*, no. 56.

612 'Silica and the metal oxides used in glassmaking'. In *GC*, no. 93, May 1949.

613 *and* HAYNES, E. B. 'The "Amen" glasses'. In *CONN*, Jly–Dec 1942, p. 47–51, *illus*.

614 'Horridge on Jacobite emblems'. In *GN*, 1947, p. 24–5. Comment on and summary of the *GC* paper no. 56.

615 HOUGHTON, John. 'List of glasshouses in operation in England in 1696'. In Elville, E. M. *English table glass.* Country Life, 1951, p. 77.

616 *A collection of letters for the improvement of*

husbandry and trade. London, 1681–3 and 1692–1703.

617 HOWARD, Alexander L. *comp. The Worshipful Company of Glass Sellers of London from its inception to the present day*. Northwood, Rawlinson, 1940, 152p., *illus*.

618 HOWE, Bea. 'The charm of old marbles'. In *CL*, Dec 1969, p. 1593, *illus*.

619 'Distinctive patterns in Victorian table glass'. In *ADCG*, Jly 1967, p. 62–4, *illus*.

620 'Old glass ships'. In *ADCG*, May 1964, p. 45–6, *illus*.

621 'Skill of the wandering glass-blowers'. In *CL*, 1957, p. 159–60, *illus*.

622 'Varied forms of Victorian art glass'. In *ADCG*, Sept 1968, p. 90–2, *illus*.

623 'Variety of Victorian flower vases'. In *CL*, Dec 1957, p. 1374–5, *illus*. Includes glass vases.

624 'Variety of Victorian glass'. In *CL*, Apr 1957, p. 824–5, *illus*.

625 'The Victorian cult of the fern' [glass ornaments, etc.]. In *CL*, Oct 1962, p. 898–9, *illus*.

626 HUDSON, J. Paul. 'Seventeenth-century glass wine bottles and seals excavated at Jamestown'. In *CJGS*, 1961, p. 78–89, *illus*. Includes some English examples.

627 'George Ravenscroft and his contribution to English glassmaking'. In *A*, 1967, p. 822–31, *illus*.

628 HUGHES, George Bernard. 'The art of the glass punch bowl'. In *Country Life Annual*, 1965, p. 88, 90, *illus*.

629 'Beauty of English cased glass'. In *CL*, June 1963, p. 1322–3, *illus*.

630 'Chronology of English candlesticks: summary of major changes'. In *A*, 1930, p. 234–7, *illus*.

631 *Collecting antiques*. 2nd ed. Country Life, 1960. First pub. 1949. Contents include English millefiori paperweights, p. 300–10, *illus. (col.)*.

632 'Cordial and dram glasses'. In *Antiques Rev.*, 1950, Pt 4, p. 21.

633 'Cordial and dram glasses of Old England'. In *ADCG*, Sept 1946, p. 16–18. *illus*.

634 *Country Life collectors' pocket book*. Country Life, 1963. Glass, p. 135–75, *illus*.

635 'Crystallo ceramie illustrated by examples at Buckingham Palace'. In *AP*, Jan–June 1953, p. 183–5, *illus*.

636 'A cure for gluttony'. In *CL*, Apr 1957, p. 643, *illus*. Surfeit water glasses.

637 'Dating of English wine glasses'. In *The British Antique Trades and Collectors' Directory*, Luton, Woodhouse, n.d. [*c*. 1950], p. 15–19, *illus*.

638 'Decanters for the admiral's table'. In *CL*, Oct 1960, p. 722–3, *illus*.

639 'Decorated drinking glasses' [tumblers]. In *CL*, May 1958, p. 525–6, *illus*.

640 'Decorating the Georgian dessert table' [sweetmeat stands, etc.]. In *CL*, May 1959, p. 1144–5, *illus*.

641 'Discovered in the cellars' [bottles]. In *CL*, June 1955, p. 1575–6, *illus*.

642 'Drinking glasses for Orange Lodges'. In *CL*, Aug 1958, p. 312–13, *illus*. Orange Lodges were clubs formed in honour of William III, Prince of Orange.

643 'Eighteenth-century drinking glasses collected by Mr Herbert F. Elkington'. In *CONN*, Jly–Dec 1952, p. 112–17, *illus*.

644 'England's first crystal glass' [Verzelini]. In *CL*, Sept 1968, p. 700–1, *illus*.

645 'English champagne and strong ale glasses'. In *A*, Aug 1931, p. 92–5, *illus*.

646 'English crystal cameos'. In *CL*, June 1949, p. 1304–5, *illus*.

647 'English drinking cans'. In *CL*, Apr 1959, p. 836–7, *illus*. Includes examples in glass.

648 'English glass'. In *Connoisseur Concise Encyclopedia of Antiques*, 1954, v. I, p. 75–83, *illus.*, *bibliog*.

649 *English glass for the collector, 1660–1860*. Lutterworth, 1958, 251p., *illus.*, *bibliog*. Contents include: Crystallo ceramie, p. 199–205; Moulded and pinched glass, p. 149–59; Pressed glass, p. 160–71.

650 'English millefiori paperweights'. In *AP*, Jan–June 1952, p. 191–3, *illus*.

651 'English rummers and firing glasses'. In *A*, Feb 1931, p. 113–16, *illus*.

652 *English, Scottish and Irish table glass. From the sixteenth century to 1820*. Batsford, 1956, 410p., *illus.*, *bibliog*. Contents include: Candlesticks, tapersticks, girandoles and girandole candlesticks, p. 315–35, *illus.*; Serving bottles, ... squares and carafes, p. 257–83, *illus.*; Tumblers, fruit and salad bowls, p. 337–50, *illus*.

653 'Fine ware from Scottish glass-houses'. In *CL*, Aug 1961, p. 386–7, *illus*.

654 'Flint-glass in the collection of His Majesty the King'. In *Antiques Rev.*, 1948, Pt I, p. 11–14, *illus*.

655 'Flint glass candlesticks'. In *Antiques Rev.*, 1949, Pt 3, p. 35–6, *illus*.

656 'Georgian armorial glass'. In *CL*, Dec 1957, p. 1271–4, *illus.* Includes Beilby glasses.

657 'Georgian rummers'. In *AP*, Jly–Dec 1955, p. 81–3, *illus.*

658 'The girandole-candlestick'. In *CL*, Jan 1957, p. 188–9, *illus.*

659 'Glass' [1810–30]. In *Connoisseur Complete Period Guides: Regency Period*, 1968, p. 1157–60, *illus.*

660 'Glass epergnes for Georgian dessert'. In *CL*, Feb 1960, p. 371, *illus.*

661 'Glass lamps that lit humble homes' [open-flame chamber lamps]. In *CL*, Jly 1962, p. 69, *illus.*

662 'Glass pyramids on the dessert table' [salvers, etc.]. In *CL*, Mar 1964, p. 716–17, *illus.*

663 'Glass rolling-pins'. In *CL*, Feb 1951, p. 319, *illus.*

664 'Glass toddy-lifters'. In *CL*, Dec 1953, p. 1958–9, *illus.*

665 'Glass toddy rummers'. In *CL*, Oct 1957, p. 868–9, *illus.*

666 'Glasses for jelly and custard'. In *CL*, Nov 1959, p. 768–9, *illus.*

667 'Glasses for Orangemen: souvenirs of revolt'. In *The Times*, Aug 5th 1961, *illus.*

668 'Glasses for the syllabub'. In *CL*, June 1959, p. 1270–2, *illus.*

669 'Golden oranges in cut-glass bowls'. In *CL*, Feb 1964, p. 332–3, *illus.*

670 'The hey-day of Bristol enamel glass'. In *CL*, Mar 1961, p. 512–13, *illus.*

671 'The hey-day of Irish decanters'. In *CL*, Aug 1964, p. 510–11, *illus.*

672 'Irish glass'. In *Connoisseur Concise Encyclopedia of Antiques*, v. 3, 1957, p. 91–9, *illus.*, *bibliog.*

673 'Jacobite drinking glasses'. In *GC*, nos. 51 *and* 52.

674 'Jacobite drinking glasses'. In *CL*, May 1944, p. 418–19, *illus.*

675 'Label decanters of Georgian times'. In *CL*, Apr 1961, p. 764–5, *illus.*

676 *Living crafts.* Lutterworth, 1953. The glass-blower, p. 173–82, *illus.*

677 'Loops and frills of Georgian glass'. In *CL*, Mar 1970, p. 570 *and* 574, *illus.* Sweetmeat glasses.

678 *More about collecting antiques.* Country Life, 1952.
Contents include: Enamel and milk-white opaque glass, p. 78–85; Old English wine bottles, p. 86–93; Open-flame glass lamps, p. 94–103; *all illus.*

679 'Music from vessels of glass'. In *CL*, Nov 1961, p. 1138–9, *illus.*

680 'Naval history in glass'. In *CL*, Mar 1968, p. 759–60, *illus.* Engraved rummers, Frigate glasses, etc.

681 'Old English champagne glasses'. In *CL*, May 1952, p. 1496–7, *illus.*

682 'Old English champagne and ale glasses'. In *CL*, June 1946, p. 1082–3, and 1180–1, *illus.*

683 'Old English cider glasses'. In *CL*, Jly 1956, p. 22–3, *illus.* and in *Wine and Spirit Trade Rev.*, Jly 1958, p. 914–18, *illus.*

684 'Old English cruets' [some of glass]. In *CL*, Jan 1955, p. 178–80, *illus.*

685 'Old English cut glass'. In *ADCG*, May 1947, p. 16–18, *illus.*

686 'Old English decanters'. In *AP*, Jly–Dec 1943, p. 137–40, *illus.*

687 'Old English decanters'. In *ADCG*, June 1948, p. 40–2, *illus.*

688 'Old English decanters and their labels'. In *A*, 1929, p. 475–80, *illus.*; and in *Old Furniture*, 1929, p. 227–33, *illus.*; and in *Chambers's Jnl.*, Sept 1937, p. 667–8.

689 'Old English dessert sweetmeat and jelly glasses'. In *CL*, Dec 1944, p. 1078–9, *illus.*

690 'Old English gilded glass'. In *CL*, Dec 1952, p. 1952–3, *illus.*

691 'Old English glass candlesticks'. In *Old Furniture*, 1929, p. 204–11, *illus.*

692 'Old English glass candlesticks' [including Irish urn-stemmed moulded examples]. In *AP*, Jan–June 1945, p. 45–7, *illus.*

693 'Old English wine fountains'. In *CL*, Feb 1955, p. 390–1, *illus.*

694 'Old English wine glasses'. In *AP*, Jly–Dec 1942, p. 129–31, *illus.*

695 'Old Irish glass'. In *AP*, Jan–June 1947, p. 46–9, *illus.*

696 'Orange glasses for Georgian dessert'. In *CL*, Mar 1960, p. 690–1, *illus.*

697 'Punch and toddy glasses'. In *AP*, Jly–Dec 1953, p. 174–6, *illus.*

698 'A rainbow with a sparkle: Stourbridge glass'. In *CL*, Dec 1964, p. 1498–1503, *illus. in colour.*

699 'Simple mystery of crystal cameos'. In *CL*, Jly 1966, p. 183–4, *illus.*

700 'Square bottles for sundry uses' [spirit decanters, medicine bottles, etc.]. In *CL*, May 1963, p. 1007, 1009, *illus.*

701 'Surfeit water glasses'. In *Wine and Spirit Trade Record*, Sept 1958, p. 1194–6; *illus.*

702 'Tea-caddies made of glass'. In *CL*, Sept 1961, p. 564–5, *illus.*

703 'Tea-time cordials'. In *CL*, Dec 1955, p. 1530–1, *illus.*

704 'Tricks in the tavern' [trick glasses]. In *CL*, Mar 1957, p. 424–5, *illus.*

705 'Water jugs for the Georgian table'. In *CL*, June 1965, p. 1538–9, *illus.*

706 'Wine glass coolers and finger bowls'. In *CL*, June 1953, p. 1976–8, *illus.*

707 HUGHES, Therle. *Homes and Gardens Guide: Glass.* Homes and Gardens, 1965. 15p., *illus.*

708 *More small decorative antiques.* Lutterworth, 1962.
Contents include: Crystal cameos, p. 178–84; Tumblers and beakers, p. 185–96, *illus.*

709 *Small decorative antiques.* Lutterworth, 1959.
Contents include: Glasses to dress the dessert, p. 157–68, *illus.*

710 'Tumblers and beakers'. In *Homes and Gardens*, Mar 1966, p. 92–3, *illus.*

711 'Variety in dessert glasses'. In *ADCG*, Feb 1966, p. 33–6, *illus.*

712 HULME, E. Wyndham. 'English glass-making in the sixteenth and seventeenth centuries'. Three articles in *The Antiquary*, v. 31, 1895. Crystal glass from Bowles to Mansel, p. 68–72; Glass-making at the Restoration, p. 102–6; The invention of flint glass, p. 134–8, *diags.*

713 'The French glass-makers in England in 1567'. In *The Antiquary*, v. 34, 1898, p. 142–5.

714 'Note on Knole [Kent] glassmaking'. In *The Antiquary*, v. 41, 1905, p. 164.

715 'Old English glasses'. In *The Antiquary*, v. 34, 1898, p. 112–18. Includes a review of Hartshorne's *Old English glasses.*

716 HUME, Ivor Noel. 'Bottled treasure from the Goodwins'. In *CL*, Feb 1955, p. 570–1, *illus.*, *map*. Eighteenth-century ale bottles washed up at Sandwich, Kent.

717 'A century of London glass bottles, 1580–1680'. In *Connoisseur Year Book*, 1956, p. 98–103, *illus.*

718 'Collection of glass from Port Royal, Jamaica'. In *Historical Archaeology*, 1968, p. 5–34, *illus.*

719 'English glass wine bottles'. In *AP*, Jan–June 1956, p. 155–6, *illus.*

720 'A friend of Elizabethan ale glasses'. In *CONN*, Sept–Dec 1968, p. 259–61, *illus.* An excavation at Honey Lane Market, near Cheapside.

721 'The glass wine bottle in Colonial Virginia'. In *CJGS*, 1961, p. 91–118, *illus.*, *diags.* Includes continental and English examples.

722 'A lyttle bottell: charm of apothecaries phials'. In *ADCG*, Oct 1954, p. 32, *illus.*

723 'Medieval bottles from London'. In *CONN*, Jan–June 1957, p. 104–8, *illus.*

724 'Neglected glass' [apothecary and medicine bottles]. In *CL*, Sept 1954, p. 716–17, *illus.*

725 'Ornamental glass bird fountains of the eighteenth century'. In *A*, Aug 1966, p. 208–10, *illus.*

726 'Relics from the Wine Trade's own church'. In *Wine and Spirit Trade Record*, Feb 1958, p. 158–64, *illus.*

727 'Report from America on Tudor and early Stuart glasses found in London'. In *CONN*, May–Aug 1962, p. 269–73, *illus.*, *bibliog.*

728 'A seventeenth-century Virginian's seal: detective story in glass'. In *A*, Sept 1957, p. 244–5.

729 'Some English glass from Colonial Virginia'. In *A*, Jly 1963, p. 68–71, *illus.*

730 'To corking and wiring'. In *Wine and Spirit Trade Record*, June 1958, p. 772–6, *illus.*

731 'Wine bottle treasures'. In *Wine and Spirit Trade Record*, 1956, p. 288–94; 580–6; 868–70; 1010–18; *all illus.*

732 'Wine relics from the colonies' [bottles]. In *Wine and Spirit Trade Record*, Aug 1952, p. 1052–8, *illus.*

733 HUMPHREYS, Gregor Norman. 'Development of the twist stem drinking glass'. In *A*, Mar 1929, p. 191–5, *illus.*

734 'Hundred years of British glass making from 1824 to 1924'. In *National Glass Budget*, v. 79, no. 21, 1963, p. 4; 10–12. A history of Chance Bros.

735 HUNTLEY, R. 'English royalty in glass'. In *American Collector*, Sept 1943, p. 12–13, *illus.*

736 HURST, D. Gillian. 'Post-Medieval Britain in 1966 – Glass'. In *Post-Medieval Archaeology*, v. 1, 1967, p. 118–19. Excavations of the sixteenth–seventeenth-century site at Alfold, Surrey.

737 HURST, Ruth, 'Rare glass from the City of Liverpool Museum'. In *The Liverpool Bulletin*, v. 14, 1967, p. 16–31, *illus.*

738 INTERNATIONAL COMMISSION ON GLASS. *English, French and German dictionary of glass making.* Classified with indices. Charleroi, 1965, 233p.

739 [1968]. *Proceedings ed.* by E. J. Gooding. Pitman, 1969, *illus.* The Eighth Congress took place in London.

740 'International Exhibition, London, 1862: catalogue of the exhibition'. In *Art Jnl. (Supplementary volume)*, 1862. British glass, p. 106–16, *illus.*; several references to

British manufacturers, e.g. Osler, p. 258, Pellatt, p. 14 *and* 128.

741 'Irish glass exports' [1780–1811]. In *GN*, 1952, p. 24–5.

742 JABCKOWSKI, Janusz. 'W. E. S. Turner – na tle epoki'. *Szkło i Ceramika* 15, no. 5, 1964, p. 113–17. An obituary of Professor W. E. S. Turner.

743 'Jacobite drinking glasses'. In *The Times*, Sept 22nd 1962, p. 11, *illus.*

744 'Jacobite glass'. In *The Evening Argus*, Jan 22nd 1970, p. 13, *illus.*

745 'Jacobite glass' [Lord Torphichen's Collection]. In *CL*, Feb 1929, p. 29, *illus.*

746 JANNEAU, Guillaume. *Modern glass*. Studio, 1931. English glass, Plates 102–12.

JANSON, S. E. *see* SCIENCE MUSEUM.

747 JERNINGHAM, Charles E. 'The Oxburgh glasses'. In *CONN*, May–Aug 1908, p. 17–18, *illus.* Eleven Jacobite glasses 'discovered' at Oxburgh Hall in 1907.

748 JEUDWINE, W. R. 'Early English drinking glasses' [from a private collection]. In *AP*, Jan–June 1956, p. 207–10, *illus.*

749 JOHNSON, Stanley Currie. *Collecting old glass-ware*. Country Life, 1922, 32p., *illus.*

750 JOKELSON, Paul. *100 of the most important paperweights* [? London], 1966, 239p., *illus.*

751 *Sulphides: the art of cameo incrustation*. New York, Nelson, 1968, 159p., *illus.* (some col.).

752 JONES, Dorothy Lee. 'The glass of Thomas Webb and Son'. In *Bull. of the National Early American Glass Club*, Mar 1962, p. 5–11, *illus.*

753 JONES, Vera. 'English Bristol glass'. In *Antiques Jnl.*, Oct 1966, p. 18–20, *illus.*

754 JOYCE, Day. 'Mary Gregory glass'. In *ADCG*, June 1958, p. 58–60, *illus.*

755 KEEN, Geraldine. 'The Times-Sotheby index: 5. English glass' [analysis of prices 1950–68]. In *CONN*, Jan–Apr 1969, p. 95–7, *illus.* A revised version of the article in *The Times*.

756 KELLER, Joseph. *A collection of patterns for the use of glass decorators* [working notes and drawings]. MS. in the Brierley Hill Public Library Collection.

757 KENWORTHY, Joseph. *Bolsterstone glass house and its place in the history of English glass making* [from 1670]. Sheffield, 1914, 45p., *illus.* (Early History of Stocksbridge and District, Handbook no. 6).

758 'Glassmaking at Bolsterstone near Sheffield from about AD 1650 to 1750'. In *TSGT*, 1918, p. 5–12, *illus.*

759 KENYON, G. H. *Glass industry of the Weald.* Leicester University Press, 1967, 231p., *illus.*, *bibliog.*

760 'Petworth [Sussex] town and trades, 1610–1760: Glassmaking'. In *Sussex Archaeological Collections*, 1961, p. 106–8.

761 'Some comments on the medieval glass industry in France and England'. In *TSGT (News and Reviews)*, 1959, p. 17–20, *bibliog.*

762 'Some notes on the glass industry in England prior to 1567'. In *Jnl. of the British Soc. of Master Glass Painters*, 1956–7, p. 103–7.

763 'A Sussex yeoman family as glassmakers'. In *Sussex Notes and Queries*, v. 7, 1939, p. 171–3.

764 'A Sussex yeoman family as glassmakers and some notes on Wealden glass'. In *TSGT (News and Reviews)*, 1951, p. 6–11.

765 'Wealden glass: some notes'. In *Sussex Notes and Queries*, v. 13, 1950, p. 58–61.

766 KEYES, Homer Eaton. 'Cameo glass' [George Woodall vases, etc.]. In *A*, Sept 1936, p. 109–12, *illus.*

767 'Bristol opaque-white glass'. In *A*, Apr 1938, p. 109–12, *illus.*

768 KIDDLE, A. J. B. 'Advertisements in the seventeenth and eighteenth centuries' [concerning the glass trade]. In *GC*, nos. 76 *and* 77.

769 'Extracts and advertisements from London and Irish newspapers, 1747–1779'. In *GC*, no. 18.

770 'William Absolon, Junior, of Great Yarmouth'. In *Trans. of the English Ceramic Circle*, v. 5, Pt 1, 1960, p. 53–63.

771 'Kidd's process for silvering and ornamenting glass' [Mr Kidd of Poland Street, London]. In *Art Jnl.*, 1850, p. 202.

KING, J. *joint author see* COYSH, A. W. and KING, J.

772 KING, W. 'Flämisches glas und seine beziehungen zum englischen glas' [The relationship between Flemish and English glass]. In *Pantheon (Munich)*, Apr 1931, p. 158–60, *illus.* With English translation.

773 KING, William. 'English glass'. In *British Museum Quarterly*, 1934, p. 145–6.

774 'English glass goblet [*c.* 1690–1700] in the British Museum'. In *AP*, Jan–June 1949, p. 131, *illus.* The goblet was presented to the British Museum by the Glass Circle in memory of John Maunsell Bacon, founder of the Circle.

775 'King's Champion' [a commemorative goblet for the coronation of George IV]. In *CL*, Oct 1963, p. 798–9, *illus.*

776 'King's Lynn glass: an exciting venture' [the

modern glass factory]. In *Pottery Gazette and Glass Trade Rev.*, 1967, p. 1049–51, *illus.*

777 KINNEY, Kay. *Glass craft: designing, forming, decorating.* Pitman, 1962, 179p., *illus.*

778 KISCH, *Sir* Cecil. 'Engraved goblets by Laurence Whistler' [a gift to Trinity College, Oxford]. In *CONN*, Jan–June, 1957, p. 154–6, *illus.*

779 KLEINFELDT, Kay. 'Georgian decanters'. In Ray, Cyril, *ed. The complete imbiber, 5.* Vista Books, 1962, p. 155–60, *illus.*

780 KNOWLES, John A. 'Henry Gyles, glass-painter of York'. In *Walpole Soc. Publications*, 11, 1923, p. 47–72.

781 'Medieval processes of glass manufacture'. In *Glass*, 1927, p. 343, 345, 349, 391, 395, 397, 399, *illus.*

782 LARDNER, Dionysius. *Cabinet cyclopaedia.* Longmans, Rees, etc., 1832. v. 26 [by George Richardson Porter]. 'A treatise on the origin, progressive improvement and present state of the manufacture of porcelain and glass'. Glass, p. 125–327, *illus.*

LARGERBERG, Ted *and* LARGERBERG, Vi. *photographers see* MANLEY, C. C.

783 LATHAM, Jean. 'Collecting dressing table accessories' [glass toilet bottles, etc.]. In *ADCG*, Nov 1967, p. 57–60, *illus.* (*some col.*).

784 'Collecting glass friggers'. In *ADCG*, Jan 1966, p. 41–3, *illus.*

785 LAUGHTON, J. K. 'Sir Robert Mansell [1573–1656]'. In *Dictionary of National Biography*, v. 36, 1893, p. 88–9.

786 LAURENCE, Ninha V. 'Three old wines' [including a 'Byng' glass]. In *CONN*, Jly–Dec 1930, p. 173, *illus.*

787 LAVER, James. *Victoriana.* Ward, Lock, 1966. Victorian glass, p. 164–74, *illus.*

LAVINGTON, Margaret, *joint author see* GRAY, H. *and* LAVINGTON, Margaret.

788 LAWRENCE, G. F. 'Glass from London excavations'. In Churchill, Arthur, Ltd, *Catalogue of old English Glass, 2nd ed.,* 1937, p. 11–12.

789 'Laurence Whistler's four seasons' [engraved glass scenes]. In *CL*, June 1968, p. 1695, 1697, *illus.*

790 LAYCOCK, C. H. 'Bristol rollers' [rolling-pins]. In *Devon and Cornwall Notes and Queries,* Jan 1920, p. 36–8; Apr 1920, p. 73–6; Jly 1920, p. 104–5; Jan 1921, p. 158–9.

791 LAZARUS, Peter. 'The antique glass of Wales'. In *ADCG*, Jly 1969, p. 86–9, *illus.*

792 'The story of English drinking glasses' [six articles]. In *ADCG*, 1969.
Contents: (1) Balusters, Feb, p. 74–8; (2) Plain stems and Newcastle glasses, Mar, p. 82–6; (3) Air twists, incised stems and composite stems, Apr, p. 77–81; (4) Opaque, mixed and colour twist stems, May, p. 56–60; (5) Faceted and cut stems and sweetmeats, June, p. 102–6; (6) Specific types, Aug, p. 78–84; *all illus.* (*some col.*).

793 LEEDS, E. Thurlow. 'Glass bottles of the Crown Tavern, Oxford'. In *Oxoniensia*, v. 14, 1952, p. 87–9, *illus.*

794 'On the dating of glass wine bottles of the Stuart period'. In *The Antiquary*, v. 50, 1914, p. 285–90, *illus.*

795 'Seventeenth- and eighteenth-century wine bottles of Oxford taverns'. In *Oxoniensia*, v. 6, 1941, p. 44.

796 LEEDS CITY ART GALLERY [*Catalogue of*] *An exhibition of glass, or glass-making as a creative art through the ages. Nov 1961.* Compiled by Robert J. Charleston, Hugh Wakefield *and others*, Leeds City Art Gallery, 1961, 60p.

797 LEFFINGWELL, B. H. 'Bibliography pertaining to glass paperweights and addenda'. In *Bull. of the Paperweight Collectors' Assn.*, June 1958 and June 1963.

798 'Paperweights for the advanced collector'. In *Antiques Jnl.*, Mar 1964, p. 20–7, *illus.*

799 LE VERRIR, William. 'London and other glass at the Antique Dealers' Fair' [1935]. In *AP*, Jly–Dec 1935, p. 159–63, *illus.*

800 LEWIS, Geoffrey D. 'The Catcliffe glassworks' [near Rotherham]. In *Industrial Archaeology*, v. 1, 1964, p. 206–11, *illus., bibliog.*

801 *The South Yorkshire glass industry.* Sheffield City Museum, 1964, 6p., *illus., bibliog.*

802 'The South Yorkshire glass industry'. In *GC*, no. 136.

803 LEWIS, J. Sydney. *Old glass and how to collect it.* Werner Laurie, [1916], 225p., *illus.* Includes catalogue of auction prices, p. 191–225.

804 LIDSTONE, Marjorie. 'Glass perspective: a survey of glass production through the ages'. In *AC*, 1957, p. 238–43, *illus.*

805 LITTLE, Tenison. 'Irish glass, its appeal and some cherished misconceptions'. In *AC*, 1963, p. 19–22, *illus.*

806 LLOYD, Ward. *Investing in Georgian glass.* Barrie & Rockliff: The Cresset Press, 1969, 160p., *illus.* (*some col.*).

807 'Loan exhibition of English glass' [at the Victoria

and Albert Museum, 1968]. In *CL*, Jly 1968, p. 38–9, *illus.*

808 LOCKHART, R. Stevenson. 'Harold Gordon – Scots glass engraver'. In *Studio*, Aug 1950, p. 50–1, illus. Engraved tumblers.

809 LONDON MUSEUM. *The Garton collection of English table glass* [in the London Museum], by John Hayes. HMSO, 1965, 40p., *illus.* A collection of 437 specimens presented by Sir Richard Garton (1857–1934).

LOEWENSTEIN, K. L. *joint author see* LYNTON, Paul *and* LOEWENSTEIN, K. L.

810 LONDON: PATENT OFFICE. *Subject list of works on the silicate industries* [ceramics and glass]. London, 1914.

811 LUKINS, Jocelyn. 'Glass rolling pins'. In *ADCG*, May 1970, p. 65–8, illus. (*some col.*).

812 LYMBERY, R. S. 'Problems and prospects of future glass collecting'. In *GC*, no. 67.

813 LYNTON, Paul *and* LOEWENSTEIN, K. L. 'Musical glasses'. In *TSGT* (*News and Reviews*), 1951, p. 17–22.

814 McC[ORMACK], J. 'Rare tankard – glass-making in Newcastle' [inscribed G. TYZACK]. In *CONN*, Jan–Apr 1922, p. 165–6, *illus.*

815 'A Ravenscroft glass'. In *CONN*, Jly–Dec 1932, p. 321, *illus.*

816 MACDONALD-TAYLOR, Margaret. 'Lighting the Georgian house: chandeliers of wood and glass'. In *CL*, Aug 1963, p. 498–9, *illus.*

817 MACKAY, James. 'Air twist glass'. In *The Financial Times*, Dec 13th 1969, p. 8, *illus.*

818 'Baluster wine glasses'. In *The Financial Times*, May 18th 1968, p. 8, *illus.*

819 'Burmese glass' [fairy lights]. In *The Financial Times*, Nov 30th 1968, p. 8, *illus.*

820 'Collecting Nailsea glass'. In *The Financial Times*, Jly 12th 1969, p. 8, *illus.*

821 'Glass paperweights'. In *The Financial Times*, Mar 15th 1969, p. 8, *illus.*

822 MACKAY, James A. *Antiques of the future.* Studio, 1970. Includes glass and glass paperweights, p. 54–77, *illus.*

823 McKEARIN, Helen. 'Eighteenth-century advertisements of glass imports into the Colonies and the United States'. In *GN*, 1954, p. 13–21, and 1955, p. 15–25, *illus.*

824 MACLEOD, Catriona. 'Late eighteenth-century Dublin finger bowls in the National Museum of Ireland'. In *Royal Soc. of Antiquaries of Ireland*, 96, 1966, p. 140–6, *illus.*

825 MacMULLEN, H. T. 'Waterford glass'. In *CL*, Aug and Sept 1946, p. 398–400 and 444–5, *illus.*

826 MACNAGHTEN, Patrick. 'Glass lustre' [mer-

cury glass]. In *Ideal Home*, Nov 1959, p. 125, 127, *illus.* Describes the Thesiger Collection.

827 'Through a glass lightly'. In *CL*, Apr 1969, p. 937, *illus.* Comments on the exhibition of Laurence Whistler's engraved glasses at Agnews, 'A point on glass', Apr–May 1969.

828 MADEIRA, Louis C. 'Historic English toasting glasses'. In *A*, 1954, p. 128–30.

829 'Making of glassware: historical survey'. In *Pottery Gazette*, 1950, p. 869–72, *illus.*

830 'Manchester exhibition of British industrial art, 1846'. In *Art Union*, 1846, p. 42, *illus.* The exhibition included items by Richardson of Stourbridge.

831 MANCHESTER PUBLIC FREE LIBRARY. *Catalogue of books on ceramics, glass-ware, ornamental metal-work, enamels and jade in the Free Reference Library*, compiled by F. Bentley Nicholson. Manchester Public Free Library, 1908, 20p. (Occasional lists, no. 8.)

832 MANKOWITZ, Wolf. *The Portland Vase and the Wedgwood copies.* Deutsch, 1952, 76p., *illus., bibliog.*

833 MANLEY, C. C. *Collectible glass. Book 4: British* [coloured] *glass.* The C. C. Manley Collection at Brierley Hill photographed by Ted and Vi Largerberg. Port Richey, Florida, 1969, 18p., *illus.* (col.).

834 'English iridescent glass'. In *The Spinning Wheel*, Feb 1969, p. 14–16, 54, *illus.*

835 MANN, M. 'Harrison Williams Waterford glass'. In *Studio* (*American ed. – 'International Studio'*), 95, Feb 1930, p. 39–43, *illus.*

836 MANNING, John. 'Jacob Verzelini: Elizabethan glass-maker'. In *AP*, Apr 1964, p. 299–302, *illus.*

837 MARSH, Tracy H. 'English heroes honoured in glass'. In *Hobbies*, May 1963, p. 86, *illus.*

838 'Glass terminology'. In *Hobbies*, Oct 1964, p. 85–92.

839 'Royalty in glass' [Queen Victoria's Jubilee]. In *Hobbies*, Jly 1963, p. 84–5, *illus.*

840 MARSHALL, E. J. 'Collecting English drinking glasses in the twentieth century'. In *AP*, Jan–June 1951, p. 165–8, *illus.*

841 MARSHALL, H. R. 'Tassie's coloured glass intaglios'. In *GC*, no. 92, Apr 1949, 13p.

842 MARSHALL, Monica. 'English glass for beginners'. In *GC*, no. 127.

843 MARSON, Percival. *Glass and glass manufacture.* Revised and enlarged by L. M. Angus-Butterworth. 4th ed. Pitman, 1949, 145p., *illus.* First pub. 1918.

844 MATTHEWS, W. C. 'Old glass collecting'. In *Chambers's Jnl.*, June 1933, p. 431–4.

845 MAXWELL, H. W. 'The early connection of

the glass works at Nailsea and Bristol'. In *GC*, no. 95.

846 MAYERS, Colin. 'Glass Congress [London, 1968]: history and design'. In *Pottery Gazette and Glass Trade Rev.*, 1968, p. 1058–61, *illus.*

847 MEIGH, Edward. 'The Society of Glass Technology: Golden Jubilee: a brief history'. In *Glass Technology*, 1966, p. 147–80, *illus.*

MEIGH, Edward, *ed. see* GOODING, F. J. and MEIGH, Edward, *eds.*

MEIGH, Edward *see* SOCIETY OF GLASS TECHNOLOGY, SHEFFIELD.

848 MELTON, James. 'Glass candelabra and lustres'. In *Connoisseur Concise Encyclopaedia of Antiques*, v. 3, 1957, p. 165–70, *illus.*

849 MERRET, Christopher. *The art of glass*. London, 1662. A translation with additions of Antonio Neri's *L'Arte Vetraria*, pub. Florence, 1612.

850 *The art of glass ed.* by *Sir* T. Phillipps. Middle Hill (Worcs.), 1826, Folio priv. print.

851 METEYARD, Eliza. *The life of Josiah Wedgwood*. 2 v. Hurst and Blackett, 1866. Reference to the Barberini [Portland] Vase, v. 2, p. 575–83, *illus.*

852 MICHAELIS, Ronald F. 'Old bottle seal finds'. In *ADCG*, Oct 1964, p. 51–2, *illus.*

MIDDLEMAS, Keith, *joint author see* DAVIS, Derek C. *and* MIDDLEMAS, Keith.

853 'Milk glass'. In *The Times*, Jly 16th 1960, p. 9.

854 MILLS, John Fitzmaurice. 'Problems and solutions II' [The care of glassware]. In *CONN*, Nov 1968, p. 165.

855 'Mr Pargeter's art productions in glass' [Red House Glass Works, Stourbridge]. In *The Reliquary*, 18, 1877–8, p. 57–8.

856 'Mr Pargeter's "Milton Vase"' [Red House Glass Works, Stourbridge]. In *The Reliquary*, 19, 1878–9, p. 243, *illus.*

857 'Modern glass'. In *Art Jnl.*, 1889 (p. 3–4 of Art and Industries Supplement, between p. 31 and 32), *illus.*

858 MONRO, Helen. 'The art of glass engraving'. In *Jnl. of the Royal Soc. of Arts*, 1960, p. 477–95, *illus.*

859 'Glass engraving' [contemporary – Whistler, etc.]. In *Studio*, Oct 1960, p. 122–9, *illus.*

860 MONSON-FITZJOHN, G. J. *Drinking vessels of bygone days from the Neolithic age to the Georgian period*. H. Jenkins, 1927. Includes: Old glass, p. 128–38; Saxon glass, p. 15–16, *illus.*

861 MOODY, B. E. 'The origin of the "reputed quart" and other measures' [bottles, etc.]. In *Glass Technology*, 1960, p. 55–68, *illus.*

862 MOORE, John, *comp. Worshipful Company of*

Glass Sellers of London, incorporated 1664. Priv. print, 1899, 61p., *ports.*

863 MOORE, N. Hudson. *The collector's manual.* New York, Tudor, 1935. Includes antique glassware, p. 76–101, *illus.* First pub. 1905.

864 'How about Waterford glass?' In *A*, Sept 1923, p. 116–20, *illus.*

865 *Old glass, European and American.* Hodder and Stoughton, 1935, 394p., *illus.* Contents include: Bristol glass, p. 152–68; Irish glass, p. 174–203; Nailsea, p. 169–73, *illus.* First pub. New York, Stokes, 1924.

866 'More Ravenscroft glass'. In *GN*, 1953, p. 21–3, *illus.*

867 'Musical glasses'. In *The Times*, Feb 15th 1964, p. 11, *illus.*

868 NAGEL, Fred A. 'Enchanting paperweights signed P.Y.'. In *Bull. of the Paperweight Collectors Assn.*, 1968, p. 3–8, *illus.*

869 'Nailsea glass jugs'. In *CONN*, May–Aug 1906, p. 48–50, *illus.*

870 NAPIER, Ivan. 'Colour tints in English . . . and Irish glass'. In *GC*, no. 45.

871 'Frans Greenwood and his glass'. In *GC*, no. 58.

872 'King's Lynn glass'. In *GC*, nos. 29 *and* 34.

873 'Newcastle glass'. In *GC*, no. 39.

NERI, Antonio *see* MERRETT, Christopher.

874 NESBITT, Alexander. 'Glass'. In *Encyclopedia Britannica*, 9th ed., 1879, v. 10, p. 647–55.

875 *Notes on the history of glass-making prepared as an introduction to the catalogue of the collection of glass of various periods formed by the late Felix Slade. . . .* London (priv. print.), 1869, 50p., *bibliog.*

see also (1) CHAFFERS, W.
            (2) VICTORIA AND ALBERT MUSEUM.

876 'New glass technology gallery' [at the Science Museum]. In *Pottery Gazette and Glass Trade Rev.*, 1968, p. 752–3, *illus.*

NEW SOUTH WALES ART GALLERY, SYDNEY, *see* ART GALLERY OF NEW SOUTH WALES, SYDNEY.

NICHOLSON, F. Bentley, *compiler see* MANCHESTER FREE PUBLIC LIBRARY.

877 NOPPEN, J. G. 'Eighteenth-century English glass'. In *AP*, Jan–June 1934, p. 179–86, *illus.*

878 'Eighteenth-century English ale glasses'. In *AP*, Jan–June, 1935, p. 3–9, *illus.*

879 'English glass drinking vessels'. In *AP*, Jly–Dec 1933, p. 77–83, *and* p. 225–31, *illus.*

880 'The Manderson Collection of eighteenth-century glass'. In *AP*, Jan–June, 1935, p. 327–31, *illus.*

881   'On collecting antique glass for use'. In *AP*, Jly–Dec 1938, p. 241–3, *illus.*

882   'A series of old English decanters'. In *AP*, Jly–Dec 1935, p. 74–9, *illus.*

883   NORMAN-WILCOX, G. 'A compendium of drinking glasses with Jacobite engravings'. In *A*, Jly 1932, p. 11–14, *illus.*

884   'English glass: baluster stems, an historical summary'. In *A*, Nov 1932, p. 174–6, *illus.*

885   NORTHWOOD, John. [Catalogue of the] *Borough of Stourbridge Glass Collection.* Stourbridge, 1954, 36p.

886   *John Northwood I: his contribution to the Stourbridge flint glass industry, 1850–1902.* Stourbridge, Mark and Moody, 1958, 134p.

887   'The reproduction of the Portland Vase'. In *TSGT*, 1924, p. 85–92, *illus.*

888   'Stourbridge cameo glass'. In *TSGT* (*News and Reviews*), 1949, p. 106–13, *illus.*

889   'Note on milk glass: Bristol and continental types'. In *A*, Oct 1928, p. 319–21, *illus.*

890   NYMAN, Ben. *The Nyman Collection of cameo glass, porcelain enamelling and pâte-sur-pâte.* 2 v. [priv. print.?], 1957, *illus.*

891   ODDY, R. 'Scottish glasshouses'. In *GC*, no. 151.

892   O'DEA, W. T. *A short history of lighting.* HMSO, 1958, 40p., *illus.*
       Includes lamps, shades, etc.

893   'Old and new glasses'. In *The Times*, 1911, Nov 11th p. 6 *and* Nov 17th p. 6.

894   'Old English bottles'. In *CL*, Dec 1921, p. 778–80, *illus.*

895   'Old English glassware – unique and priceless collection at Brierley Hill'. In *Pottery Gazette*, 1950, p. 70–5, *illus.*

896   'Old English tumblers – pictorial engravings on glass'. In *ADCG*, Jan 1959, p. 27–9, *illus.*

897   'Old glass: hints to the collector'. In *The Countryman*, 1936, p. 524–5.

898   OLD WATERFORD SOCIETY. *Exhibition of Waterford glass, 1952* [Catalogue]. [Waterford?], 1952.

899   'Opaque glass'. In *The Times*, Aug 18th 1956, p. 9, *illus.*

900   'Open-flame gas lamps'. In *The Times*, Nov 30th 1963, p. 11, *illus.*

901   ORD, P. R. 'Observations on glass cutting by diamond'. In *TSGT*, 1957, p. 245–58, *illus.*

902   ORMSBEE, Thomas H. 'English glass'. In *Encyclopedia Americana*, 1968 ed., v. 12, p. 692–3.

903   OSWALD, Adrian, *and* PHILLIPS, Howard. 'A Restoration glass hoard from Gracechurch Street, London'. In *CONN*, Jly–Dec 1949,

p. 30–6, *illus.* Discovered in 1940 and later presented to the Guildhall Museum.

904   OWEN, Hugh. *Two centuries of ceramic art in Bristol: a history of the manufacture of the 'true porcelain' by R. Champion, with a biography.* London, 1873, 419p., *illus.* Includes glass.

905   *Oxford Junior Encyclopedia.* Contents include 'Table glass', v. 11, 1955, p. 435–7, *illus.*
       PAINTER, K. S. *see* BRITISH MUSEUM.

906   PALMER, M. A. 'English glass in the Cecil Higgins Museum, Bedford'. In *AP*, Jly–Dec 1950, p. 39–42, 47, *illus.*

907   PAPE, T. 'An ancient glass furnace at Eccleshall, Staffordshire'. In *Antiquaries' Jnl.*, v. 14, 1934, p. 141–2, *plan.*

908   'An Elizabethan glass furnace' [at Bishop's Wood, Staffordshire]. In *CONN*, Jly–Dec 1933, p. 172, 175–7, *illus.*, *plans.*

909   'Medieval glassworkers in North Staffordshire'. In *Trans. North Staffordshire Field Club*, v. 68, 1933–4.

910   'Paris International Exhibition, 1878'. In *Art Jnl.*, 1878 (Supplement, 104p., at end).
       Contents include frequent mention and illustration of English and continental glass exhibits.

911   'Paris Universal Exhibition, 1867'. In *Art Jnl. Supplementary volume: 'Paris Exhibition'*, 1867.
       Contents include: 'The glass domestic and decorative' [with illustrations and descriptions of British items], by George Wallis, p. 77–107.

912   PARKES, Judith. *Antique collecting with BP, 2nd ed.*, 2 v., BP Shell-Mex, 1969. First pub. 1967.
       Contents include: Glass, v. 1, p. 40–51, *illus.*

913   PEAKE-ANDERSON, Constance. 'Glass of today'. In *Studio*, Aug 1931, p. 72–97, *illus.*

914   PELLATT, Apsley. *Curiosities of glassmaking with details of the processes and productions of ancient and modern ornamental glass manufacture.* D. Bogue, 1849. 146p., *illus.*
       The material in this book was originally a series of lectures given at the Royal Institute.

915   *Flint glass manufactures (models and specimens exhibited at the Great Exhibition, London, 1851).* London, 1851.

916   'Glass for fancy use and household purposes'. In *The Technologist (London)*, 1864, 4, p. 120.

917   *Memoir on the origin, progress and improvement of glass manufactures: including an account of the patent Crystallo-ceramie, or glass incrustations.* B. J. Holdsworth, 1821. 42p., *illus.* (*col.*).

918 'Pellatt, Apsley' [obituary notice]. In *ILN*, May 16th 1863, p. 546.

919 'Pellatt Apsley' [obituary notice]. In *The Times*, Apr 20th 1863, p. 12.

920 'Pellatt [Apsley] and Co. A service of table glass . . . executed for the Prince of Wales'. In *Art Jnl.*, 1863, p. 59.

921 'Pellatt and Wood'. In *Art Jnl.*, 1875, p. 56–7. A short description of the firm.

922 PELLATT, Frederick. 'The manufacture of glass'. In *Jnl. of the Franklin Inst.*, v. 42, 1846, p. 271.

923 PERCIVAL, MacIver. *The glass collector: a guide to old English glass.* H. Jenkins, 1918, 347p., illus., bibliog.

924 'Perkes and Co.'s. [Stoke-on-Trent] engraved glass'. In *The Reliquary*, 1875, p. 167.

925 PERRETT, J. Bernard. 'The eighteenth-century chandeliers at Bath'. In *CONN*, Jly–Dec 1938, p. 187–92, illus.

926 'The evolution of the English glass chandelier'. In *AP*, Jly–Dec 1939, p. 101–4, illus.

PERROT, P. N. *see* (1) CORNING MUSEUM OF GLASS.
(2) 'Survey of contemporary glass'.

927 PETER, Mary. *Collecting Victoriana.* Arco, 1965. Contents include: Victorian glass, p. 108–29, illus.

928 PEVSNER, N. 'English qualities in English glass'. In *CL*, Jly 1941, p. 109, illus.

929 PHILLIMORE, John. 'A famous bridge [Wearmouth] in pottery and glass'. In *AP*, Jan–June 1941, p. 6–9, and p. 35–7, illus.

PHILLIPPS, *Sir* T. *ed. see* MERRET, Christopher.

930 PHILLIPS, Howard. 'Learning to look at glasses. Illustrated by a select group of English glasses, 1730–1770'. In *AC*, 1959, p. 63–8, illus.
joint author see OSWALD, Adrian, *and* PHILLIPS, Howard

931 PHILLIPS, John Pavin. 'The Society of Sea-Sergeants' [South Wales]. In *GN*, 1950, p. 15–17. Glasses exist bearing the emblem of this Society and are possibly connected with the Welsh Jacobites.

932 PILKINGTON BROTHERS, LTD. *Pattern book of ornamental glass.* St Helens, 1896. 62p., illus.

933 *Pilkington Glass Museum* [Catalogue of the Collection]. St Helens, 1969, illus. Loose sheets in card folder.

934 'Pilkington Museum of glass'. In *AC*, 1964, p. 250–1, illus.

PINDER-WILSON, R. H. *see* BRITISH MUSEUM.

935 PLESCH, Peter H. 'English and continental glass in the collection of Dr and Mrs Peter H. Plesch'. In *CJGS*, 1965, p. 79–82, illus.

936 POLAK, Ada. 'English connections in Norway's old glass industry'. In *AP*, Jly–Dec 1952, p. 17–20, illus.

937 *Modern glass.* Faber, 1962, 94p., illus., bibliog. (Faber Monographs on Glass). Contents include: English glass, p. 33, 58–62, 77–80.

938 'A Newcastle glass blower in eighteenth-century Norway'. In *GC*, no. 98.

939 'Notes on glass chandeliers'. In *GC*, no. 112.

940 PONTIL, *pseud.* 'Glass age'. In *CONN*. Contents: Early English and Dutch glasses, Jan–Apr 1918, p. 213–16; Balusters, tear glasses, etc., May–Aug 1918, p. 132–8; Various wine glasses, Jan–Apr 1919, p. 33–7, and May–Aug 1919, p. 75–80, all illus.

941 'Two Ravenscroft sealed goblets'. In *CONN*, Jan–June 1933, p. 200, illus.

[PORTER, George Richardson] *see* LARDNER, Dionysius.

942 'Portrait glasses of Prince Charles Edward in enamel colours'. In *GN*, 1956, p. 21–6, illus.

943 POWELL, A. C. 'Glassmaking in Bristol'. In *Trans. of the Bristol Archaeological Soc.*, v. 47, 1925.

944 POWELL, Harry James. 'The development of coloured glass in England'. In *TSGT*, 1922, p. 249–55.

945 *Glassmaking in England.* C.U.P., 1923, 183p., illus. Includes: Old London and provincial glasshouses, p. 86–111.

946 'Happy hunting grounds of a [glass] designer'. In *CL*, Sept 1922, p. 44–6, illus.

947 'Whitefriars Glass Works: notes of a flint-glass manager from 1875 to 1916'. In *TSGT*, 1918, p. 241–6.

948 , *and others. Principles of glassmaking . . . together with a treatise on Crown and sheet glass by H. Chance . . . and plate glass by* H. G. Harris, London, 1883, 186p.

949 POWELL, JAMES AND SONS (WHITE-FRIARS) LTD. *Whitefriars glass Catalogue.* J. Powell and Sons, Ltd, n.d. [1938?] illus.

950 *Whitefriars handmade crystal* [Catalogue]. Wealdstone, J. Powell and Sons Ltd, n.d. [1948?] 72p., illus., map.

951 'Powells', The Whitefriars Studios'. In *Jnl. of the Soc. of Master Glass Painters*, v. 13, 1959–60, p. 321–5, illus.

952 PRENTISS, E. L. 'The manufacture of cut-glass'. In *Brush and Pencil*, v. 16, 1905, p. 131.

953 'Pressed glass'. In *The Times*, Jly 23rd 1966, p. 13.

954 PRESTON, Eric, HOLLAND, A. J., *and*

TURNER, W. E. S. 'Study of the brilliance exhibited by lead crystal glass'. In *TSGT*, 1935, p. 125–38, *illus.*

955 PRICE, R. 'Notes on the evolution of the wine bottle'. In *Trans. of the Glasgow Archaeological Soc.*, v. 6 (New Series), Pt 1, p. 116.

956 PRICE, R. K. 'The Price family of glassmakers'. In *GC*, no. 133.

957 PROSSER, R. B. 'Apsley Pellatt (1791–1863)'. In *Dictionary of National Biography*, v. 44, 1895, p. 264–5.

958 PRYOR, G. R. 'Scientific aids to the identification of antique paperweights'. In *Antiques Rev.*, Dec 1953–Feb 1954, p. 19–20, *illus.*

959 PURSER, C. J. 'Brief history of the Wear Glass Works'. In *TSGT*, 1946, p. 198–200.

960 'Queen's gift to the [French] President'. In *CL*, Apr 1957, p. 698–9, *illus.* Three goblets engraved by Laurence Whistler.

961 RACKHAM, Bernard. *Catalogue of . . . [the Schreiber Collection] presented to the [Victoria and Albert] Museum in 1884.* 3 v., HMSO, 1924.
Contents include: Glass, v. 3, p. 79–86, *illus.*

962 'Ceramics and glass'. In *Georgian Art.* Batsford, 1929. (Burlington Magazine Monograph – III). Glass, p. 41–2, *illus.*

963 'An early diamond-engraved glass at South Kensington'. In *BUR*, Jan–June 1929, p. 68–9, 73, *illus.* A letter by Buckley commenting on the article follows on p. 162.

964 'The glass collections of the Victoria and Albert Museum . . .'. In *TSGT*, 1934, p. 308–22, *illus.*

965 *A key to pottery and glass.* Blackie, 1940, 180p., *illus.*

966 'Three Elizabethan glasses'. In *BUR*, Jan 1913, p. 22–7, *illus.*

967 'Verzelini and his followers'. In *BUR*, Jly–Dec, 1925, p. 182–7, *illus.*

RAMSEY, L. G. G. *ed. see Connoisseur Complete Encyclopedia of Antiques.*

968 RAMSEY, William. *History of the Worshipful Company of Glass Sellers of London.* London, 1898.

969 'Rare Jacobite glasses in the collection of Col. W. Churchill Hale'. In *CONN*, May–Aug 1963, p. 141–5, *illus.*

970 RAVENSCROFT, William. *Some Ravenscrofts.* Milford-on-Sea, T. E. Stone, 1929, 87p.

971 'Ravenscroft diary'. In *GN*, 1950, p. 13–14.

972 'Ravenscroft "sealed" goblet *c.* 1677'. In *AP*, Jan–June, 1943, p. 161, *illus.* An item from the Collection of R. F. Ratcliff, sold to Cecil Davis in 1943.

973 READ, Herbert. 'The Bles Collection of English and Irish glass'. In *BUR*, Jly–Dec, 1923, p. 247–8, *illus.*

974 'Cross-currents in English porcelain, glass and enamels'. In *Trans. of the English Ceramic Circle*, v. 1, 1934, no. 4, *illus.*

975 'English glasses in the collection of Mr John M. Bacon'. In *CONN*, Sept–Dec 1926, p. 201–8, *illus.*

976 READE, Brian. *Regency antiques.* Batsford, 1953. Contents include: Glass, p. 185–203, *illus.*

977 'Reminiscences of Ben Richardson' [of Stourbridge]. In *Pottery Gazette and Glass Trade Rev.*, 1952, p. 108–9, *illus.*, *port.*

978 'Remission of the glass duties'. In *Art Union*, 1845, p. 80.

979 'Reproduction of the Portland Vase' [by Northwood and Pargeter of Stourbridge]. In *The Reliquary*, v. 17, 1876–7, p. 241–3.

980 'Return of the soul' [Jacobite glasses]. In *GN*, 1952, p. 22–3, *illus.*

981 REVI, Albert Christian. 'Cameo glass'. In *Crockery and Glass Jnl.*, Feb 1958, p. 48, *illus.*

982 'English patented paperweights'. In *Bull. of the Paperweight Collectors' Assn.*, June 1964, p. 43–6, *illus.*

983 'Modern glass paperweights'. In *Bull. of the Paperweight Collectors' Assn.*, June 1961, *illus.*

984 *Nineteenth-century glass: its genesis and development.* Revised ed. New York, Nelson, 1969, 301p., *illus.* (*some col.*).

985 'Novelty type cameo glass'. In *The Spinning Wheel*, Apr 1957, p. 24–5, *illus.*

986 'Ruby glass'. In *The Spinning Wheel*, Mar 1961, p. 20, 22, *illus.*

987 'Stevens and Williams' Silveria Glass'. In *The Spinning Wheel*, Aug 1958, p. 28, 30, *illus.*

988 'Threaded glassware'. In *The Spinning Wheel*, Jly 1958, p. 14–16, *illus.*

989 'E. Varnish and Company's silvered glassware'. In *The Spinning Wheel*, Mar 1964, p. 16, *illus.*
see also CORNING MUSEUM OF GLASS.

990 REYNOLDS, Ernest. *The plain man's guide to antique collecting.* M. Joseph, 1963. Contents include: Glass, p. 125–32, *illus.*

991 RICHARDSON, A. E. *Georgian England: a survey of social life, trades, industries and art . . . 1700 to 1820.* Batsford, 1931. Contents include: Ornamental glass, p. 144–6, *illus.*

992 RIDLEY, Ursula. 'The history of glass making on Tyneside'. In *GC*, no. 122.

993 'The history of glass making on the Tyne and

Ware'. In *Archaeologia Aeliana* (Newcastle), v. 40 (Series 4), 1962, p. 145–62, *illus.*

994 'The Ridley connection with industry'. In *AP*, Oct 1962, p. 610–13, *illus., port.* Matthew Ridley bought Howdon Pans Glassworks from the Henzell family in 1759.

995 RISLEY, *Sir* John Shuckburgh. 'Commemorative glass'. In Bles, Joseph, *Rare English glasses of the seventeenth and eighteenth centuries*, 1925, p. 157–76, *illus.*

996 'A Frans Greenwood goblet'. In *BUR*, Jly–Dec 1922, p. 297–8, *illus.*

997 'Georgian electioneering glasses'. In *BUR*, Jly–Dec 1920, p. 220, 225–33, *illus.*

998 'Georgian rummers'. In *BUR*, Jan–June 1921, p. 270–82, *illus.*

999 'Jacobite wine-glasses, some rare examples'. In *BUR*, Jan–June 1920, p. 276–87, *illus.*

1000 'Exhibition of Oxburgh and Berkley glasses' [Jacobite]. In *BUR*, Jly–Dec 1920, p. 51–2.

1001 'Old English glasses with white spiral stems'. In *BUR*, Jan–June 1919, p. 219–31, *illus.*

1002 'Sea-power under George III illustrated on contemporary glass'. In *BUR*, Jly–Dec 1919, p. 203–10, *illus.*

1003 'A wine glass commemorating a famous eighteenth-century election'. In *CONN*, Sept–Dec 1918, p. 160–2, *illus.* The Wenman and Dashwood wine glass.

1004 ROBERTSLAW, Ursula. 'Where all that glitters is lead'. In *ILN*, Dec 29th 1969, p. 22–3, *illus.* Modern Waterford glass.

1005 ROBERTSON, R. A. 'Admiral became glass maker – Sir Robert Mansell's stormy passage'. In *ADCG*, May 1956, p. 20–2, *illus.*

1006 'Blowpipe creates elegance: the glass technique'. In *ADCG*, Oct 1955, p. 16–18, *illus.*

1007 *Chats on old glass*. Benn, 1954. 180p., *illus., bibliog.*

1008 *Chats on old glass. Revised with a new chapter on American glass by Kenneth M. Wilson, curator, Corning Museum of Glass*. New York, Dover, 1969. 167p., *illus., bibliog.* Contents include: George Hay (founder of Scottish glassmaking), p. 58–60.

1009 'Drink in beauty: glass through the centuries' In *ADCG*, June 1956, p. 39–41, *illus.*

1010 'Early English glass making: foreign craftsmen revived industry'. In *ADCG*, Mar 1956, p. 17–19, *illus.*

1011 'Eighteenth-century triumph – trends in English glass'. In *ADCG*, Dec 1960, p. 34–6, *illus.*

1012 'Foundations of a noble tradition – English glass'. In *ADCG*, Nov 1960, p. 24–6, *illus.*

1013 'Glass to see in Scotland'. In *ADCG*, May 1963, p. 48–9, *illus.*

1014 'His name endures in glass – Verzelini's uphill fight in London'. In *ADCG*, Apr 1956, p. 28–30, *illus.*

1015 'Symbolism in Jacobite glass'. In *ADCG*, Oct 1956, p. 21–3, *illus.*

1016 ROBINSON, J. B. Perry. 'Glass of today and how to choose it for use and decoration in the home'. In *Studio*, Oct 1935, p. 202–8, *illus.* English and Swedish glass.

1017 'Rodney decanters for seafarers'. In *The Times*, Mar 16th 1963, p. 11, *illus.*

1018 ROGERS, Horace M. *The making of a connoisseur*. Estates Gazette, 1951. Contents include: Romance of old English and Irish glass, p. 250–77, *illus.*

1019 ROGERS, Millard F. 'The European and American Glass Collection'. In *AP*, Jly–Dec 1967, p. 478–85, *illus.*

1020 ROHAN, Thomas. *Old glass beautiful: English and Irish*. Mills and Boon, 1930. 144p., *illus.*

1021 ROSE, Jeffrey, A. H. 'The Apsley Pellatts'. In *GC*, no. 150.

1022 'Apsley Pellatt, Jnr., 1791–1863'. In *CONN*, Sept–Dec 1963, p. 232–3, *illus.*

1023 'Glass and the House of Hanover'. In *GC*, nos. 117 *and* 123.

1024 'James and William Tassie'. In *GC*, no. 153.

1025 ROSS, Euan. 'Traditions of English glass'. In Crompton, Sidney, *ed.* English glass, 1967, p. 7–38, *illus.*

1026 ROWNTREE, Diana. [Contemporary] 'Glass table ware'. In *Architectural Rev.*, Sept 1956, p. 197–200, *illus.*

1027 ROYAL SCOTTISH MUSEUM. *English glass* [in the Royal Scottish Museum]. Edinburgh, HMSO, 1964, 32p., *illus.*

1028 RUDD, T. *Old English drinking glasses*. Southampton, Rudd, n.d. [*c.* 1910?], 9p., *illus.*

1029 RUEFF, André E. 'Collections of English glass in America'. In *Brooklyn Museum Quarterly*, 1–2, 1914, p. 119–41, *illus.*

1030 RUGGLES-BRISE, Sheelah, *Lady*. 'The Buggin Bowls'. In *GC*, no. 63.

1031 'Glass in letters, lists and literature'. In *GC*, no. 35.

1032 'Glass in sixteenth-century wills and inventories'. In *GC*, no. 48.

1033 'Glass fragments of the seventeenth century found near All Hallows Church, Lombard Street'. In *GC*, no. 63A.

1034 'Jelly glasses at dinner two centuries ago'. In *GC*, no. 62.

1035 'List of sealed bottles from seventeen museums'. In *GC*, no. 25.

1036 'List of sealed bottles from eighteen private collections'. In *GC*, no. 26.

1037 'More bottle seal discoveries'. In *CL*, Oct 1952, p. 1315–16, *illus.*

1038 *Sealed bottles.* With illustrations by Barbara Ashley. Country Life, 1949, 175p., *bibliog.*

1039 'Sealed wine bottles and bottle-decanters'. In *GC*, no. 24.

1040 'Symposium of bottle-decanters'. In *GC*, no. 69.

1041 'Wine in England through the ages'. In *GC*, no. 16.

1042 RUSSELL, G. Gordon. *Collection of seventeenth- and eighteenth-century English drinking glasses.* [Catalogue?]. Sydney (Australia), 1964. *Illus.*

1043 'S for Savoy?' In *CONN*, Jan–June 1960, p. 271., *illus.* The Shuckburgh Roemer sold in 1960 for £1,300.

1044 SALZMAN, Louis F. *English industries of the Middle Ages. New ed.* O.U.P., 1923. Spine title: 'Medieval English industries'. A second ed. of *English industries of the Middle Ages . . . 1913.*
Contents include: Glass, p. 183–93, *illus.*

1045 [Sussex] 'Glass'. In *Victoria County History of Sussex,* v. 2, 1907, p. 254–5.

1046 SANCTUARY, C. T. 'Evolution of the decanter, 1700–1830'. In *AP*, Jly–Dec 1947, p. 113–15, *illus.*

1047 'On collecting glass'. In *AP*, Jly–Dec 1950, p. 186–8, *illus.*

1048 'Opaque white glass'. In *AP*, Jan–June 1951, p. 73–6, *illus.* Mainly Bristol glass.

1049 'Some early glasses'. In *AP*, Jly–Dec 1957, p. 14–17, *illus.*, and Jan–June 1958, p. 18–20, *illus.*

1050 SANDILANDS, D. N. 'Chapters in the history of the Midlands glass industry'. In *TSGT (Proc.),* 1931.
Contents: The early history of glass-making in the Stourbridge area, p. 219–27; Birth of Birmingham's glass industry, p. 227–31; Last fifty years of the Excise Duty on glass, p. 231–45; The Spon Lane Works, p. 245–51.

1051 'Sarah Siddons: a study in identity'. In *GN*, 1956, p. 19–20, *illus.*

1052 SAVAGE, George. *Glass.* Weidenfeld and Nicolson, 1965. 128p., *illus. (some col.),* (Pleasure and Treasures).
Contents include: English and Irish glass, p. 95–114.

1053 *Antique collectors' handbook. 2nd ed.* Spring Books, 1969.
Contents include: Glass, p. 132–9, *illus.*

1054 *Art and antique restorers' handbook. 2nd ed. rev.* Barrie and Rockliff, 1967.
Contents include: Restoring glass, p. 48–50.

1055 SCHALCH, E. A. 'The charm of old bottles'. In *Wine and Spirit Trade Record,* 1958, p. 1356–62, *illus.*

1056 SCHOFIELD, Robert E. 'Josiah Wedgwood and the technology of glass manufacture'. In *Technology and Culture,* v. 3, 1962, p. 285–97.

1057 SCHRIJVER, Elka. *Glass and crystal.* 2 v., Merlin, 1964, 1966, *illus., bibliog.* First pub. Bossum (Netherlands), 1963.
Contents: v. 1: From the earliest times to 1850; v. 2: From the mid-nineteenth century to the present. Includes English glass.

1058 SCIENCE MUSEUM. *Descriptive catalogue of the collection illustrating glass technology by S. E. Janson.* HMSO, 1969, 55p., *illus.* Includes bottles and glassware.

1059 SCOTT, Amoret *and* SCOTT, Christopher. 'Blue glass from Bristol'. In *CL*, Feb 1961, p. 327, *illus.*

1060 *Antiques as an investment.* Oldbourne, 1967.
Contents include: Glass, p. 74–85.

1061 SCOTT, GREENWOOD AND SON, LTD. *A handbook on pottery and glassware: a revised ed. of 'A textbook for salespeople . . .'.* Scott, Greenwood, 1933, 72p., *illus.* First pub. 1923.

1062 *Making pottery and glassware in Britain . . . reprinted from the Pottery and Glass Trade Rev.* Scott, Greenwood, n.d., 96p., *illus.* Includes a glossary of terms.

1063 *Recipes for flint glass making by a Bristol glass master and mixer. . . .* Scott, Greenwood, 1900, 62p., *bibliog.*

1064 SEABY, Wilfred A. 'Finest Irish Williamite glass'. In *CL*, Dec 1965, p. 1635–6, *illus.*

1065 *Irish Williamite glass: a study of wheel-engraved examples from the eighteenth and early nineteenth centuries.* Belfast, Ulster Museum, 1965, 18p., *illus., bibliog.*

1066 'Williamite engraved glassware'. In *GC*, no. 154.

1067 SEAGO, T. Taylor. 'From the glassmaker's idle moments' [friggers]. In *CL*, Oct 1963, p. 1058–9, *illus.*

1068 'Glasshouse friggers'. In *Pottery Gazette,* 1946, p. 524, *illus.*

1069 SECCOMBE-HETT, G. V. A. 'Label decanters'. In *GC*, no. 119.

1070 SELBY, Edward. 'Jacobite glass – historic memorials to a lost cause'. In *ADCG*, Mar 1962, p. 31–32, *illus.*

1071 SELLERS, Maud. 'Glass' [making in York]. In *Victoria County History of York,* v. 2, 1912, p. 429–31, *illus.*

1072 'Glass works' [in Durham]. In *Victoria County History of Durham*, v. 2, 1907, p. 309–11.

1073 SERRE, F. de. 'Jacobite glasses at Olympia'. In *CL*, Jly 1928, p. 149–51, *illus*.

1074 , J. de [? possibly the same as above]. 'Irish glass'. In *CL*, Sept 1927, p. 454, *illus*.

1075 SHAND, P. Morton. 'The architecture of wine'. In *Architectural Rev.*, Sept 1929, p. 101–18, *illus*.
Bottles, including English and continental examples.

1076 SHEFFIELD CITY MUSEUM. *South Yorkshire glass* [Catalogue]. Sheffield Museum, 1963, 17p.

1077 SHEFFIELD UNIVERSITY. Department of Glass Technology. *List of books, pamphlets, and periodicals in the library*. Sheffield University, 1922, 31p.

1078 SHEPPARD, T. 'Hull and its glassworks'. In *Hull Museum Publications*, nos. 53, 74 and 151.

1079 SHULL, Thelma, *Victorian antiques*. New York, Tuttle, 1963.
Contents include: Bristol glass, p. 237–42, *illus*.

1080 [SIMMS, Rupert]. *Contributions towards a history of glass making and glass makers in Staffordshire, with an extraordinary tale entitled 'A legend of the glasshouse', founded on fact altered from the original by R. S. (Re-printed from the 'Midland Counties Express'. Wolverhampton)*. Wolverhampton, Whitehead, 1894, 16p.

1081 SIMON, André Louis. *Bottlescrew days. Wine drinking in England during the eighteenth century*. Duckworth, 1926, 273p., *illus*.
Contents include: Wine glasses and wine bottles, p. 226–42.

1082 'Champagne glasses'. In *GC*, no. 85.

1083 'Collecting wine: John Pierpont Morgan's cellar-book'. In *CONN*, Sept–Dec 1962, p. 227–30, *illus*. Bottles and glasses.

1084 'The evolution of the wine bottle'. In *GC*, no. 27.

1085 *The history of champagne*. Ebury Press, 1962.
Contents include: Champagne glasses, p. 155–9, *illus*.

1086 *The history of the wine trade in England*, 3 v. Wyman, 1906–9. Mention of bottles and glasses.

1087 'Old bottles – origins of corkscrews'. In *GC*, no. 71.
see also 'Wine Trade Loan Exhibition'.

1088 SKINNER, Basil. 'James and William Tassie'. In *Museums Jnl.*, Nov 1960, p. 200–4, *illus*.

1089 SMITH, *Sir* H. Llewellyn. 'Symposium on the form, design, and decoration of glass'. In *TSGT*, 1934, p. 89–95.

1090 SMITH, J. C. Varty. 'Concerning old pattern books'. In *The Queen*, Sept 18th 1915. From Ford's Glasshouse, Edinburgh.

1091 SMITH, R. S. 'Glassmaking at Wollaton [Notts.] in the early seventeenth century'. In *Trans. of the Thoroton Soc.*, 1962, p. 35–66.

1092 SMITH, R. Weaver. 'Art of glass'. In *ADCG*, Oct 1948, p. 17–19, *illus*.

1093 'The beginnings of English glass and the rise of Bristol'. In *ADCG*, Nov 1948, p. 15–17, *illus*.

1094 'Bottle glass and Nailsea'. In *ADCG*, Dec 1948, p. 22–4, *illus*.

1095 Engraved drinking glasses'. In *ADCG*, Feb 1949, p. 28–30, *illus*.

1096 'Irish and other cut glass'. In *ADCG*, Mar 1949, p. 25–7, *illus*.

1097 'Old English wine and ale glasses'. In *ADCG*, Jan 1949, p. 19–21, *illus*.

1098 'Old glass and its makers'. In *ADCG*, Aug 1948, p. 27–9, *illus*.

SMITH, Robert Henry Soden. *see* VICTORIA AND ALBERT MUSEUM.

1099 SOCIETY FOR THE PROMOTION OF CHRISTIAN KNOWLEDGE. *The manufacture of glass*. S.P.C.K., 1845, 35p., *illus*. (Useful arts and manufactures of Great Britain).

1100 SOCIETY OF GLASS TECHNOLOGY. *Glass and W. E. S. Turner, 1915–1951; edited by E. J. Gooding and Edward Meigh*. Sheffield, S.G.T., 1951, 144p., *illus*.

1101 *International Commission on Glass: world list of periodicals dealing with glass*. Sheffield, S.G.T., 1952. Duplicated typescript.

1102 *List of books, pamphlets and periodicals in the library*. Sheffield, S.G.T., 1922, 16p.

1103 'Society of Glass Technology Golden Jubilee'. In *Pottery Gazette and Glass Trade Rev.*, 1966, p. 1230–3, *illus.*, *ports*.

1104 SOLON, Louis M. E. 'Contribution towards a bibliography of the art of glass. Pt. 1: Glassmaking and technology; Pt. 2: History of the art, stained glass . . . glass painting'. In *Trans. of the English Ceramic Soc.*, 1912–13, p. 65–77 and p. 285–324.

1105 'Some interesting specimens of Scottish glass'. In *Wine and Spirit Trade Rev.* June 1958, p. 762–6, *illus*.

1106 SPIERS, Claude H. 'Pharmaceutical and medical glass'. In *GC*, no. 126.

1107 STANLEY, Federick. 'Newcastle glass: a rewarding choice'. In *ADCG*, Aug 1967, p. 63–4, *illus*.

1108 'Scotland's best in antiques'. In *ADCG*, Apr 1964, p. 44–6, *illus.* Jacobite and Scottish glass.

1109 STANNUS, *Mrs* E. Graydon. 'How to recognize old Irish glass'. In *CL*, Nov 1926, p. 133, *illus.*

1110 *Old Irish glass. New ed.* Connoisseur, 1921, 15p., *illus.* (Connoisseur Series of Books for Collectors).

1111 STEEVENSON, Muriel. 'Afterthoughts' [on Jacobite glass]. In *GC*, nos. 86 *and* 87.

1112 'Amen and Fiat'. In *GC*, no. 11.

1113 'Historical aspects of the Jacobite glasses'. In *GC*, no. 5.

1114 'The Jacobite Club'. In *GC*, no. 116.

1115 'Jacobite clubs'. In *GC*, nos. 7, 59, 60 *and* 61.

1116 'Jacobite emblems: the Rose'. In *GC*, no. 12.

1117 'Jacobite emblems: Pt. 1: the Rose; Pt. 2: the Thistle'. In *AP*, Jan–June 1940, p. 102–5, and Jly–Dec 1940, p. 41–4, *illus.*

1118 'More clubs'. In *GC*, no. 101.

1119 'More emblems on Jacobite glasses'. In *GC*, no. 13.

1120 'Pruning the Jacobite rose'. In *GC*, no. 144.

1121 'Some Jacobite toasts'. In *GC*, no. 17.

1122 STENNETT-WILSON, Ronald A. *The beauty of modern glass.* Studio, 1958, 128p., *illus.* (*some col.*). Includes English glass.

1123 'Contemporary glass'. In *Art and Industry.* Dec 1958, p. 188–93, *illus.*

1124 STEUBEN GLASS INC. *British artists in crystal.* New York, Steuben, 1954, 24p., *illus.* Includes the work of Whistler, Minton, Piper, etc.

1125 STONE, Peter *and* STONE, Jon. 'The early eighteenth century in England'. In *ADCG*, Oct 1953, p. 17–19, *illus.*

1126 'The English pioneers' [in glass]. In *ADCG*, Aug 1953, p. 20–2, *illus.*

1127 'From Victoria to the present day'. In *ADCG*, June 1954, p. 32–3, *illus.*

1128 'Ravenscroft and English crystal'. In *ADCG*, Sept 1953, p. 24–6, *illus.*

1129 'Rococo colour'. In *ADCG*, Nov 1953, p. 23–5, *illus.* Opaque and painted glass, etc.

1130 'Stourbridge: the manufacture of glass (Tour in the manufacturing districts)'. In *Art Union*, 1846, p. 102–7, *illus.* Includes Richardson, Thomas Webb, etc.

1131 'Stourbridge [glass] Collection opened'. In *The Times*, Feb 4th 1954, p. 8.

1132 STOURBRIDGE GLASS MANUFAC-TURERS. *Detailed catalogue of the exhibits of a loan exhibition of Stourbridge glass . . . held for the Stourbridge Festival of Britain Exhibition, 1951.* Stourbridge, 1951, 28p., *illus.*

1133 *Stourbridge Official Guide.* Stourbridge, 1966 [and other years]. Includes a descriptive note on the permanent glass exhibition, p. 62–3, *illus.*

1134 'Stourbridge public [glass] collection'. In *The Times*, Jly 28th 1954, p. 5.

1135 STRAUSS, Jerome. 'Chinoiserie on glass'. In *A*, 1952, p. 414–17, *illus.*

1136 'English glass at the Brooklyn Museum'. In *Bull. of the Brooklyn Museum*, no. 4, 1957, p. 1–6, *illus.*

1137 *Glass drinking vessels from the collection of Jerome Strauss and the Ruth B. Strauss Memorial Foundation* [Exhibition Catalogue]. New York, Corning, 1955.

1138 'A vintner's drinking glasses'. In *A*, 1961, p. 102–5, *illus.*

1139 STUART, James. 'Letter from London: the Winifred Geare glass'. In *A*, 1966, p. 808, 816, *illus.*

1140 STUART, Sheila. 'Antique glass for the table'. In *ADCG*, Dec 1964, p. 52–4, *illus.*

1141 'Charm of old glass'. In *ADCG*, Mar 1948, p. 13–15, *illus.*

1142 'Elegant ways of illumination'. In *ADCG*, Jly 1964, p. 39–41, *illus.*

1143 *Small antiques for the small home.* Yoseloff, 1968. Contents include: glass, p. 23–36, *illus.*

1144 *A dictionary of antiques.* Chambers, 1953. Contents include: Glass and the English tradition, p. 165–97, *illus.*

1145 'How we got the decanter'. In *ADCG*, Feb 1964, p. 36–8, *illus.*

1146 'Old English glass'. In *ADCG*, Apr 1962, p. 33–5, *illus.*

1147 *Antiques for the modern home.* Chambers, 1962. Contents include: Old glass, p. 85–96, *illus.*

1148 'Old glass: early designs in Great Britain'. In *Chambers's Jnl.*, Dec 1947, p. 733–4.

1149 'When Johnson went drinking'. In *ADCG*, June 1962, p. 38–40, *illus.*

1150 'Sudden rise in value of English glass'. In *Art Digest Newsletter*, Apr 1968, p. 7–8.

1151 'Surfeit glasses'. In *The Times*, Dec 23rd 1961, p. 9, *illus.*

1152 'Survey of contemporary glass'. In *Craft Horizon*, Nov 1960. Contents include: 'New directions in glass-making' by P. Perrot; 'The fluid breath of glass' by J. Burton, etc.

1153 [TAIT, Hugh]. 'English glassmaking'. In *CL*, June 1927, p. 107–10, *illus.*

1154 TAIT, Hugh. 'The Pilkington Museum of

Glass'. In *CONN*, Sept–Dec 1964, p. 230–7, *and* Jan–Apr 1965, p. 20–5, *illus.* (*some col.*).

1155 'A review of post-medieval European glass acquired since the outbreak of the Second World War [by the British Museum]. In *British Museum Quarterly*, 1963–4, p. 28–33, *bibliog.*

1156 'Wolff glasses in an English private collection' [Mr J. G. Littledale]. In *CONN*, May–Aug 1968, p. 99–108, *illus., bibliog.*

see also BRITISH MUSEUM.

1157 'Talk on Beilby and other glasses exhibited by members'. In *GC*, no. 83.

1158 TALLIS, John. *History and description of the Crystal Palace and Exhibition of the World's Industry* ['*Great Exhibition*'] *in 1851*, 3 v., J. Tallis and Co., 1851.
Contents include: Description of glass including British items, v. 1, p. 76–83, *illus.*; Note on Osler's Crystal Fountain, v. 3, p. 21–2.

1159 TAYLOR, I. *Scenes of British wealth in produce, manufacture and commerce . . . new ed.* John Harris, 1832.
Contents include: Newcastle glass, p. 227–33.

1160 TAYLOR, Marjorie V. 'Glass [making in Worcestershire]. In *Victoria County History of Worcestershire*, v. 2, 1906, p. 278–81.

1161 THESIGER, Ernest. 'Collecting mercury glassware'. In *The Listener*, Dec 1958, p. 985–6, *illus.* Silvered or lustre glass.

1162 'Thomas Webb – a century and a quarter'. In *Pottery Gazette and Glass Trade Rev.*, 1962, p. 274–7, *illus.*

THOMSON, G. *ed. see* WIHR, Rolf.

1163 THORPE, William Arnold. 'The aesthetics of flint'. In *Apollo Annual*, 1948, p. 82–5, *illus.*

1164 'Anglo-Irish glass'. In *CL*, v. 61, 1927, p. 40–4, *illus.*

1165 'Antecedents of the [Glass] Circle'. In *GC*, no. 66.

1166 'The Beginnings [and rise] of English cut glass'. In *CONN*, Jly–Dec 1930, p. 226–34, *and* p. 307–13, *illus.*

1167 'The Beilby glasses'. In *CONN*, May–Aug 1928, p. 10–23, *illus.*

1168 'Bristol rollers . . .'. In *ADCG*, Aug 1947, p. 19–20, *illus.*

1169 [British glassware]. In *Chambers's Encyclopaedia*, 1967 ed., v. 6, p. 386–8, *illus.* (*some col.*).

1170 'Codes of work in glass history'. In *Jnl. of the Royal Soc. of Arts*, 1948, p. 460–77, *illus.*

1171 *Collections of glass at Brierley Hill Public Library: a handlist.* Brierley Hill Public Library, 1949, 48p., *illus.*

1172 'The Dagnia tradition in Newcastle glass'. In *CONN*, Jly–Dec 1933, p. 13–25, *illus.*

1173 'Development of cut-glass in England and Ireland'. In *A*, 1930, p. 300–3, *and* p. 408–11, *illus.*

1174 'The diversions of the diamond'. In *GC*, no. 80.

1175 'Drinking glasses commemorative of William III'. In *AP*, Jan–June 1926, p. 165–70, *and* 210–16, *illus.*

1176 'Early English glasses in the collection of Lady Davy'. In *CL*, Jly 1928, p. 111–12, *illus.*

1177 'Early glass cutters such as Thomas Betts, Jerom Johnson, Ackerman, etc.'. In *GC*, no. 84.

1178 *English glass. 3rd ed.* Black, 1961, 305p., *illus., bibliog.* (Library of English Art). First pub. 1935, 2nd ed. 1949.
Contents include: The period of monopolies [Mansell], p. 114–34; Mr Jacob [Verzelini], p. 94–113; Medieval Wealden glass, p. 82–93.

1179 'English glass in Mr W. T. Wiggins-Davies's collection'. In *CONN*, Jly–Dec 1930, p. 3–8, *illus.*

1180 'English glasses' [Lady Davy's Collection]. In *CL*, Mar 1928, p. 76–80, *illus.*

1181 'English glassware in the seventeenth century'. In Churchill, Arthur, Ltd., *Catalogue of old English glass, 2nd ed.*, 1937, p. 13–22. This article is reprinted in *GN*, 1956, p. 27–36.

1182 *English and Irish glass with an introduction.* Medici Soc., 1927, 35p., *illus.* (*some col.*).

1183 'The evolution of the decanter'. In *CONN*, Jan–June 1929, p. 196–202, *and* 271–81, *illus.*

1184 'The glass sellers' bills at Woburn Abbey'. In *TSGT*, 1938, p. 165–205, *illus., facsims.*

1185 'The Henry Brown collection of English glass. Pt. 1: Preference for balusters; Pt. 2: Decline and decoration'. In *AP*, Jly–Dec 1928, p. 141–8 *and* 208–14, *illus.*

1186 'An historic Verzelini glass' [dated 1586]. In *BUR*, Jly–Dec 1935, p. 150–7, *illus., bibliog.*

1187 *A history of English and Irish glass.* 2 v. Medici Soc., 1929, *illus., bibliog.*
Contents include: Abjects, orts and imitations, p. 301–7; Dagnia family tree, p. 145; Ravenscroft, p. 116–33; special types of glassware, p. 313–34; terminology of glass, p. 335–40; Sussex [glass]: the French tradesmen, p. 51–8.

1188 *A history of English and Irish glass* Holland

Press, 1969. Facsimile reprint of the 1929 edition. In one volume, limited to 500 copies.

1189 'The Hoare bills for glass'. In *GC*, no. 89, Jan 1949, 24p.

1190 'Jacobite glass in the collection of Mr C. Kirkby Mason'. In *AP*, Jan–June 1926, p. 14–22, *illus.*

1191 'The Lisley group of [eight] Elizabethan glasses'. In *CONN*, Jly–Dec 1948, p. 110–17, *illus.*

1192 'Memorable English glass in the Cecil Higgins collection'. In *BUR*, Jly–Dec 1938, p. 155–62, *illus.*

1193 'A newly discovered Verzelini glass' [inscribed 'Wenyfrid Geares' and the Vintners' Company's arms, belonging to the Earl of Northumberland in 1930]. In *BUR*, Jan–June 1930, p. 256–7, *illus.*

1194 'Nipt diamond waies – a symposium of members' pieces'. In *GC*, no. 68.

1195 'Prelude to European cut-glass'. In *TSGT*, 1938, p. 5–37, *illus.*

1196 'The Rees Price collection of English glass' [Jacobites, etc.]. In *AP*, Jly–Dec 1925, p. 250–8, *illus.*

1197 'The Roscoe collection of English glass' [Wm. Malin Roscoe of Liverpool]. In *CONN*, Jly–Dec 1935, p. 205–9, *illus.*

1198 'The Scudamore flute'. In *AC*, 1932, p. 361–2, *illus.*

1199 'The social history of the Portland Vase'. In *GC*, nos. 137, 138 *and* 139.

1200 'Some types of Newcastle glass'. In *A*, 1933, p. 206–9, *illus.*

1201 'Towards a classification of Nailsea glass'. In *A*, 1932, p. 13–16, *illus.*

1202 'Water-glass' [Letter discussing the term with two subsequent letters from readers]. In *CL*, Nov–Dec 1951, p. 1470, 1473, 1637, 2172 *and* 2175.

1203 'The white Beilbys'. In *The present state of glass studies*, Pt 2, *AC*, 1962, p. 135–7, *illus.*

1204 'The Wiggins-Davies collection of English glass'. In *CONN*, Jly–Dec 1930, p. 86–9, *illus.*

1205 TILLEY, Frank. 'The Marshall collection in the Ashmolean Museum, Oxford' [II: Glass]. In *AC*, 1959, p. 35–8, *illus.*

1206 'The Times Weekly Review: survey of the British glass industry'. In *The Times*, Nov 8th 1956.

1207 'Toddy rummers'. In *The Times*, Oct 24th 1959, p. 9, *illus.*

1208 TRAPPNELL, Alfred. *Catalogue of Bristol and Plymouth porcelain, with examples of Bristol glass and pottery*. . . . Bristol and London, A. Amor, 1905, 95p., *illus.* Glass, p. 70–3.

1209 'Traquair Amen glass'. In *GN*, 1951, p. 12–13, *illus.*

1210 TRENCHARD, C. 'English glass bottles'. In *AC*, 1935, p. 185–6, *illus.*

1211 TRETHOWAN, Harry. 'James Humphries Hogan, R.D.I.: an appreciation'. In *Studio*, May 1948, p. 156–7, *illus.* J. H. Hogan was Art Director of the Whitefriars Glass Works.

1212 'Truly modern and truly cut' [recent Webb Corbett designs]. In *Pottery Gazette and Glass Trade Rev.*, 1963, p. 1268–9, *illus.*

1213 TURLEIGH, Edward. 'The Adam tradition'. In *ADCG*, June 1952, p. 43–5, *illus.*

1214 'Air-twist·stems'. In *ADCG*, Jan 1952, p. 21–3, *illus.*

1215 'Candlesticks'. In *ADCG*, Feb 1952, p. 24–6, *illus.*

1216 'The charm of Nailsea'. In *ADCG*, Jly 1952, p. 20–2, *illus.*

1217 'Colour and decoration'. In *ADCG*, Apr 1952, p. 24–6, *illus.*

1218 'Contrivance of table ware'. In *ADCG*, Aug 1951, p. 30–2, *illus.*

1219 'Early English crystal'. In *ADCG*, Oct 1951, p. 21–3, *illus.*

1220 'The enjoyment of light'. In *ADCG*, Jly 1951, p. 29–31, *illus.*

1221 'Evolution of the decanter'. In *ADCG*, Mar 1952, p. 27–9, *illus.*

1222 'Georgian grace' [in glass]. In *ADCG*, Aug 1952, p. 24–6, *illus.*

1223 'The heritage of technique'. In *ADCG*, Sept 1952, p. 27–9, *illus.*

1224 'Line and form'. In *ADCG*, Dec 1951, p. 27–9, *illus.*

1225 TURNER, William E. S. 'The British glass industry: its development and its outlook'. In *TSGT*, 1922, p. 108–46.

1226 'A notable British seventeenth-century contribution to the literature of glassmaking' [Neri-Merret's *Art of glass*, 1662]. In *Glass Technology*, 1962, p. 201–13, *illus.*

1227 'Mr John Northwood's plaque of Aphrodite'. In *TSGT*, 1924, p. 92–3, *illus.*

1228 'The Society of Glass Technology'. In *Jnl. of the American Ceramic Soc.*, 1923, p. 181–3.

1229 'The tercentenary of Neri-Merrett's *The art of glass*'. In *Advances in Glass technology*, Pt 2, New York, 1963, p. 181–201, *illus.*

joint author see PRESTON, Eric, HOLLAND, A. J., *and* TURNER, William E. S.

1230 'Tyne Glass House'. [South Shore Flint Glasshouse?]. In *GN*, 1955, p. 7, *illus.*

1231 ULLYETT, Kenneth. 'English blown glass'. In *ADCG*, Nov 1947, p. 19–20, *illus.*

1232 'Old Masonic drinking glasses'. In *ADCG*, Jly 1965, p. 55–7, *illus.*

1233 UNWIN, Max. 'A treatment for the preservation of glass'. In *Museums Jnl.*, 1951–2, p. 10.

1234 VAN DE GOOTE, D. 'Old glass from the Green Isle' [Ireland]. In *CL*, May 1922, p. 134, *illus.*

1235 VAN LEDDEN HULSEBOCH, C. J. 'A report on signatures' [On glasses engraved by David Wolff]. In Buckley, Wilfred, *D. Wolff and the glasses he engraved*, 1926, p. 33–7.

1236 'Vases of "Clutha" glass by Messrs James Couper and Sons, Glasgow' [coloured glass]. In *Art Journal*, 1892, p. 376–7, *illus.*

1237 'Verzelini glasses at Corning: a rare acquisition, together with a Butler Buggin bowl'. In *AC*, 1963, p. 236, *illus.*

1238 'Verzelini goblet inscribed "God save Quyne Elisabeth 1586"'. In *AP*, Jan–June 1935, p. 375–6, *illus.*

1239 VICKERS, Eric J. 'Technical aspects of the photography of glass'. In *TSGT*, 1936, p. 110–18, *illus.*

1240 VICTORIA AND ALBERT MUSEUM. *A descriptive catalogue of the glass vessels in the South Kensington Museum. With an introductory notice by Alexander Nesbitt.* Chapman and Hall, 1878, 218p., *illus.* (*some col.*).

1241 *English glass.* [Compiled by] R. J. Charleston. HMSO, 1968, 15p., *illus.* (Victoria and Albert Museum Large Picture Book Series).

1242 *Exhibition of English glass* [Catalogue]. Victoria and Albert Museum, 1968, 44p., *bibliog.*

1243 *Fifty masterpieces of pottery, porcelain, glass vessels . . .* 2nd ed. HMSO, 1963, 102p., *illus.* First pub. 1950.

1244 *Glass . . .* by Alexander Nesbitt. Chapman and Hall, 1878, 143p., *illus.* (South Kensington Museum Art Handbooks).

1245 *Glass: a handbook for the study of glass vessels of all periods and countries and a guide to the Museum collection* by W. B. Honey. HMSO, 1946, 241p., *illus.*, *bibliog.* English glass, p. 95–126.

1246 *Glass table-ware.* HMSO, 1952, 28p., *illus.* (Small Picture Book Series No. 1).

1247 *Glass table-ware.* [Exhibition catalogue]. HMSO, 1957, 32p., *illus.*

1248 *A list of books in the National Art Library . . . illustrating glass, etc.* [With prefatory note by Robert Henry Soden Smith]. Victoria and Albert Museum, 1887, 47p.

1249 *A picture book of English glass.* HMSO, 1926, 24p., *illus.*

1250 *Victorian and Edwardian decorative arts.* HMSO, 1952, 40p., *illus.* (Small Picture Book Series No. 34).

1251 'Victorian glass shades'. In *The Times*, Feb 11th 1967, p. 11, *illus.*

1252 'Victorian ornamental glass'. In *The Times*, Nov 7th 1964, p. 11, *illus.*

1253 'Visit to the Brierley Hill Glass Collection'. In *Pottery Gazette and Glass Trade Rev.*, 1964, p. 66–7, *illus.*

1254 VITRARIUS, *pseud.* 'A "find" in seventeenth-century glass: the Butler Buggin bowls'. In *AC*, 1937, p. 318–20, *illus.* Includes a pedigree of Butler-Buggin families.

1255 W. H. P. *and* E. B. H. [E. Barrington HAYNES]. 'An English tazza bowl and its implications'. In *AP*, Jan–June 1944, p. 158–61, *illus.*

1256 WAKEFIELD, Hugh. 'The development of design for pressed glassware as exemplified in British sources'. In *International Commission on Glass*, Comptes rendus, 2, Bruxelles, 1965 (Paper 208) p. 1–5, *illus.*

1257 [English glass from 1850]. In *Encyclopaedia Britannica*, 1970 ed., v. 10, p. 463–6, *illus.*

1258 'Glasswares by Apsley Pellatt'. In *A*, 1965, p. 85–8, *illus.*

1259 'The history of glassmaking'. In *Pottery Gazette and Glass Trade Rev.*, 1957, p. 95–100, *illus.*

1260 *Nineteenth-century British glass.* Faber, 1961, 64p., *illus.* (*some col.*). (Faber Monographs on Glass – 1).

1261 'Pottery, porcelain and glass' [1830–60]. In *Connoisseur Complete Period Guides: Early Victorian*, 1968, p. 1403–9, *illus.*

1262 'Richardson glass'. In *A*, 1967, p. 632–5, *illus.*

1263 'Victorian glass'. In *GC*, no. 110.

WAKEFIELD, Hugh, *comp. see* LEEDS CITY ART GALLERY.

1264 WAKEFIELD, R. *The old glasshouses at Stourbridge and Dudley. A short history of the local glass trade and glasshouses from the earliest times.* Revised. Reprinted from the *Stour Gazette*. Stourbridge, Stour Press, 1934, 37p., *illus.*

1265 WALKER, Vera E. 'Sixty years of glass, 1780–1840 . . .'. In *AC*, 1964, p. 79–82, *illus.*

WALLIS, George *see* PARIS UNIVERSAL EXHIBITION, 1867.

1266 WALLIS, W. Cyril. 'An unrecorded "Amen" glass in the Royal Scottish Museum, Edinburgh'. In *CONN*, Jly–Dec 1952, p. 105, *illus.*

1267 'Some Jacobite drinking glasses'. In *Scotland's Mag.*, Aug 1945, p. 22–3, *illus.*

1268 WARING, John Burley. *Masterpieces of industrial art and sculpture at the International Exhibition, 1862.* Day & Son, 1863. Glass, vol. 1.

1269 WARREN, Phelps, *Irish glass: the age of exuberance.* Faber, 1970, 155p. *illus. (some col.),* bibliog. (Faber Monograph on Glass).

1270 'Waterford glass – the story of a revival'. In *Pottery Gazette and Glass Trade Rev.*, 1964, p. 735–8, *illus.*

1271 'Waterford revisited'. In *Pottery and Glass*, Nov 1958, p. 326–7, *illus.*

1272 WATKINS, Laura Woodside. 'Early American advertisements of English glass'. In *GC*, no. 55.

1273 WAY, Herbert W. L. 'Apsley Pellatt's glass cameos'. In *CONN*, Jan–Apr 1922, p. 78–82, *illus.*

1274 'Apsley Pellatt's glass cameos in the collection of Mrs Applewhaite-Abbott'. In *CONN*, Sept–Dec 1923, p. 3–10, *illus.*

1275 'Glass paperweights'. In *CONN*, Sept–Dec 1920, p. 222–7, *illus. (some col.).*

1276 'Mrs Applewhaite-Abbott's collection of coloured glass'. In *CONN*, Sept–Dec 1922, p. 212–20, *illus.*

1277 'Old English wine glasses'. In *CONN*, Sept–Dec 1909, p. 187–8, *illus.*

1278 WEBB, Michael. 'Looking at design: glass for glass's sake'. In *CL*, Nov 1964, p. 1448–51, *illus.*

1279 WEBB, THOMAS AND SONS (Webb's Crystal Glass Co. Ltd). *A descriptive booklet illustrating the art of making 'Webb's Handmade Crystal Tableware'.* Stourbridge, Thomas Webb and Sons [1928], 8p., *illus.*

WEEDEN, Cyril, *joint author, see* EVANS, Wendy and WEEDEN, Cyril.

1280 WEISSBERGER, Herbert. 'The Rea collection of English and Irish glass'. In *Carnegie Mag.*, Mar 1957, p. 87–9, *illus.*

1281 WELCH, Charles. 'Glass' [-making in Middlesex]. In *Victoria County History of Middlesex*, v. 2, 1911, p. 155–8.

1282 WENHAM, Edward. *Antiques A to Z.* Bell, 1954. Glass, p. 70–9.

1283 WESTERLING, E. M., 'Nailsea glass and its ancestry'. In *AP*, Jan–June 1936, p. 257–63, *illus.*

1284 WESTROPP, Michael Seymour Dudley. 'Glassmaking in Ireland'. In *Proc. Royal Irish Academy*, 29, Pt. 3, 1911, p. 34–58, *illus.*

1285 'Irish cut-glass'. In *A*, 1928, p. 476–9, *illus.*

1286 'Moulded glass'. In *A*, 1928, p. 538–43, *illus.*

1287 *Irish glass: an account of glass-making in Ireland from the sixteenth century to the present day.* H. Jenkins, [1920], 206p., *illus.*
see also DUBLIN MUSEUM OF SCIENCE AND ART.

1288 WESTWOOD, Mary G. 'Old glass paperweights'. In *ADCG*, Dec 1948, p. 30–1, *illus.*

1289 WHISTLER, Laurence. *Engraved glass, 1952–1958.* Hart-Davis, 1959, 38p., *illus.*

1290 *The engraved glass of Laurence Whistler.* Cupid Press, 1952, 47p., *illus.*

1291 'Point engraving on glass'. In *GC*, no. 121.

1292 *A point on glass: engraved goblets by Laurence Whistler with three glasses by his son Simon Whistler: illustrated catalogue* [of an exhibition]. Agnew, 1969, 25p., *illus.*

1293 'Some engraved glasses by David Peace'. In *CONN*, May–Aug 1968, p. 175–7, *illus.*
see also 'The Queen's gift . . .'.

1294 WHITE, Gleeson. 'Domestic glass making in London' [mainly Whitefriars]. In *Art Jnl.*, 1896, p. 21–4, *illus.*

1295 WHITE, H. H. 'New views of old glass: English and American wine bottles of the seventeenth century'. In *A*, Jly–Oct 1933, p. 26, 68, 108 *and* 146, *illus.* English bottles, p. 68 (Aug.).

1296 WHITE, Margaret E. *European and American glass in the Newark Museum's collections.* Newark (New Jersey) Museum [1955], 32p., *illus., bibliog.*

1297 WHITEFRIARS GLASS LTD. *Whitefriars: three centuries of glassmaking.* [Catalogue]. Colchester, 1965, 54p., *illus. (some col.).*

1298 'Whitefriars glassworks: the two hundred and fiftieth anniversary'. In *AP*, Jly–Dec 1930, p. 361–7, *illus., port.*

1299 WIDMAN, Dag. 'En anglo-irish Cristallskol' [English and Irish glass]. In *Femtio Ar-Femtio Masterverk, Stockholm, National Museum*, 1961, p. 138–41, *illus.*

1300 WIHR, Rolf. 'Repair and reproduction of ancient glass'. In Thomson, G. *ed. Recent advances in conservation.* Butterworth, 1963, p. 152–5, *illus.*

1301 WILKINSON, O. N. *Old glass: manufacture, styles, uses.* Benn, 1968, 200p., *illus., bibliog.*

1302 WILKINSON, R. *The hallmarks of antique glass.* Richard Madley, 1968, 220p., *illus. (some col.).*
Contents include: English coloured glass, p. 117–51; repair, restoration, reproduction and faking of antique glass, p. 189–217.

1303 WILKINSON, Reginald. 'The art of the glass cutter'. In *ADCG*, Apr 1965, p. 49–51, *illus.*

1304 'Williamite glasses'. In *The Times*, Aug 5th 1961, p. 9, *illus.*

1305 'Williamite glasses'. In *GN*, 1946, p. 5–7, *illus.*

1306 WILLIAMS, Guy Richard. *Collecting cheap china and glass.* Corgi, 1969, 125p., *illus.*

1307 *The home-lover's guide to antiques and bric-a-brac*, Corgi, 1967. Glass, p. 66–78.

1308 WILLIAMS, Jane *and* BACON, John Mansell. 'Glass found at Alfold with notes on Jean Carré. In *GC*, no. 48A.

1309 WILLIAMSON, Reginald P. Ross. 'Jacobite drinking glasses'. In *The Windsor Magazine*, no. 493, 1936, 5p., *illus.*

1310 WILLIAMS-THOMAS, R. S. 'Bloom on old glass'. In *GN*, 1952, p. 26–7.

1311 WILLS, Geoffrey. 'Another Portland Vase' [in Bohemian glass by Zach of Munich, *c.* 1860]. In *AP*, Jan–June 1956, p. 121.

1312 'Bristol and Nailsea glass'. In *Connoisseur Concise Encyclopaedia of Antiques*, v. 4, 1959, p. 85–91, *illus.*

1313 *Country Life pocket book of glass.* Country Life, 1966, 317p., *illus.*, *bibliog.*
Contents include: English glass . . . to 1900, p. 160–243.

1314 *English and Irish glass.* Guinness Signatures, 1970.
Contents: Bottles to 1720; Bottles from 1720; Candlesticks and lustres; Chandeliers; Commemorative goblets; Drinking Glasses, Pts 1 and 2; Eighteenth-century coloured glass; Enamelled and engraved glass; Ewers and decanters; Irish glass; Modern glass; Novelties and friggers; Table wares; Victorian glass, Pts 1 and 2. All these sections originally appeared separately as 16p. pamphlets during 1968. *All illus. (some col.).*

1315 'Footware ornaments'. In *CL*, Dec 1953, p. 2043–4, *illus.*

1316 'Glass and the [National Art Collections] Fund'. In *AP*, Jly–Dec 1964, p. 504–7, *illus. (some col.)*. Includes English glass.

1317 'Sale by candle'. In *AP*, Jly–Dec 1957, p. 125. Discusses a large candle glass in Truro Museum.

1318 'Sealed glass bottles'. In *Connoisseur Concise Encyclopedia of Antiques*, v. 4, 1959, p. 257–60, *illus.*

1319 WILMER, Daisy. *Early English glass: a guide for collectors of table and other decorative glass of the sixteenth and seventeenth centuries . . . 2nd ed.* Upcott Gill, 1911, 282p., *illus.*
Contents include a list of contemporary sale prices.

1320 WILMOTH, Victor J. 'Engineering history in glass'. In *Civil Engineering and Public Works Rev.*, Jly 1968, p. 774–6, *illus.*

1321 WILSON, G. H. 'Heroic age in glass'. In *CL*, June 1928, p. 817–18, *illus.*

1322 'Old English ale glasses'. In *CL*, Sept 1926, p. 405–6, *illus.*

1323 'Old English coloured glass'. In *CL*, Mar 1929, p. 74–6, *illus.*

1324 'Old English glass'. Pt 1: Certain types of stem; Pt 2: Firing glasses and toddy lifters. In *CL*, 1926, Jan, p. 179–80, *and* Feb, p. 457–8, *illus.*

1325 'Old English glass rummers'. In *CL*, Jly 1927, p. 105–6, *illus.*

1326 'Old English masonic glass'. In *CL*, Mar 1927, p. 507–8, *illus.*

1327 WILSON, Kenneth M. 'Musical glasses'. In *A*, 1961, p. 478–9, *illus.*

1328 WINBOLT, S. E. 'Note on medieval glass-making'. In *CONN*, Jly–Dec 1935, p. 91–2, *illus.* The Surrey–Sussex industry.

1329 'The Surrey-Sussex glass industry'. Nine articles in *Sussex County Magazine*, 1931: p. 286–91; 335–40; 414–18; 470–3; 562–7; 599–604; 688–94; 742–8; 826–30. *All illus.*

1330 'Sussex medieval glass: an aftermath'. In *Sussex County Magazine*, 1935, p. 787–92, *illus.*, *map.*

1331 'Wealden glass: the old Surrey-Sussex industry'. In *TSGT*, 1932, p. 254–71, *illus.*, *map.*

1332 *The Surrey–Sussex glass industry (A.D. 1226–1615).* Hove (Sussex), Combridge, 1933, 85p., *illus.*, *maps*, *bibliog.* Chapters 1–9 are the *Sussex County Magazine* articles of 1931. Contents include a list of dates in the history of Wealden glass, p. 72–4.

1333 WINCHESTER, Alice. 'Three centuries of European glass at the Corning Museum'. In *Connoisseur Year Book*, 1955, p. 58–65, *illus.*

1334 'Wine-glass engraved with Turk's head'. In *CL*, Jly and Oct 1955, p. 250, *illus.*, and p. 733–4. Two letters, the second from G. B. Hughes.

1335 'Wine Trade Loan Exhibition' [Catalogue, *ed.* by André Simon]. London, 1933. An exhibition at the Vintners' Hall, 1933.

1336 WINKWORTH, W. W. 'Cut-glass in the collection of Robert Frank, Esq.'. In *Old Furniture*, 1927, p. 188–94, *illus.*

1337 'Moulded and blown glass in the collection of Robert Frank, Esq.'. In *Old Furniture*, 1928, p. 35–9, *illus.*

1338 'Seventeenth-century glass in the Clements Collection'. In *BUR*, Jan–June 1924, p. 289–94, *illus.*

1339 WITTS, James R. 'The Jacobites – political sentiment in glass'. In *ADCG*, Dec 1959, p. 35–7, *illus.*

1340 WOOD, Eric S. *Collins Field Guide to archaeology*. Collins, 1963.
Contents include: Glassworks in Britain, p. 130–2, 276.

1341 'A medieval glasshouse at Blunden's Wood, Hambledon, Surrey'. In *Surrey Archaeological Collections*, v. 62, 1965, p. 54–79, *illus.*

1342 WOOD, H. M. 'The family of Dagnia of Newcastle'. In *Archaeologia Aeliana* (3rd series, Newcastle), v. 17, p. 229–43.

1343 WOOD, Violet. 'Rose-red cranberry glass'. In *ADCG*, Mar 1965, p. 32–4, *illus.*

1344 *Victoriana*. Bell, 1960.
Contents include: Glass, p. 77–94, *illus.*

1345 'Wood Bros. Glass Co. Ltd [Barnsley] centenary'. In *Glass*, 1928, p. 208, 214.

1346 'Woodall [George] designs for art manufactures'. In *Art Jnl.* 1880, p. 173, *illus.* Enamelled glass vases.

1347 'Woodall glass'. In *GN*, 1948, p. 22–3, *illus.*

1348 WOODHOUSE, C. Platten. *Victoriana collectors' handbook*. Bell, 1970.
Contents include: Glass: Chapter 7, *illus.*

1349 WOODWARD, H. W. 'The literature of glass (including that of the Stourbridge district)'. In *GC*, no. 131.

1350 WORNUM, R. S. H. 'The industries of Brierley Hill'. In *Brierley Hill Official Handbook*, 1956–7, p. 42–59, *illus.*

1351 WORSLEY, Katharine. 'Cut stems'. In *GC*, no. 149.

1352 'Opaque white twists' [1755–80]. In *GC*, no. 143.

1353 WORTHING MUSEUM AND ART GALLERY. *Exhibition catalogue of English drinking glasses, 1675–1825.* Summer 1968. Compiled by L. M. Bickerton. Worthing Museum, 1968, 38p., *illus.* Duplicated typescript. About one-quarter of the exhibits were from the original Hartshorne Collection. Hartshorne was at one time Curator of Worthing Museum.

1354 WYLDE, C. H. 'Mr Charles Edward Jerningham's Collection of English glasses in the Victoria and Albert Museum'. In *BUR*, Jan–Mar 1904, p. 131–42, *illus.*

1355 WYMER, Norman. *English town crafts*. Batsford, 1949.
Contents include: The glass blower, p. 44–9, *illus.*

1356 WYNN-PENNY, W. E. 'English wine and spirit glasses of the late seventeenth and early eighteenth centuries'. In *CONN*, Jan–Apr 1902, p. 159–63, *illus.*

1357 'Loan collection of eighteenth-century glass at the Victoria and Albert Museum'. In *CONN*, Jan–Apr 1913, p. 211–21, *illus.*

1358 'Mr John Webb Singer's Collection of English eighteenth-century drinking glasses'. In *BUR*, Sept–Dec 1903, p. 59–69, and p. 144–54, *illus.*

1359 YARWOOD, Doreen. *The English home . . .* Batsford, 1956, 393p., *illus.* Frequent references to glassware.

1360 YOUNG, G. A. 'Holyrood glass'. In *Scotland's Mag.*, Aug 1961, p. 26–9, *illus.*

1361 YOUNG, Sidney. *History of the Worshipful Company of Glass Sellers of London.* London, 1913, 76p., *illus.*

1362 YOUNGER, William. *Gods, men, and wine.* M. Joseph, for the Wine and Food Soc., 1966, 526p., *illus. (some col.)., bibliog.*
Contents include: Glasses and bottles, p. 348–55.

1363 YOXALL, *Sir* James Henry. *Collecting old glass, English and Irish.* Heinemann, 1916, 109p., *illus.* (Collector's Pocket Series).

1364 'Gentle glass-makers come'. In *Cornhill Mag.*, Jan 1915, p. 80–4; *and Living Age*, Apr 3rd 1915, p. 33–7. Huguenot glassmakers in Sussex.

1365 *More about collecting.* New ed. London, 1921, 339p., *illus.* First pub. 1913. Mention of English and Irish glass.

ADDENDUM PART I

1366 BICKERTON, Leonard Marshall. 'Glass in the Ipswich Museums'. In *East Anglian Magazine*, Mar 1971.

1367 BOND, Harold Lewis. *An encyclopedia of antiques.* New York, Tudor, 1946, 389p., *illus., bibliog.*
Contents include: Glass, p. 183–225. Mainly American, but several references to English and continental glass.

1368 BRETT, Gerard. 'The pedestal bowl: its probable origin and purpose'. In *CONN*, May–Aug 1967, p. 174–5, *illus.*

1369 BURTON, Elizabeth. *The Georgian at home, 1714–1830.* Longmans, 1967.
Contents include: Glass, p. 166–75.

1370 CONNOISSEUR. *The Connoisseur new guide to antique pottery, porcelain and glass.* Edited by L. G. G. Ramsey. Connoisseur, 1961, 192p., *illus.* Includes glass, p. 85–124.

Material later used in the *Connoisseur Period Guides.*

1371 CORNING MUSEUM OF GLASS. Corning Glass Centre. Descriptive brochure. Corning, 1952, *illus.*

1372 EASTLAKE, Charles L. *Hints on household taste.* 4th ed. Longmans, 1878.
Contents include: Table glass, p. 241–57, *illus.*

1373 EVANS, Wendy. 'Contemporary English artistic glass making'. Paper read at the Fifth Congress of the International Assn. for the History of Glass, Prague, 1970.

1374 FINDLAY, Ian. *Scottish crafts.* Harrap, 1948.
Contents include: Glass, p. 110–13, *illus.*

1375 'Forest House, Bournemouth'. In *AC*, 1936, p. 167–70, *illus.* Includes a collection of English glass.

1376 GILL, William. 'Georgian wine glasses'. In Hogg, Anthony, ed., *Wine Mine: A First Anthology*, Souvenir Press, 1970, p. 74–9, *illus.*

1377 GIRLING, F. A. *English merchants' marks.* O.U.P., 1964.
Contents include: Bottle seals, p. 112–14, *illus.*

1378 'Glass Houghton Glassworks'. In *South Yorkshire Jnl. of Industry and Social History*, Pt 1, 1948.

1379 HARDEN, D. B. 'A glass bowl from Pagan's Hill, Chew Stoke' [Somerset]. In *Medieval Archaeology*, 1959, p. 104–8.

1380 HARDING, Arthur. *Collecting English antiques.* W. and G. Foyle, 1963 (Foyle's Handbooks).
Contents include: Glass, p. 79–89.

1381 HARRIS, J. R. *Origins of the St Helens glass industry.* Pilkington Glass Museum, 1969. Reprinted from *Northern History.*

1382 HOGAN, D. E. Paper on the Du Haugh and the Haughton Green glasshouse. Pilkington Glass Museum, 1969.

1383 HOLLAND, Margaret. 'Irish glass'. In *Antiques Dealer*, May 1967, p. 37–40, *illus.*

1384 HUDSON, Kenneth. *Industrial archaeology: an introduction.* John Baker, 1966.
Contents include: Glass, p. 111–14.

1385 HUGHES, G. Bernard. 'Old English cut glass'. In *CL*, Dec 1945, p. 1138, *illus.*

1386 HURST, Ruth. 'Excavation of French forest glasshouse sites at Bickerstaffe and Denton, Lancs.' Paper read at the Fifth Congress of the International Assn. for the History of Glass, Prague, 1970.

1387 KENWORTHY, Joseph. *The broken earthenware of Midhope Potteries.* 1928. Includes

material on Bolsterstone and Gawber Glassworks.

1388 KLAARENBEEK, F. W., *and* STEVELS, J. M., eds. *Bibliography of glass literature.* International Commission on Glass, 1964. 117p.

1389 LADY LEVER ART GALLERY, PORT SUNLIGHT. *Chinese porcelain and Wedgwood pottery with works of ceramic art: a record of the collection in the Lady Lever Art Gallery, Port Sunlight, formed by . . . Viscount Leverhulme, [compiled] by R. L. Hobson.* Batsford, 1924.
Contents include: 'Tassie', with a catalogue (nos. 2275–333) of the Tassie glass pastes, p. 217–19.

1390 LONDON MUSEUM. *Glass in London. A catalogue by D. B. Harden of the Museum's Summer Exhibition, 1970.* HMSO, 1970.

1391 McDONALD, L. J. Paper on Ravenshead – the first cast-plate glass company. Pilkington Glass Museum, 1969.

1392 McNAB, Jessie. 'Glassware'. In *Collier's Encyclopedia*, 1967 ed., p. 143–52, *illus.* English glass, p. 148.

1393 'Manufacture of blown domestic glassware'. In *Pottery Gazette*, 1950, p. 1668–9, *illus.*

1394 MORTIMER, Martin C. F. 'Dating an early glass chandelier'. In *CONN*, Jly–Dec 1970, p. 172–4, *illus.*

1395 'Nailsea Glass'. In *Evening Argus*, Jly 9th 1970, p. 16, *illus.*

1396 O'FALLON, J. M. 'Glass'. In *Chambers's Encyclopedia*, 1930 ed., v. 5, p. 241–51, *illus.*, *bibliog.* General article.

1397 'Glass engraving as an art'. In *Art Jnl.*, 1885, p. 309–14, *illus.*

1398 REVI, Albert Christian. 'Iridescent glass'. In *The Spinning Wheel*, 1959, Mar, p. 14–17; Apr, p. 16, 18–19; June, p. 18–21; *all illus.*

1399 TAIT, Hugh. *The Pilkington Glass Museum guide.* Pilkington Glass Museum. *Illus.* Material from the *Connoisseur* articles of 1964/5.

1400 WAKEFIELD, Hugh. 'Venetian influences on English glass in the nineteenth century'. Paper read at the Fifth Congress of the International Assn. for the History of Glass, Prague, 1970.

1401 WILKINSON, R. 'Antique glass as décor'. In *Antiques for Decoration* (Antique Finder Ltd), 1970, p. 20–2, *illus.*

ADDENDUM PART II

1402 ALFORD, B. W. E. 'The flint and bottle glass industry in the early nineteenth century

[Phoenix Glassworks, Bristol]'. In *Business History*, 10, Jun 1968, p. 12–21.

1403 'Art at auction, 1969–1970'. The year at Sotheby's and Parke-Bernet, 1969–70, edited by Philip Wilson. Macdonald, 1970. Contents include: Glass, p. 414–19, *illus.* (*some col.*).

1404 COYSH, A. W. *The antique buyer's dictionary of names.* David & Charles, 1970. Contents include: Names in glass manufacture, etc., p. 123–38.

1405 CURTIS, R. A. *and* MILLER, Martin. *The Lyle official antiques review.* Worthing, Jakta Press, 1970. Contents include: Glass, p. 316–23, *illus.*

1406 CUSHION, John. 'Pleasing glass for the modest collector'. In *Antiques Finder*, 1970–1, p. 29–30, *illus.*

1407 LAVINE, Sigmund A. *Handmade in England. The Tradition of British craftsmen.* New York, Dodd, Mead & Co., 1968. Contents include: Glass, p. 39–65, *illus.*

1408 LUCAS, J. W. 'Scotland's coloured glassware'. In *Scotland's Mag*, Jly 1968, p. 9–11, *illus.*

1409 MACKAY, James. 'English enamelled glass'. In *Financial Times*, Nov 11th 1970, p. 8, *illus.*

1410 MACLEOD, Catriona. 'Irish volunteer glass'. In *Jnl. of the Military History Soc. of Ireland*, vol. 7, no. 28, 1966.

1411 SPECK, G. E. *and* SOUTHERLAND, E. *English antiques.* Ward Lock, 1969. Contents include: Glass, p. 66–83, *illus.*

1412 TURNBULL, George *and* HERRON, Anthony. *The price guide to English eighteenth-century drinking glasses.* Clopton, Woodbridge, Antique Collectors Club, 1970. 359p., *illus.*

1413 'World of Waterford'. In *Pottery Gaz. & Glass Trade Rev.*, Dec 1969, p. 1965–8, *illus.* The modern factory.

Principal British and American Collections Open to the Public

British Isles

Notes

The specimens recorded are of English, Irish or Scottish provenance unless otherwise indicated.

Complete vessels only are recorded unless otherwise indicated.

The number of specimens is given in parentheses after each category. In some cases the figures are approximate.

The number of drinking glasses recorded includes all countries and all periods.

Opening hours are at least 10 a.m. to 4 p.m. each weekday unless otherwise indicated but some of the smaller museums close at lunch-time.

ABERDEEN. Art Gallery and Regional Museum, Schoolhill, Aberdeen
Eighteenth century (13); nineteenth century (176). Includes Cromar Watt (nineteenth-century Venetian glasses) and Miss Leslie Thomson Bequests. Drinking glasses (153). Photographs 35p for 6 in. × 4 in. print; quantity reductions.

BARNARD CASTLE. Bowes Museum, Barnard Castle, County Durham
Small collection of eighteenth- and nineteenth-century English and French glass, including glass produced for the Paris Exhibition of 1867. Photographs 25p for 8 in. × 6 in. print; colour transparencies 15p.

BATH. Victoria Art Gallery, Bridge Street, Bath, Somerset
Eighteenth century (450); nineteenth century (50); continental, sixteenth and seventeenth centuries (13), eighteenth and nineteenth centuries (115 including about 100 Bohemian). Drinking glasses (485) include colour twists and a Frigate glass. Most of the collection is from the J. M. Carr Bequest; small selections are on display from time to time; the remainder may be seen by arrangement. Photographs 50p for 8 in. × 6 in. print.

BEDFORD. Cecil Higgins Art Gallery, Castle Close, Bedford
Sixteenth and seventeenth centuries (43); eighteenth century (70); nineteenth century (63); continental, sixteenth to nineteenth centuries (56). Drinking

glasses (152) include important sealed Ravenscroft specimens, Anglo-Venetian, engraved (including Frigates) and colour-twist glasses. The original Cecil Higgins Collection has been added to by purchases from other famous collections. Open 11 a.m. to 6 p.m. Photographs 27½p each.

BELFAST. Ulster Museum, Stranmillis, Belfast 9, Northern Ireland
The collection of about 650 items contains a large proportion of Irish glass. Seventeenth century (3); eighteenth century (260); nineteenth century (340); continental, sixteenth and seventeenth centuries (4), eighteenth century (6), nineteenth century (40), some Eastern material. Drinking glasses (250); includes an important group of Williamites and a goblet attributed to Hawley Bishopp. Includes bequests by – Margaret Garrett, and Leslie Stevenson and H. A. P. McCormick. *Literature* 'Irish Williamite glass' by W. A. Seaby; 'Irish glass' by Phelps Warren. Most of the collection is in store pending opening of extension in 1971. Photographs 27½p for 8 in. × 6 in. print; colour transparencies of important pieces at 22½p to £1·58 according to size and availability.

BIRMINGHAM. City Museum and Art Gallery, Congreve Street, Birmingham 3
Eighteenth century (about 100); nineteenth century (about 120); continental, sixteenth and seventeenth centuries (45), eighteenth and nineteenth centuries (42). Drinking glasses (about 200), including a small collection of 'façon de Venise'. Important items include the Elgin Vase by John Northwood Senior and stained-glass windows designed by Burne-Jones and executed by Morris. The Department of Archaeology contains some fragments of Near Eastern glass, about 275 Roman and some fragments of medieval. Includes bequests by Miss F. M. Thomason and Miss May Morris. Photographs 27½p to £2·13 according to size and availability; colour transparencies to order at 75p each.

BLACKBURN. Museum and Art Gallery, Library Street, Blackburn, Lancs.
Eighteenth century (18); nineteenth century (42); continental, nineteenth century (24). Drinking glasses (23) include a Jacobite. Other specimens include Nailsea glass and French paperweights. Photographs 15p each.

BOURNEMOUTH. Russell-Cotes Art Gallery and Museum, East Cliff, Bournemouth, Hampshire
Small collection of some 36 specimens, including 6 of the eighteenth century and 11 continental. Open 10 a.m. to 6 p.m. in the summer, 10.30 a.m. to 5 p.m. in the winter.

BRADFORD. Cartwright Hall, Bradford 9, Yorkshire
Seventeenth century (6, wine bottles); eighteenth century (57); nineteenth century (180). Drinking glasses (71). Most of the collection is available on application only to the Keeper, Bolling Hall.

BRIERLEY HILL. Glass Collection, Public Library, Moor Street, Brierley Hill, Staffordshire
Roman (18); eighteenth century (45); nineteenth century (540); twentieth century (100); continental, nineteenth century (70). Drinking glasses (233). This extremely important collection of nineteenth-century English glass, especially that produced in the West Midlands, includes two cameo vases by George Woodall, two by Alphonse Lecheverel, a gilt loving cup by Jules Barbe, a wheel-engraved cameo standing bowl by F. Zach and the Stevens & Williams patents. Important bequests and donations include the Skidmore Westwood and Stevens & Williams Collections. Literature *see* Bibliography no. 1171. Open afternoons only (Wed. and Sun. excepted).

BRISTOL. City Museum, Queen's Road, Bristol 8, Somerset
A small collection of beads and fragments of glass from Iron Age, Roman,

Saxon and medieval sites in the Bristol area. The most important specimen is a Saxon bowl from Pagan's Hill, Chew Stoke. Colour transparency of Pagan's Hill bowl 10p.

City Art Gallery, Queen's Road, Bristol 8, Somerset
Seventeenth century (7); eighteenth century (250); nineteenth century (60); American, nineteenth and twentieth centuries (8); continental, seventeenth century (2), eighteenth century (10), nineteenth century (25), twentieth century (15). Drinking glasses (about 200). Collection includes vase and beaker decorated in Giles manner, Privateer glass and other specimens associated with the Bristol glass trade. Photographs from 25p to 33p, transparencies, where available, 10p.

Harvey's Wine Museum
The Museum covers the history of wine-making and includes some excellent specimens of seventeenth- to nineteenth-century drinking glasses. There are plans to extend this section of the Museum.

BURY ST EDMUNDS. Moyses Hall Museum, The Cornhill, Bury St Edmunds, Suffolk
Collection of 13 unguentaria (from Suffolk) and one glass jar of Romano-British period.

BUXTON. Museum, Terrace Road, Buxton, Derbyshire
Seventeenth century (1); eighteenth century (39); nineteenth century (12). Drinking glasses (29).

CAMBRIDGE. Fitzwilliam Museum, Trumpington Street, Cambridge
Pre-Roman and Roman (350); seventeenth century (120); eighteenth century (631); nineteenth century (17); continental, seventeenth century (50), eighteenth century (17), other seventeenth- and eighteenth-century specimens (25). Drinking glasses (656), including a Verzelini goblet and a signed Beilby goblet. Other important specimens are two with the Ravenscroft seal and a fourteenth-century Syrian mosque lamp. Collection includes the Donald Beves Bequest. Most pre-medieval glass is on display but only a small proportion of later glass. Access to the seventeenth–nineteenth-century material in store by application only. The Museum closes at 4 p.m. October to March inclusive. Photographs from 20p to £1·00 according to size and availability.

CANTERBURY. Royal Museum, Beaney Institute, High Street, Canterbury, Kent
Roman (19 complete vessels); Saxon (13 complete vessels); seventeenth century (1); eighteenth century (14); nineteenth century (5). Drinking glasses (21). In addition there is a collection of wine bottles, apothecaries' bottles and glass fragments. Colour transparencies of 5 Roman pieces 10p each.

CARDIFF. National Museum of Wales, Cathays Park, Cardiff, Glamorgan, Wales
Collection of excavated Roman glass from Caerleon and post-Roman sherds from Dinas Powys; seventeenth century (1); eighteenth century (148); nineteenth century (52); continental, nineteenth century (5). Drinking glasses (134). Important specimens include two Venetian plates painted with scenes of Venice, c. 1741. Photographs 22p to £2·20 according to size and availability. Colour transparencies of six specimens only.

CARLISLE. Museum and Art Gallery, Tullie House, Castle Street, Carlisle, Cumberland
Roman (20).

CHELTENHAM. Art Gallery and Museum, Clarence Street, Cheltenham, Gloucestershire
Phoenician (5); Roman (11); eighteenth century (202); nineteenth century (about 150); continental (14). Drinking glasses (184). The collection includes 63

examples of Bristol glass, engraved glasses, cider decanter and glass suitably engraved, Jacobites, paperweights, bottles and flagons.

DONCASTER. Cusworthy Hall Museum, Doncaster, Yorkshire
A small collection of some 50 specimens of documentary importance relating to the South Yorkshire glass industry. No drinking glasses.

EDINBURGH. Royal Scottish Museum, Chambers Street, Edinburgh, Scotland
Pre-Roman (40); Roman (480); Frankish (4); seventeenth century (20); eighteenth century (299); nineteenth century (223); twentieth century (191); American, nineteenth and twentieth centuries (25); continental, seventeenth century (65), eighteenth century (160), nineteenth century (340), twentieth century (48); Oriental, eighteenth and nineteenth centuries (164). Drinking glasses (510). Includes the Andrew Hunter Bequest. This extensive collection of some 2,800 specimens contains many of great importance. For details see *English glass picture book,* Royal Scottish Museum, London, HMSO, 1964. Photographs 20p to 73p according to size; £5·25 if no negative exists.

EXETER. Royal Albert Memorial Museum, Queen Street, Exeter, Devon
Roman (4); seventeenth century (11); eighteenth century (88); nineteenth century (27); Cyprus (30); continental, seventeenth–nineteenth centuries (69). Drinking glasses (70). Includes a bequest by H. H. Clarke and one by Miss C. R. Arden of the important 'Exeter' flute, *c.* 1660. Photographs 25p to £1·00 according to size and availability.

GATESHEAD. Shipley Art Gallery, Prince Consort Road, Gateshead, Co. Durham
Contains an important collection of Gateshead pressed glass (48 specimens) including the Hill Collection and the Lady Ridley Bequest.

GLASGOW. Art Gallery and Museum, Glasgow C3, Scotland
Pre-Roman and Roman (207); seventeenth century (97); eighteenth century (515); nineteenth century (124); Spanish, sixteenth century (15), seventeenth century (21), eighteenth century (18), nineteenth century (29); other continental countries, seventeenth century (16), eighteenth century (59), nineteenth century (84); Cyprus (100+); other countries (50). These figures include specimens in the Burrell Collection which contains a series of goblets, *c.* 1700; also Cyprus glass bequeathed by Sir R. Hamilton Lang and the Miss J. C. C. Macdonald Bequest of drinking glasses. The collection of 83 pieces of Hispanic glass is of considerable interest. Many specimens are in store and may only be seen by appointment. Photographs from 25p according to size and availability.

GLOUCESTER. City Museum and Art Gallery, Brunswick Road, Gloucester
Roman (2 + 250 excavated fragments); seventeenth century (9 + 250 excavated fragments from glasshouse sites); eighteenth century (127); nineteenth century (167). Drinking glasses (28). Collection includes the Stanley Marling Bequest of Bristol and decorated glass; outstanding specimens include examples of gilt decoration in the style of Isaac Jacobs and James Giles. Many specimens are in store and may be seen only by appointment.

HOVE. Central Library and Museum, Church Road, Hove, Sussex
Seventeenth century (1); eighteenth century (73); nineteenth century (78). Drinking glasses (82). All the Museum collections are at present in store; the glass collection includes bequests from Dr J. A. Rooth, Mrs Fryer, H. S. Edlin and Walter Williamson.

IPSWICH. Museum, High Street, Ipswich, Suffolk
Roman (10); Saxon (5); sixteenth–seventeenth centuries (about 20 excavated fragments); eighteenth century (467); continental, sixteenth–seventeenth centuries (2); Egyptian (3). Drinking glasses (about 450). Includes Frank Tibbenham

Bequest of eighteenth-century drinking glasses (about 100 on display at Christ-church Mansion, remainder in store). Outstanding specimens include a Nuremberg engraved goblet by G. F. Killinger, the Holeyfurnass Bowl dated 1768 and locally excavated glass from Roman times to the seventeenth century. Stored material may be seen by appointment only. Photographs 20p to £2·10.

LINCOLN. Usher Art Gallery
Seventeenth–eighteenth centuries (122, mostly of the eighteenth century); nineteenth century (12). Drinking glasses (122). The collection was made by the late C. L. Exley and is lent by G. R. G. Exley. Photographs subject to permission of owner, £1·25 to £1·50 according to size.

LIVERPOOL. City Museum, Department of Archaeology
Pre-Roman (30); Roman (400); Saxon (28); Persian (22). Bequests include the Mayer Collection and the Newberry Collection of Persian glass. Outstanding specimens include a Saxon claw beaker from Kent and Roman glass discs ornamented in gold-leaf. Most of the glass is in store and may be seen by appointment only. Photographs are available and will be quoted for on receipt of requirements.

LONDON. British Museum, London W.C.1
Contains one of the world's most outstanding and extensive collections of glass of all periods. The catalogue to the 1968 exhibition 'Masterpieces of glass' (see Bibliography) gives an indication of the range and importance of the Museum's collections.

Guildhall Museum, Gillett House, 55 Basinghall Street, E.C.2
Most of the glass in the Guildhall Museum consists of fragments excavated within the City of London. Where two figures are given in the following summary the first relates to total specimens however fragmentary, the second to complete vessels. Roman (500/50); Saxon (3/1); medieval (75/5); seventeenth century (325/120); eighteenth century (170/145); nineteenth century (50); twentieth century (50); continental, seventeenth century (125/10), eighteenth century (5/2). Drinking glasses (350/60). Most of the complete vessels of the seventeenth to nineteenth centuries are wine bottles (many with seals) and apothecaries' bottles. The fragmentary material recovered from a cellar in Gracechurch Street, probably that of a glass-seller's shop destroyed in 1666, is of particular importance. Other fragments include those of a Verzelini tazza and of two Ravenscroft sealed wine glasses. Photographs 17p and 22p from existing negatives. Colour transparencies, where available, 10p.

London Museum, Kensington Palace, W.8
Roman (85, including fragments and jewellery); Saxon (1 beaker + fragments and beads); medieval (14 including fragments and beads); seventeenth century (50); eighteenth century (550); nineteenth century (250); continental, seventeenth century (several wine-glass stems). Drinking glasses (c. 350, including fragments). Outstanding specimens include the Parr Pot, a lattimo jug dating to 1546–7 and the Chesterfield Flute, c. 1640–60. Also included is the Sir Richard Garton Bequest of 437 specimens. *Literature see* Bibliography nos. 809 and 1380. Glass not on display may be seen by arrangement. Prints from existing negatives 15p to £1·05; charge for new negative 85p; colour transparencies 50p.

Science Museum, South Kensington, S.W.7
Models of furnaces; equipment used in glassmaking, by hand or machine; displays illustrating the properties and uses of glass. Photographs 5p to 75p from existing negatives.

Victoria and Albert Museum, South Kensington, S.W.7
Contains one of the world's greatest collections of glass, in excess of 3,000 speci-

mens and especially strong in English glass of the seventeenth to twentieth centuries. Egyptian, Roman, medieval European and Islamic glass, Venetian and German glass and specimens from other European countries of sixteenth to nineteenth centuries are also well represented. There is a collection of twentieth-century glass which includes American and Scandinavian factories. The principal guide is by W. B. Honey (Bibliography no. 1245). Important gifts and bequests include those by C. Rees-Price, Mrs Jeanie H. R. Price, Francis Buckley and the gift by Mrs Buckley of the Wilfred Buckley Collection. Photographs of important pieces 25p; a limited number of colour transparencies is available.

MANCHESTER. City Art Gallery, Mosley Street, Manchester
Contains some 600 eighteenth-century English drinking glasses including the following bequests: Leicester Collier, 1917; Lloyd Roberts, 1920; Tylecote, 1965. Published in *Glass in the Manchester City Art Galleries* (picture book); Oliver Wilkinson, *Old glass* and *Journal of Glass Studies*, vol. III (article by W. D. Hall). The entire collection is at present in store; photographs of those illustrated in the Glass picture book 25p for 6 in. × 8 in. prints.

Manchester Museum, The University, Manchester
Egyptian (170); Roman Empire (240); Late Roman or Coptic (22, from Egypt); Arabic, eleventh to thirteenth centuries (13). Drinking vessels (32 cups, 1 tumbler). Important bequests include the Sharp Ogden Collection and Robinow Collection. Most of the collection is in reserve and may be seen by appointment only with the Keeper, Department of Archaeology. Photographs to order; no charge if for research purposes.

NEWCASTLE. Laing Art Gallery, Higham Place, Newcastle-upon-Tyne 1
Medieval (loan collection of phials and bottles from the London Museum); eighteenth century (15); nineteenth century (470); continental, nineteenth century (5); Oriental (7). Drinking glasses (110). Outstanding specimens include unsigned Beilby glasses and decanter; signed Gallé vases.

NORWICH. Castle Museum, Norwich, Norfolk
Roman (6 + fragments); Saxon (1 + fragments); eighteenth century (100); nineteenth century (50); continental, eighteenth century (5). Drinking glasses (100). Contains an important series of some 25 glasses of the 'Lynn' type and a series of 12 specimens attributed to Absolon of Great Yarmouth. About half the collection is in store and may be seen by appointment only.

NOTTINGHAM. Museum and Art Gallery, The Castle, Nottingham
Contains a small collection of Roman bottles and phials and of English eighteenth and nineteenth century drinking glasses and bottles. Important specimens include a Venetian tazza with enamel *putti* and the Bles Bowl, English lead glass, c. 1685.

OLDHAM. Art Gallery and Museum, Union Street, Oldham, Lancashire
Roman (2, from Palestine); medieval (2 fragments); eighteenth century (50); nineteenth century (70); Bohemian, nineteenth–twentieth centuries (9). Drinking glasses (120). Collection includes bequests from Francis Buckley and Eli Ormerod. Much of the collection is in store and may be seen by appointment only. Photographs by arrangement.

OXFORD. Ashmolean Museum, Department of Antiquities, Beaumont Street, Oxford
Pre-Roman (50, from Mediterranean area and Persia); Roman (about 750 complete vessels, only 5 to 10 pieces from Britain, remainder from the Continent and Near East); Saxon (20, half from British sites, remainder Frankish); seventeenth–eighteenth centuries (400, including about 200 wine bottles and a further 200 assorted bottles and flasks).

Ashmolean, Department of Eastern Art
Contains a small collection of glass objects from the Near and Far East, including examples of Syrian enamelled ware from Fustāt (Old Cairo).

Ashmolean, Department of Western Art
Seventeenth–eighteenth centuries (about 650, including some continental specimens and a series of early Venetian glasses). The collection includes the following important gifts and bequests: C. D. E. Fortnum (15, Venice and Bohemia); Sir Bernard Eckstein (125, decorated drinking glasses); W. S. Susman (63, drinking glasses); H. R. Marshall (458, English drinking glasses). The principal strengths of the collection are the engraved, stippled and enamelled drinking glasses of the eighteenth century, including Jacobites. Students may have access to the collections by appointment. Photographs 30p from existing negatives, £1·05 from new negatives; colour transparencies 37p.

RAWTENSTALL. Museum, Whitaker Park, Rawtenstall, Lancashire
Roman (14 of varied provenance); eighteenth century (85); continental (38, of all periods). Most of the specimens are from the Peers Groves Collection, the majority of which is in store. They may be seen by appointment. The Museum is open from 2 p.m. to 5 p.m. only, except Saturday, 10 a.m. to 5 p.m.

ST HELENS. Pilkington Glass Museum, Prescot Road, St Helens, Lancashire
The Museum, recently established by Pilkington Bros has been designed to illustrate the history and manufacture of glass from Egyptian times to the present day. Its collections include many important glasses. Pre-Roman (20); Roman (37); medieval (43); seventeenth century (9); eighteenth century (30); nineteenth century (18); twentieth century (3); American, twentieth century (2); continental, seventeenth century (23), eighteenth century (9), nineteenth century (11). Drinking glasses (68). Outstanding specimens include a Bohemian Humpen dated 1625; a flagon and bowl from the Sittingbourne Treasure (late first century); a Nuremberg Humpen of 1691; sealed Ravenscroft posset pot, c. 1677; wine glass engraved by Jacob Sang, 1759; portrait glass of Prince Charles Edward in enamel colours, c. 1770. Open weekdays 10 a.m. to 5 p.m., weekends 2 pm. to 4.30 p.m., Wednesdays (April to October) 10 a.m. to 9 p.m. Photographs 20p to 25p; colour transparencies 13p (5 in. × 4 in. transparencies £3).

SHEFFIELD. City Museum, Weston Park, Sheffield, Yorkshire
Roman (43 from Mediterranean area); Saxon (53, glass beads); eighteenth century (186); nineteenth century (82); twentieth century (59); continental, seventeenth century (24), eighteenth century (16), nineteenth century (5). Drinking glasses (184). The collections include important material from south Yorkshire glasshouses. Outstanding specimens include a loving cup made at Bolsterstone by Frank Morton (d. 1732), the earliest documented piece from this factory. Gifts and bequests include the Bateman Collection of Saxon glass beads and the Kenworthy Collection of eighteenth-century glass made at Bolsterstone. Open 10 a.m. to 5 p.m. (June–Aug 10 a.m. to 8.30 p.m.) Photographs and transparencies by arrangement.

STAFFORDSHIRE *see* BRIERLEY HILL

STOURBRIDGE. Council House, Mary Stevens Park, Stourbridge, Worcestershire
Resulting from a temporary exhibition in 1951 as part of the Festival of Britain, an important collection of nineteenth- and twentieth-century glass has been built up, housed in a display area at the Council House. More than 500 specimens are on display, including a bequest of 300 pieces made in his family's glassworks by Benjamin Richardson of Wordsley Hall and a gift of 140 pieces by John Northwood from his private collection.

Outstanding specimens include glasses engraved by William Fritsche and J. T. Fereday, examples of the work of George Woodall and Stourbridge paper-weights formerly in the collection of ex-King Farouk. Open weekdays, normal office hours.

STROUD. Museum, Lansdown, Stroud, Gloucestershire
Contains some eighteenth- and nineteenth-century glass and fragments from the glassworks at Woodchester which produced window, bottle and table glass from 1590 to 1615. There is also a collection of about 100 local beer and mineral bottles. The most outstanding specimen is a locally excavated flagon of early eighteenth century date, and almost certainly made at the Grandchamp Factory, Amblève, Belgium. Open weekdays 10.30 a.m. to 1 p.m., 2 p.m. to 5 p.m.

TRURO. Royal Institution of Cornwall, The County Museum, Truro, Cornwall
Contains 8 specimens of Roman glass, a good collection of bottles of the seventeenth to nineteenth centuries, two English Privateer glasses and several other pieces of English and Irish glass of the eighteenth and nineteenth centuries.

WINCHESTER. City Museum, The Square, Winchester, Hampshire
The collection consists of excavated material and includes a Roman glass flagon, medieval glass lamp, a Venetian bowl and numerous bottles and other vessels of the eighteenth century.

Hampshire County Museum Service, Chilcomb House, Chilcomb Lane, Winchester, Hampshire
Seventeenth century (3); eighteenth century (52); nineteenth century (90); twentieth century (4). Drinking glasses (50). Includes a tazza of c. 1665, possibly from the Duke of Buckingham's Greenwich glasshouse. May be seen by appointment only. Photographs, taken to order, £1·05.

WORTHING. Museum and Art Gallery, Chapel Road, Worthing, Sussex
Roman (6); Saxon (11 + fragments); eighteenth century (45); nineteenth century (94); twentieth century (8); continental, eighteenth century (4), nineteenth century (3). Drinking glasses (96). The most outstanding specimens are in the group of 11 vessels from Highdown Saxon cemetery, including a goblet with wheel-engraving of a hunting scene and Greek inscription (Late Roman/Alexandria); a ribbed amber bottle with opaque-white trail decoration (Near East, eleventh–twelfth century), excavated locally, is also of interest. There is a general collection of eighteenth- and nineteenth-century drinking vessels and some sealed bottles. Photographs 20p, or 40p if negative does not already exist; colour transparencies 13p if in print; others can be taken to special order.

United States of America

The major collections of English and American drinking glasses are in the following museums:

BOSTON. The Museum of Fine Arts, 469 Huntington Avenue, Boston, Massachusetts

CHICAGO. Art Institute of Chicago, Michigan Avenue at Adams Street, Chicago, Illinois

HARTFORD. Wadsworth Atheneum, 25 Atheneum Square North, Hartford, Connecticut

NEW YORK. The Corning Museum of Glass, Corning Glass Centre, Corning, New York

NEW YORK. The Metropolitan Museum of Art, New York

PHILADELPHIA. Museum of Art, Benjamin Franklin Parkway at 26th Street, Philadelphia, Pennsylvania

TOLEDO. Toledo Museum of Art, Monroe and Scottswood, Toledo, Ohio

Index

Abbreviations
T   Text page reference.
B   Entry number in
      bibliography.
P   Plate number.